# ME[ET]
# AT THE
# BORDER

Amanda & Amar ~

    Happy travelling the
world, love-birds!! ☺
    This is an autographed
copy of one of our favourite
travel writers' works ~
    Enjoy! ♡

Ann
Ashwani
───→
2015

Warm Regards,

[signature]

# MEET ME
# AT THE
# BORDER

INDER RAJ AHLUWALIA

Om Books International

First published in 2012 by

# OM

Om Books International

Corporate & Editorial Office
A-12, Sector 64, Noida 201 301
Uttar Pradesh, India
Phone: +91 120 477 4100
Email: editorial@ombooks.com
Website: www.ombooksinternational.com

Sales Office
4379/4B, Prakash House, Ansari Road
Darya Ganj, New Delhi 110 002, India
Phone: +91 11 2326 3363, 2326 5303
Fax: +91 11 2327 8091
Email: sales@ombooks.com
Website: www.ombooks.com

ISBN: 978-93-81607-18-3

10 9 8 7 6 5 4 3 2 1

Printed at Thomson Press, India

# Contents

# Introduction

One of the burdens of my life as an international travel writer has been answering people's repeated queries about the 'most beautiful' country I have ever visited. My stock answer has been that it is hard to single out a particular country. And it is.

Or is it?

I mean, should I not be thinking of the innate charms I have seen in some select spots that have wrapped themselves around me like an octopus' tentacles, and enveloped me in a dream-like world? Should I not be thinking of the culture that seeps through almost every facet of a country, and shrouds everything to the point that it almost drags you down with its sheer weight and intensity? Should I not be thinking of the thousands of men and women I have met across the globe, and of those I have managed to get close to, and those with whom I have broken bread?

I *do* think of all this often enough. But is merely thinking of these myriad elements enough? Isn't there much more to this stunning script that has become part and parcel of my life and daily existence? Isn't there another dimension that needs to be addressed? Isn't there a need for more ground to be broken? It is a richly confused legacy that needs richly confused minds to delve into, understand, and appreciate.

I guess I am 'richly confused' enough. How else can I explain the immense pleasure I have got from the life I have led so far? It has been a rich experience, and I have felt the need to share it in detail with others. That's what I have done. I have charted my exciting journey as an international travel writer, a journey I embarked upon three decades ago, and presented the scenarios and people I encountered across the globe through the four seasons of each year. I have threaded together the moments, passions and adventures, and the comical interludes that have made the canvas of my life so colourful and interesting.

A wise man once said it is better to laugh at yourself rather than have others do it for you. I have been involved in incidents that would make a dancing girl blush. One such incident immediately comes to mind. Way back in 1983, I happened to visit Singapore to attend the Travel Agents of India Annual Convention as a young and zippy lad with just a couple of years of writing experience. As part of general city sightseeing, the delegates were taken to Haw Paw Villa, or Tiger Balm Gardens as it is also known. As our motley group was alighting from the bus, our guide said we would stop there for 20 minutes, and cautioned each alighting delegate to look after his wallet. When it was our turn — myself and another young travel writer — the good man said with a twinkle in his eyes, "Gentlemen, you just look after yourselves!" Deeply embarrassed, we looked around to see if anyone had heard this, and of course, everyone around had!

While in the 'confession mode', I must mention that no account of my travels, and indeed of my life itself, would be complete without mention of the impact my being a Sikh has had on my personality, character, and life's adventures. And it must be showing because all through my travels around the world these past thirty-odd years, I have received more smiles — I call them 'goodwill miles' — than I have merited. There have been literally hundreds of occasions on which people have just smiled at me for no real reason at all.

Imagine an international travel convention with 1200 delegates from the world over, and just *one* of them wearing a turban. You *stick out* like a beacon! And that's the way it has been with me for years now. I have felt thousands of pairs of eyes peering at me through umpteen two-hour banquet dinners and cocktail receptions. Most times, and in most places, the reactions have been extremely pleasant. The delegates have sought me out, engaged me in conversation, asked me to join in at their table, and tried to unravel the mysteries of my being!

The list of questions is endless. Is my turban for show, or is it part of my religion? Do I wear it all the time? Does it come readymade or do I tie it every day? How long is it? Does its colour have a special significance?

I'd be lying if I didn't confess to a feeling of smug satisfaction at this, especially pertaining to the women who smiled and 'chatted' me up. And I'd be lying if I didn't admit to intense flirtation on my part. Shameful as it sounds, the fact is that I've used my physical appearance as a weapon of seduction.

There has been no dearth of inspiration in my life. My late parents, in their own distinct way, spurred me on to achieve what I was seeking through my writing. They never professed to understand exactly what I was doing with my life — I think they thought of me as some sort of drifter really — but were supportive enough. They never questioned my methods and seemed to accept the fact that there probably was a method to my madness. And as I grew in stature and my writing became more visible and impactful, they developed a sense of pride in my work. They never tired of talking proudly of my writing and travels behind my back. "Your parents are very proud of you" was the message repeatedly relayed to me by their circle of friends. They were the sort of parents I would wish everyone to have.

And then there is the inscrutable S.P. Dutt — affectionately known to his cronies as 'Speedy' — with whom I have shared a laugh or two, over a drink or three. (*He* doesn't drink, by the way!) He tosses what I have dubbed his 'signature' phrase at me, "Young man, tell us about yourself!" And I toss back my stock answer, "There's little to tell and plenty to hide." Upon which he showers me with compliments about my 'superlative talents' as a travel journalist, and my 'enormous success'. We both come away happy. He, because he has done what he does best, which is praise others. And I, because I am relieved that at least one person on this planet has been fooled by me.

Anil Katoch and his wife, Nupur, have sort of adopted me and insist I give them a shout whenever I need anything. Their grouse against me is that I didn't move into their apartment to spend more time together. Just knowing that people like them are around for me helps. Manika Chopra has remained unchanged in character, and maintained her friendship with me for some 25 years in spite of being hit by the modern catastrophy called 'big money', which can severely dent friendships. And there's my uncle, Jagmohan Singh, who has kept tabs on my health and general welfare.

Talking of this planet, there are stunningly beautiful places with awesome assets — each a carefully kept secret — lands of great beauty enhanced by physical vastness, geographical diversity, historical legacies, cultural richness and distinct people with distinct lifestyles.

I am talking about unforgettable vistas of nature that include the world's highest sand dunes just minutes away from endless beaches; the world's oldest desert; an exceptional variety of wildlife in sanctuaries that are role models in environment preservation; safaris that bond us with nature; a hotel made entirely from ice and snow; an underground hotel; service that's an effortless whisper; blazing sunsets melting into lantern-lit romance; cruises that are almost sinful in terms of what they offer; meals that are the envy of royalty; thermal springs that provide instant rejuvenation; festivals that border on the sublime; people who are still living in the past.

I am dwelling on the thrill that accompanies travel. I mean *real* travel, or at least my perception of what that should be. I am talking of the intense beauty and mystique still on show at select places on our planet. I am touching upon some of the mysteries that cling to certain places and make them exotic beyond belief. I am talking about vast oceans; wide horizons; clear skies; memorable sunsets and starry nights; ethereal landscapes; silence and solitude.

But things aren't idyllic. They are just real. And reality was never meant to be simple. There is hope *and* despair, joy *and* grief, belief *and* doubt. There is a stoic tenor to the different landscapes and to the people themselves. And therein lies the beauty.

I am talking about a feeling of antiquity engendered by three-toed dinosaur footprints left more than 200 million years ago; by petrified forests where fossilised tree trunks have lain for over 240 million years; and by oceans so deep, their secrets will never really be revealed.

And yet, I have experienced it all just now.

There is a huge, wide world waiting out there. It shows many faces and many images that range from 'subtle' to 'stark'. Though I have tried to understand them all, it is the starkness that has floored me. The many gripping faces generate a sense of freedom, a sort of *déjà vu*.

I had asked myself if I could afford to miss all this. And I knew I couldn't. And thus began my journey.

This is my way of sharing it with others.

Meet me at the border!

# Etosha And I

It was a dusty little car on a dusty road on just another morning. As usual, we were running late, thanks to a rather long drawn-out breakfast lecture on the perils of falling sick while travelling, followed by an equally drawn-out but more refreshing cup of brandy-laced coffee (or was it the other way around?).

No matter which way you look at it, Africa takes a little getting used to. And I am not referring to the heat or dust. That's all a bit exaggerated anyway. It is the attitude. Old Africa hands know that when Mmangaa tells them "Jack seyz he'll join us at eight," Jack can be expected to show up some time *after* eight. Realistically, by ten!

Our guide in Namibia, Jock Erasmus wasn't too worried about our showing up late. "It's a big country," he explained by way of reason. "They'll wait for us at lunch. If not, we can always get a *kudu* (deer)." Suitably reassured, I sat back and enjoyed the view. And quite a view it turned out to be too. Part sub-Saharan, part bushveld, part plain African, the landscapes that unfolded before us as we drove along were stunning to say the least. And I know what I am talking about. I have seen a landscape or two in my time.

Two more hours of sheer highway pleasure and we pulled up at Makuti Lodge located just outside one of the park's gates, blending perfectly with the jungle and bush setting. It was a delight. As upscale as they come, the lodge offers thinly veiled luxury — a private wooded area complete with wild animals, a large swimming pool, spacious rooms, and sumptuous meals including the famed *boma* (a great African tradition where guests sit around a bonfire in circular enclosures) dinners. The talk over lunch centred on why we were here in the first place.

"I've been coming here for the past 15 years, and I can swear, nothing, absolutely nothing's changed one little bit. Has it Fred?" Now here was a lady fond of her voice, and obviously used to being heard above the crowd.

"By the way, I'm Helen and this is my husband Fred," she bellowed to all around within earshot, *her* earshot. "We're from Boston and yessiree, this place sure does take the tension right out of you, doesn't it Fred?!"

Helen talked, Fred nodded, and the rest of us listened. That's the way it went. But the lunch was as delicious as Helen was talkative.

For those of you who haven't seen it, Etosha National Park in Northern Namibia isn't just a premier Southern African sanctuary for the wild, but also a top-quality conservation project right up there with the world's best. Scenic, varied topography and excellent sightings have enhanced the park's reputation to the point where it is almost a pilgrimage centre for genuine wild-lifers.

We entered the park and Jock drove us straightaway to a nearby waterhole that just happened to be a premier animal sighting spot. All waterholes yield good sightings, but this one was renowned. Half an hour, and we had logged an impressive list of sightings that included three of the famed

Etosha elephants and a couple of giraffes. Etosha elephants, by the way, are a particular group of males who had been kicked out of the herd, and now been officially declared 'rogue'. Everyone wanted to see them but no one wanted to get up-close and personal.

The giraffes, of course, were 'normal' wild animals, Jock told us. Seeing giraffes drink is an adventure by itself as they splay their legs and lean down awkwardly to reach the water, while keeping a constant lookout for predators, especially lions.

Our dust-covered car with a cracked windscreen, gliding along the non-metal road didn't disturb the equilibrium of the jungle. Most game parks don't have the space, but here we had been driving for two hours and were still far from its centre, one reason being that there is no centre or core area. The entire park is core area and home to assorted wildlife!

The official speed limit in the park is a comparatively high 60 kmph, but the straightness of the roads, complete lack of traffic, and the leisurely breakfast brandy, collectively tilted the scales in favour of over-speeding, and we were doing an unholy 80 kmph! Every ten minutes saw the landscape change, with wooded areas giving way to open meadows and vast flatlands, forests, and bush land. The only thing that broke the basic dryness was the acacia, among the world's hardiest and most durable trees, and Africa's green lungs.

'Etosha' literally means 'the great white place of dry water', an apt description when you consider its barrenness. With an area of 22,700 square kilometres, the park is almost a country by itself in terms of vastness and physical diversity. For those who like comparisons, it is ten times the size of Luxembourg. The entire park area is encircled by electrified wire to fence in the animals. "And keep undesirables out," Jock put in softly. "Joke," he added a few seconds later.

In Etosha, like in much of Southern Africa, the light falls on shrubs and mopane grass, making animals easy to sight even from a distance. And goodness knows, there are enough of them to see. The abundant resident wildlife includes lion, elephant, leopard, cheetah, and black rhino that roam through the acacia groves and savanna. Scavengers like spotted hyena and jackal follow their hunting tracks, crying late into the night as they go about stealing whatever they can, wherever they can, and from whoever they can. Antelopes are present in thousands, and springbok, zebra, kudu, wildebeest, and impala graze on vegetation wherever they can find it. Perhaps, watching all this from a safe haven is the Damara Dik Dik, the smallest antelope in Africa.

Besides this density and rich diversity of game thriving in a near-desert environment that make Etosha amongst the highest-rated parks in game-rich Southern Africa, the stunning scenery with fairy tale landscapes are of equal delight to photographers, writers, the passionate, and the lonely. (Three guesses for the category to which I belong).

As it always does in Africa, dusk settled gently in the bush, but it was still clear enough to see things for a couple of 100 metres. The day had slipped by. It was time to leave. Visitors are obliged to leave the park by 7 p.m., so we returned to Makuti Lodge. The customary *boma* barbecue over, we retired to bed in anticipation of an early start the next morning.

Crisp sunshine, clear light, and the smell of freshly brewed coffee had us all wide awake and excited. Within minutes we were back in the park, back on the dusty road, now familiar territory. It was a glorious morning.

Sunrise in Etosha was an experience to be long cherished. The sky was criss-crossed with birds. There were great raptors that dropped out of the blue like arrows, crimson-breasted shrikes perched on several types of trees, threading the park with song, and weaver birds that build communal nests that make even big branches sag. High up in the skies, watching over the proceedings, a tawny eagle described ever-decreasing concentric circles as it prepared to swoop down on its prey.

It almost seems as if there are two Etoshas. The wet summer sees game migrating westwards as newborn animals celebrate the cycle of creation. The dry winter shows the park's other face, with game converging around natural springs and on the wide Andoni Plains. There are as many waterholes here as there are patches on a giraffe's neck, but the best game-viewing centres around select ones like Arroe, Gaus, and Klein Namatoni. This concentration of game around waterholes is one of Etosha's main assets. Sadly, while this is where the animals drink, and where you get the best sightings, this is also where many die, ambushed by crafty predators.

The best part of our trip came as a complete surprise. At the heart of the park, covering about a fifth of its total area, is the Etosha Pan, a unique and beautiful eco-system and a famous landmark in its own right. Kilometres of completely flat salt plain have created a unique geographical phenomenon. Comprising huge stretches of savanna, with flat lands of limestone and golden grass stretching as far as the eye can see, the Pan is a sight to behold. Once, there was a lake here, apparently one of the world's largest. Then, eons ago, the earth shifted and the lake drifted into the ocean, and the sun shrank the Pan, leaving behind deposits of mineral salts.

When nature's kind, rain evokes the ancient lake and surrounds it with green, but mostly the Pan remains true to its name — bone-dry, caked, parched, barren, stark and stunningly beautiful.

The Pan acquires a haunting beauty as mirages dance across its shimmering expanse, and animal tracks criss-cross its length and breadth before fading into the distance and merging with the horizon. Blue wildebeest, zebra, and springbok cross the flatlands, stirring up fine dust as they graze on the salty grass, and leave their spoor on its surface like tracks across a white moon.

And in true desert fashion there was enough dust left for us to swirl in as we drove through this unique stretch of the country with its boundless beauty.

This is where the famous aircraft scene in *Lost in Africa* had been filmed, Jock informed us. Having seen and enjoyed the film, I instantly 'connected' with the scene and the place, which further heightened its beauty for me.

Hours later, we left the Pan, and headed for Sprokieswoud (the enchanted wood). Here you see a different face of Etosha, with a small forest of moringa trees on a level plain, contrasting with the surrounding barren environs. These trees normally grow only on hillsides and their presence here is one of the park's many mysteries. A San legend tells us how the Great Builder completed his creation and then flung these moringas eastwards with their roots pointing to the sky.

We had stopped at a waterhole near the Von Lindequist Gate, and for the first time in my life, I saw as many as 50 zebras together, drinking desperately, oblivious of a pride of black striped hyenas nearby. "It isn't as if they don't fear hyenas. Deep down, almost every animal does. Hyenas are like that, and worthy of being feared," Jock whispered in my ear. "It's just that they're too damn thirsty to care." Then suddenly they began to back off from the water and loped away, stirring up whirls of dust. "Probably a lion upwind," Jock whispered in my ear again.

Etosha had been like a dream. In giving me the closest possible look at nature, it had also given me many images, but the one that is etched in my mind was of a solitary elephant standing by the pool, his image reflected in the water. Soon, others would join him, and the intricate life cycle of the jungle would be acted and re-enacted the way it has been for millions of years.

I knew that these memories would stay with me forever. I was truly impressed, almost awed by the beauty of nature exposed to me.

And I was thirsty!

# The Last European Wilderness

Out of the airport, into the open, and immediately onto a dog-sledge with 12 of the tundra's friendliest, loudest and friskiest huskies isn't bad going for one cold, grey morning.

"Mind your feet," our guide Tommy politely cautioned us, and off we went with a flourish, or at least the equivalent of a flourish in these extraordinary circumstances. "Huskies love to eat, sleep, and run," Tommy said with the seriousness such a statement deserved. We all nodded our heads in acknowledgement of this fact. After all, who were we to disagree or complain on that cold morning with the air freezing and crisp, soft snow as high as our waists, and our spirits even higher.

We followed a carefully laid-out script. Over mugs full of blueberry vodka, we had been duly apprised of the phenomenal geographical beauty and wonders of the polar region, in an informal Arctic briefing at the airport itself. Tommy Sormling and Ake Pudas, our guides from Wild Tours, would have both looked more at home in a funeral parlour rather than an adventure company. To start with, they spoke very little, in fact they hardly spoke at all unless absolutely necessary. To top things off, they both looked as if they had great human insight and had this foreboding that the world was about to come to an end. But then that was judging them a bit harshly. The fact is that they had both spent their lives conducting such tours in the tundra region, and were professionals down to their bone marrow. So there!

This morning at least they seemed in no hurry at all as they kitted us out in isothermal gear. "All types of people come here, you know, from all types of places," Ake said in that laid-back way which became his patent throughout our association.

Lesson one: never try to hurry in the Arctic. It doesn't pay. Lesson two: don't try to be macho when it comes to dealing with the cold.

It was quiet and peaceful, almost ethereal, as it always is in this remote, beautiful corner of the world. For long we were deep inside the Arctic Circle in Kiruna, the world's largest city with an area of 20,000 square kilometres — half the size of Switzerland — and big enough to accommodate the entire world's population, standing up. Snow fell incessantly and softly as we arrived in this challenging and exciting, ultimate outdoors man's paradise, a great wilderness area with large tundra regions in the north and the mighty Kebnekarse Massif in the south, with kilometres of flat, open country in between. The region's stark beauty couldn't be ignored for a second, never mind the cold.

Kiruna had welcomed us in typical fashion — with sleet and snow.

Strange as it may sound, no one in these parts bothers much about the weather. Though winter temperatures plummet to -40°, tourists go indoors mainly to sleep, spending most of their time enjoying the unique local bounties of nature so generously on offer. "While we get the best of nature here, it's not wise to take nature for granted. It might stop being so generous, so we must make the most of it. Sleep is basically for the bored, tired, or useless," Tommy volunteered softly. We all nodded in agreement, desperately stifling our yawns.

For most of summer, the sun shines without a break here, making the midnight sun a unique polar phenomenon. And the sun never sets from May 28 till mid-July, making Northern Lapland one large greenhouse. Come winter, and the sun takes a holiday from December 9, resting just under the horizon, creating five hours of daylight called the blue twilight. But even in the middle of the night, it isn't really dark, thanks to the snow, the moon, and the famous Aurora Borealis, known as the Northern Lights, which attract tourists from the world over. Japanese women have created another Arctic legend in their belief that children conceived during Aurora Borealis are born healthy and happy. Well!

The surety of snow is what established Kiruna's fame, and you can vouch for it every winter. Riksgransen and Bjorkbden are excellent winter-sports centres with downhill possibilities, off-pist skiing, snowboarding and telemark skiing. Besides, you can snow-scooter safari at Lainio, Riksgransen, and Jukkasarvi, raft in six alpine rivers, fish in an astounding 6,200 lakes, and ski from end-October through end-April. With the aid of four-wheel drives, you can also venture out into the country and see and absorb the uniqueness — the harshness and benevolence — of nature in the polar region.

There is plenty to do in this Arctic region. The tundra between Tornetrask and the Finnish border shows the region's sheer physical expanse, and the new Nordkalott Trail snakes through a vast tract of land. There are several other interesting and popular trails. Abisko's trails have day trips; Noolja has family tours; and Laktatjaffo has waffle tours. Completing the nature package are wild flowers like the Laestadius poppy, and the mountain orchid, Lappfela.

Courtesy dog-sledge rides, snow-scooter safaris, and cross-country ski trails, you can discover a thousand natural sites and the unique lifestyle of the Sami people and the nomadic reindeer herds on which this remarkable culture has survived for thousands of years. You can visit the largest and deepest iron ore mine in the world with over 400 kilometres of underground roads, or tour the northernmost rocket stations in the world. You can fish in lakes through clear, thick ice.

A popular Kiruna winter event is jig fishing (ice fishing), also known as binocular fishing, particularly enjoyable when char, trout, and grayling are running in the Rautasjaure, Rastojaure and Tornetrask lakes. You can try your hand at winter sports like downhill, cross-country skiing and snow-boarding, ice-climbing, and paragliding.

Let your imagination go. Picture yourself handling a gourmet banquet in the snow, and believe me, there's no better place than Lapland to find out just what genuine Northern cuisine is all about.

Sami barbecuing is a sort of lifestyle and adventure by itself. Suovas (reindeer meat marinated overnight in salt water, then smoked over a birchwood fire and deep-fried with mushrooms), are all-time favourites. So is fjallroding (Arctic char marinated in Absolut Citron and finely chopped chives, and served with walnut sauce). Contrary to popular belief, and certainly my own, alcohol consumption out in the open is taboo. "Big health trouble," came the answer in a chorus, every time one asked why, or reached for a hip flask.

The world doesn't really know it, but people have lived in the municipality of Kiruna since centuries, one with nature, eking out an existence in this barren, beautiful land. But Kiruna city is young, founded at the turn of the 19th century when mining started in what would become the world's largest underground mine — the kilometre-deep Kiirunavaara.

11

Things have moved on a bit and today, high-rise structures and modern shopping malls dot the cityscape. The Kiruna City Hall with its beautiful clock tower and art museum; the Hjalmar Lundbohm House, and the church with its lovely altarpiece, are all local symbols and merit a visit.

So, who lives here? As a people, the Lapps are as fascinating as they come. They always have been. You can glimpse Lapp life from close quarters at centres like the Jukkasjärvi Homestead Museum with its handicrafts collection; at the all-female staff crafts cooperative Mattarakha facility that shows crafts manufacture; and at Samegarden which features a permanent exhibition. The last weekend in January features the annual snow festival, among Europe's grandest. The five-day holiday period packs a variety of events from concerts to snow sculpture competitions, art exhibitions, theatre, and dog and reindeer races.

Tourists from the world over pour in here at the roof of the world for a variety of reasons that range from savouring the great outdoors and the distinct Lapp culture, to enjoying a rare sense of space and privacy.

Kiruna is all about images, experiences, and memories. Memories of visits to reindeer and husky farms and tea shared with farmers in sturdy, cosy wigwams; memories of the locals and their hardy lifestyle, which has apparently remained unchanged over the centuries; memories of travelling in a world seemingly devoid of people, noise or commotion. And memories of snow-scooter rides that bordered on 'suicide' risk levels, and of the snow itself, which shrouded everything as far as one could see. Time flew and experiences flooded our calendar.

The snow was like a powdery wall, shrouding everything. As we were leaving, it started to snow heavily, giving the white landscape a fresh coat. But no matter how much it snows in Kiruna, no one complains.

It wouldn't do to skip mentioning my personal experience of 'ice cold hospitality', extended at the coolest place to stay in the world.

Deep inside the Arctic Circle, situated on the shores of the Torne River, in the old village of Jukkasjärvi in Swedish Lapland, the Ice Hotel is the world's largest igloo, built entirely of ice and snow over an area of 4,000 square metres, with its lobby, rooms, walls, flooring, furniture, decorative pieces, and public areas like the Absolut Ice Bar, all made from ice and nothing else!

Imagine a hotel built from scratch every year. A new design, new suites, a brand new reception — in fact, everything crisp and new each year. The entire structure is built, incredibly, each November out of pure ice and sparkling snow.

'Jukkasjärvi' is the Lapp word for 'meeting place', and the Ice Hotel opens its freezing doors to welcome visitors from the world over, who come to wonder at its extraordinariness and beauty, enjoy its 'cool' environs and 'ice cold' hospitality, admire the midnight sun and the Aurora Borealis.

Our hotel transfer explained it all. "If you haven't done this before, hold on tight," Tommy declared solemnly. Seconds later, hanging precariously onto a dog-sledge, we were racing across the snow-covered tundra as if our lives depended on it (and indeed they did). 14 kilometres and several heartbeats later, we broke journey at a post. "We stop here for 30 minutes so the dogs can rest and we can eat some reindeer meat and hash potatoes."

An hour later we pulled up at the porch of the Ice Hotel to a 'cold but friendly' welcome.

The hotel's vast confines contain some 40 rooms including 7 suites, 120 beds, huge colonnaded halls and public galleries, the Absolut Ice Bar, a cinema and a separate chapel.

And if all this isn't enough, what the igloo building contains by way of art and design is even more amazing. The furniture, carvings and sculptures in the public areas and exhibition galleries are all made of solid ice, each piece created afresh every year by well-known artists, designers, sculptors and ice carvers. Mighty ice columns in spacious halls, pure ice chandeliers lit by fibre optics, solid ice glasses in the bar, and ice beds with reindeer skins as bedcovers — the hotel never ceases to amaze and fascinate.

You sleep on the 'bed', in inside temperatures of upto -15°. For good measure, you are given a certificate mentioning the inside and outside temperatures, stating you spent the night there, to prove to the folks back home that you have indeed lost your mind. Talk about 'cold hospitality'.

The free(zing) building materials are delivered every year at the appropriate time — 10,000 tonnes of crystal clear ice from the 'ice manufacturing plant', the Torne River, and 30,000 tonnes of pure snow generously supplied by Mother Nature. Each year, the building technique improves and the management's 'snow-how' increases.

The chapel is a delight. It was empty when I went in. Complete silence greeted me as I entered and walked down the aisle. An ice altar, ice benches and pew, and gospel carvings, lend it dignity and allow one to pray in total calm. The hotel arranges marriages, and christenings, subject to one condition: the babies must have the letters 'is' (Swedish for 'ice') in their names. So all those with names like ChrISter, ISak, DorIS, or ISabella, can get christened in the only ice chapel in the world. And if your name does have 'is' in it and you aren't married, well, I'll tell you how to go about it.

Anyone for the movies? The in-house 'cinema' is actually a large film auditorium where, seated on reindeer skin atop ice slabs, you can watch slide shows of the Northern Lights and other marvels of the Arctic region. The videos and other equipment are actually placed in a refrigerator to 'keep warm'.

After the show, a drink perhaps? The Absolut Ice Bar is where guests gather for drinks and gossip. Naturally, vodka is the favoured drink, with straight vodka copiously quaffed from tumblers made of ice. Regulars may have met the Swedish Royal couple or the Irish President. Perhaps they have also rubbed shoulders with 'super cool' models Naomi Campbell or Kate Moss or the Swedish model Marcus Schenkenberg, or the famous photographer Herb Ritts, or the Swedish rock star Jennifer Brown, or the American rock band Van Halen. There weren't any of those celebrities around the night I was there, but the crowd was interesting, enlightened and friendly.

We warmed up with an Absolut Blue, a mix of Absolut vodka and blueberry syrup. You can lean over the huge bar table of solid ice, perch on ice stools or just relax in the seating area with its ice chairs and tables, complete with ashtrays. The alcohol is stored in special cold-resistant bottles. Once used, the glasses, carved from ice, are just heaped in a corner to form a block that stays there till the entire hotel melts down.

*In sauna veritas* (In the sauna, truth is revealed). Well, this is the motto of the Swedish Sauna Academy, and the truth is, a sauna is guaranteed to warm the cockles of your heart. You can try different types of saunas, and get instructions from an expert Master of Sauna Ceremonies who will introduce you to the noble art of enjoying a real, traditional sauna.

Guests are invited on a conducted tour of the premises, given a run-down on things, and shown the icy artefacts, products of skilled sculpting, carving, and chiselling, that embellish the glacial décor and pay tribute to 'ice for art's sake'. Ake Larsson and Arne Berg gave up wood-sculpting to work on ice, and inspired ace fashion photographer Herb Ritts to shoot here. Modelling clothes created exclusively by Naomi Campbell, Kate Moss, Mark Findley, Marcus Schenkenberg, and by Gianni Versace for Absolut, pose on surrealistic ice staircases and lounge on icy armchairs at -30°.

Beddy-bye procedure is to strip and zip up into giant sleeping bags. Ten minutes of wrestling with the clothes and you are ready to hit the 'sub-zero hay'. Strangely, if you take the advice of the locals, you'll rarely feel the cold. And it can get to -35°. You sleep like the Samis, with your bed covered with reindeer hides, and sleeping bags that keep you as warm as toast.

Ready to call is an icy day, I snuggled gingerly into my bag, just my face exposed to the elements, which in this case happened to be an ambient -7° (guests often describe it as a healing kind of feeling), and waited for sleep to come. A little lamp in the room threw ghostly shadows across the floor, walls, ceiling, on the bed, and in the corridor beyond. Somewhere in the distance, someone snoring.

I tried equal parts of exercise, alcohol, spirit of adventure, and as a last resort, meditation. But sleep eluded me completely that night. Being forewarned about cameras being ruined, I had tucked mine on my chest, zipped up in the bag. No problem. I had also heeded the friendly 'bar advice' about not drinking just before retiring to bed, as the toilets were outside the igloo. No problem, there, either. But still no sleep. The night passed glacially but sleep eluded me.

'Enough,' I told myself. Things had come to a sorry pass if a seasoned traveller like myself couldn't sleep just because it was a measly -7°. Out of my sleeping bag I wriggled, into my boots, ready for action, camera in hand, determination strong in my heart.

'This isn't on. I'm trying to sleep away the night while there's an entire world waiting to be discovered,' I hissed at myself. Pitying the restfully asleep guests for missing out on such an experience, I slithered disdainfully but gingerly down the corridor.

The next hour was one that will remain etched in my memory forever. The lobby resembled nothing I had ever seen before, or have seen since. Light filtered through the ice walls, casting ghostly shadows on everything, creating an alabaster effect. Like beacons in the mist, little lamps flickered gently, marking their territory. Outside, the snow fell gently, shrouding the garden ice sculptures. Inside, the exhibits shone forth. It was pure magic. I felt completely alone, and completely privileged.

I opened the ice door latch and stepped outside into the snow that had formed a high, soft cushion. There were no other footprints, just mine. I went into the garden, walked up to the main drive, then to the door of the chapel. If it had been pure magic before, it was something more now — complete silence, complete privacy, complete peace. It was as though I were the only human being on another planet.

After that visit, I snuggled back into my bed, and fell into a restful, though short sleep.

In the morning, staff will wake you up with a hot drink of mountain berries. To set yourself up for the day, you can bake in the sauna before eating breakfast at the nearby inn. After the sauna, you are expected to go out and roll in the snow, and take my word for it, it's worth the madness.

While at the hotel, I decided to do my 'friendly Arctic' bit. "Chilly, isn't it," I politely mentioned to the lady at the reception desk.

17

"Depends on your viewpoint," she whispered back equally politely. "In these parts we like to think of it as rather cool." Her smile could have cracked ice. "Anyway, our polar sleeping bags will keep you as warm as toast." Another smile! More cracked ice!

Morning brought sunshine, and a balmy -4°.

"Comfortable night," she purred softly through her customary ice-cracker smile.

"Very comfortable," I said softly.

"You weren't cold were you," she whispered angelically. "Heeding the advice of the locals, you'll rarely feel the cold. Actually, there's really no such thing as cold weather, just bad clothing..."

"I'll pass the word around," I hissed over our goodbyes, my camera frozen, but my heart considerably thawed and soul uplifted.

The Ice Hotel had charmed me to the point of seduction. Sure, it's cooler than your average hotel. Spending the night in a freezer may not be everyone's cup of tea, but at least you never have to worry about an empty ice bucket. Or a heatstroke!

"Come again soon...," she purred sweetly as I was leaving. "Before we melt away... ."

# Opals And Nature

As first impressions went, Sandy was quite a bomb. Standing there by the runway, her hair and clothes blowing in the wind, she could have passed off as anyone except who she really was.

"Hi, I'm Sandy," she said as she offered her hand to me. "For the next couple of days you're in my charge, but don't worry, I'll look after you," she declared with a deadpan expression. "I've never lost guests. Well, almost never."

I hopped into Sandy's van for the drive into town, listening to her stories about life in the outback. A few things became clear as we got to know Sandy better. She liked to talk, liked people who listened to her, disliked people who didn't listen to her, drove well, had this peculiar sense of humour, and was an excellent guide.

What can one say about a town like Coober Pedy except that it's refreshingly different, has a name that sounds like an exotic animal, and from the air, resembles a children's playhouse with little structures neatly tucked between roads and huge patches of golden sand.

To say that Coober Pedy's not your normal, run-of-the-mill, conventional type of town is to put things extremely mildly. Consider the facts. In which other place in the world do 75 per cent of the locals actually live underground, not as a fad but because it's 'cool'. Literally so! Summer temperatures hover near the 50°-celsius mark. And then there's this amazing statistic about the locals. The town's total population of 4,500 comprises an incredible 47 nationalities.

As for the name, it does have a meaning. 'Coober Pedy' means 'white man in a hole', and the holes and the people living in them are there because it is the Australian outback's leading mining town and the opal capital of the world, mining 80 per cent of the world's opal.

Opal is the lifeblood here. The town was built and nurtured on opal, and flourishes on it both in terms of mining and tourism. Today, opal brings miners, traders, and buyers, and the romance of all this brings in the tourists, who also get to enjoy a taste of genuine rural Australian lifestyles and stunning landscapes. Which explains why I landed up here in the first place. 150 million years ago, the ocean covered this region. After the ocean receded, climatic changes lowered the underground water tables, and silica solutions were deposited in cavities and faults. Over millions of years, these solutions have formed into opal. And the story begins. Ever since the first opal was accidentally found here in 1915 by gold miners, the rush began. The boom-and-bust story saw the opal mining trade develop into a multi-million dollar industry in the 1960s and '70s, with Coober Pedy being the centre of things and developing into a modern mining town. With no topsoil, soaring temperatures, an annual rainfall of 175 mm, and water costing $5 per kilo litre, Coober Pedy has never been renowned for its lushness.

But then no one comes here for greenery. Neither the opal traders, nor the tourists.

Talking of tourists, if you see some bent over a heap of mud, rest assured they aren't praying or building sand castles.

They are indulging in the noble pursuit of 'knoodling'. The town's one and only physical pastime, knoodling involves running one's hands through the mud in search of opal. After all, what's the point in coming all this way and not trying your luck?

We saw them soon enough, and right in the heart of the town too. Scavenging for occasional, left-behind pieces, were dozens of excited 'diggers', their hands roughened, their clothes looking like they were stolen from the salvation army, and their spirits childishly high.

I did the dutiful thing. I joined in and knoodled. Having heard that most knoodlers cursed when they ended up not finding any opal, I did the dutiful thing again and cursed. Typical of me, I drew a blank. No opal, but some genuine scars on my hands. "It's there, lying about, but you rarely get to find any. But don't worry. At least it's something to tell the folks back home," Sandy said with an expansive smile.

Every town needs a legend. Coober Pedy has Yanni Athanasiadis (Sandy's boss) who came here as a young man from his native Greece to seek his fortune, and today owns and runs the Umoona Opal Mine, museum and underground complex, with an aboriginal interpretive centre, a made-to-order jewellery facility, and an underground self-catering camping. Yanni's always around, with interesting local gossip and plenty of opals to sell. "As you can imagine, things were tough when I first arrived here. Sure, we found opal but it all needed money, and money's hard to come by. Whatever I earned, I ploughed back into the business. But now I am sort of comfortable," Yanni said softly replenishing my glass with red wine, showing the sort of deftness that comes with practice and a healthy bank balance.

Apart from getting a taste of genuine Australian outback life, visitors get a first-hand look at the unique style of underground living in old mines now converted into comfortable homes. Of the three underground churches in town, the underground Catholic Church of St Peter and St Paul are particularly beautiful. There are also several other interesting places to drop in or 'under', like the underground Art Gallery, that features displays of aboriginal artefacts, or Dugout Motel, or 'Dusty Radio Station' run by children, or the Opal Cave Lookout with its splendid town views.

Not shopping for opal in Coober Pedy is like visiting Sydney and not seeing the Opera House. "Almost sinful," Yanni and Sandy proclaimed in a chorus. The town's shops stock and display more opal than anywhere else in the world, some offering opal-cutting demonstrations. With serious opal shopping done, there are also tribal art objects to pick up.

They have gone to town on tourism and it has paid off handsomely. For a place so small and remote, there are an amazing number of things to see and do, and you can choose from a variety of interesting packages. For $15 you can see 'Martin's Night Sky Presentation and Ghost Busters', a package that includes star-gazing out in the darkness of the 'Moon Plains Desert', and savour what turns out to be a very welcome complimentary glass of wine.

I just have to tell you about my local hotel. Cave service with a smile! Remember all those hotels that seem to go on and on skywards, packing over 50 storeys in their quest to dominate city skylines? Well, try this for something different. A hotel that's reached lofty heights without even getting off the ground! In fact, things move quite in the opposite direction. I got 'down' to the heart of the matter.

The award-winning Desert Cave Hotel in Coober Pedy is the world's only underground international hotel, and it is underground, burrowing deep into a hill, its rooms or 'dugouts', as they are called, actually being caves with thick uneven walls. Entering my room, I remember telling myself I had never ever encountered such complete darkness. I groped for the switch, put the light on, and literally stumbled onto the mini refrigerator so thoughtfully placed just by the side of the door.

This was one 'come-down' I didn't regret. Actually built above and below the ground, the hotel isn't just an architectural marvel but also reflects the true beauty of the Australian outback. Rather than lounging on spacious lawns, guests get to experience the rugged fun of dugout-style living.

Duly checked-in, a cup of coffee quickly downed, I was whisked away on a guided tour of the premises, my itinerary taking me alternately below and above ground level. Things looked quiet, but there was plenty happening, and plenty to see, and most of it underground. Within sandstone surrounds neatly wedged into solid rock formations, you can wander around underground and also view a superb pictorial mining display and a film with skillful sound back-ups, that reveal the dark and mysterious world, work, and lifestyle of the modern-day miner.

Awaiting anyone who cares to 'drop down', is an entire shopping arcade where you can pick up true Australian mementos in chic outlets like Decave, Opal World, and Opal Cutter at the Cave. Opal earrings and bracelets range between $50 and $500 upwards. I did my bit and bought a little bracelet, 'a real bargain for $70,' I was politely informed.

Soon it was time to quench that desert thirst and I trooped into what is the world's only underground bar that stocks anything and everything except non-alcoholic beers. Gin cocktails are recommended, and downing them at one go considered good frontier etiquette. Doubling up as an all-purpose, mixed-cuisine restaurant is the Crystal Café where food never seems to run out, and the staff never seems to go off duty. I relaxed in an atmosphere of continental *joie de vivre* and savoured the salad-of-the-day before exploring the buffet they had set out with the belief that there's no tomorrow. There is equally wholesome dining at Umberto's that boasts a formal setting but relaxed atmosphere, excellent *à la carte* food, and an elaborate wine list. Soft music wafts out of hidden speakers in the rock walls. I was one satisfied visitor. But then food always does clear away most of my blues.

Quietly suggestive, in architectural terms, is the foyer, which towers upward in a spectacle of glass and natural surrounds of rock and sandstone. In this rock-like citadel, you can enjoy facilities that include the luxury of a sauna, swimming pool, gym, and auditorium that also caters to group meetings.

'Rooms with a view' — of the total 50 rooms (average tariff $150), 19 are underground while the others are 'normal'. While the claustrophobic can live in a normal fashion and take in views of the little town, the adventurous can relax in their dugout-style rooms of natural sandstone and literally 'stare' at the solid walls.

My room resembled a vault, so solid were the walls and so complete the darkness when the door was shut. But the most overpowering feature was the silence. I felt far away from everyone and everything, completely shut off.

Having started the Desert Cave in 1988 as a family business, its owner Robert Coro has developed the hotel into a unique, award-winning institution. Opal apart, underground living and the outback are other major attractions of the region with its unique composition and great natural beauty. This also helps.

The fact that Desert Cave is the only underground large hotel complex in the world is certainly a huge boost to its status. Smug in the belief that opal — Coober Pedy's main attraction for tourists — will last for generations to come, promising good, prolonged business for the hotel, Coro nevertheless, refuses to sit back, and feels a constant need to innovate. "Nothing's rock-solid in business (no pun intended). One must constantly innovate to stay ahead."

I slept the sleep of the blessed.

The next day a beautiful world was waiting. Apart from everything else, it was an awakening of the soul. Less than an hour's drive from Coober Pedy, lies a huge world waiting to be discovered. Though often visited, it's still basically virgin territory, unspoilt, un-built, completely unblemished by man. This is an expanse of nature quite unrivalled anywhere in the world in terms of its vastness, harshness, and stark natural beauty.

A unique nature park of staggering geographical diversity, the Breakaways Reserve is a timeless land telling stories of timeless people. Located within the Arckaringa and Eromenya (Great Astesian) Basins, in one of the world's largest deserts, the Breakaways is a land apart. Spread across a vast sea of sand and rock, from the flat-topped mesas to the stormy Gibber Desert, there is stirring and stunning arid scenery, with remnants of countless ages providing a wealth of geological interest. The area is also rich in aboriginal history.

Baked by the sun for millions of years, with scanty rainfall, the region is parched beyond belief, with winds strong enough to blow humans away. The dryness and strong winds have resulted in a form of rock erosion that has carved up the mountains with sculpted precision, giving them distinct shapes and sizes, creating a moon-surface effect that is a feature of the landscape. A beautiful feature, I might add!

It was only a matter of time before Hollywood recognised the unique, pristine beauty of the Breakaways, appreciating it for what it is — one of the world's most awe-inspiring landmasses, almost tailor-made as a locale and setting for films of the 'great outdoors'! Over the years, the stunning beauty of the vast landscapes with the famed plateau-like outcrops of rock and soil of various colours and hues, has been the locale for several futuristic and science-fiction films like *Fire in the Stone*, *Priscilla, Queen of the Desert* and *Mad Max*.

Here, at the start of the 'Painted Desert', the world stands still. At no two points during the day does the desert bear the same image. The colours change literally by the hour, and the eyes play tricks as distances get distorted. It is pure and simple nature at its starkest, harshest and most beautiful. I was impressed. And humbled!

Doing the sunrise over Mount Despair is living life! It is an awakening of the senses and soul. Imagine standing in the predawn darkness on the rim of a cliff, 100 metres above the desert floor, purple black mesas below, before and behind you. Exactly above the centre of the largest one, you see Venus, the Morning Star, burning in a deep violet sky. Nothing moves. No wind, no sound, not even a whisper. There's only the cold. As the light begins to glow, almost reluctantly, on the eastern horizon, you see all around, an immense desert plain, flat as water — it is, in fact, the bed of an ancient inland sea. On and on it goes, a vast stretch without a break, without a building or any other sign of human habitation, 3,200 kilometres to the northeast until it reaches the Arafura Sea, between Australia and Papua New Guinea.

I noticed many things, but above all, I noticed the stillness. This is no place to be alone, certainly not at night. The silence is overpowering. As the light gathers, it is sublime and scary. When the low bars of cloud on the eastern horizon go from grey to molten gold, seconds before the sun's rim peers over the desert, it's the closest thing you can experience to being in outer space. Then, as the light floods the plain, stretching the horizons, things come to life. Birds begin to move: the black crow; the white cockatoo uttering dawn screams; the rainbow lorikeet, and the mighty wedge-tailed eagle, 'always there but rarely seen'. But if you try, you do see them, little black specks in a blue sky.

A new day, the tiniest little piece of eternity, has begun. The cycle of nature goes on without change. Everyone and everything around is well and truly dwarfed. And you feel an uplifting of the soul. That's really the only way I can describe it.

Roaming these vast stretches of barren land are red kangaroos; common wallaroos; euros (grey kangaroos); dingoes; and several reptiles, all with one thing in common. Over the centuries, they have all learned to adapt and survive in this harsh terrain, going without water for weeks on end.

The desert holds other attractions as well. There are conventional riches like gold and opal, and other riches like rock fossils. There are pristine views of the landscape and of the celestial world at night. There is total silence. There is peace. There is calm.

And yes, there is one other phenomena, this one man-made. Let me tell you about the Dog Fence. The longest fence ever built — over twice the length of the Great Wall of China — this 5,300 kilometres of wire and post fencing runs dead straight to the horizon in both directions. Meant to keep dingoes inside Northern Australia and out of South Australia so they won't massacre the sheep, the Dog Fence is a marvel of human endeavour for practical purposes, yet quite unsung, and almost unknown outside Australia.

It is definitely not to be missed, but make sure the wind doesn't blow your hat over the fence, as it has only one gate every 20 kilometres.

Two days had gone by. It was time to leave. Seeing us off at the airport, Sandy became nostalgic. "I know we're a bit out of the way, but do drop in again. And don't bother to bring a raincoat."

# Riviera Ruminations

The Carlton's revolving door turns, turns, turns and turns, cutting the opulent air into four equal parts. 'Folly, mystery, wonder, fascination.'

When I had first read this slogan some 25 years back, it had struck me as being weird, immodest, and not entirely belonging to what we perceive to be the 'real world', the world we live in. But back then, I didn't really know the region well. Once I did, there was nothing weird about such words and descriptions. In fact, they were about as apt as apt could be.

'Folly, mystery, wonder, fascination.' Indeed.

"After 40 years as a guide here, I feel this is the best way to describe this place," Pierre said almost apologetically, wiping his moustache. When I told him I agreed whole-heartedly, he smiled and wiped his moustache again. "It's that kind of place, you know," he said softly.

Strange and bizarre as these words may sound, they do justice to the region's character, its fortunes, its legends, and the famous personalities who have passed through this famous door of this famous hotel. Literary luminaries, mega stars, heads of government, the richest of the rich, and the most glamorous, all have been here, stayed and played here, and become part of local legends that have contributed to the hype.

The Côte d'Azur, as the French Riviera's known, has never been embarrassed by its fame. France's second most popular tourist destination after Paris, it is the world's most upscale playground, hangout of the high priests of fame and glamour, and the haunt of international movers and shakers. It is haloed holiday turf, fun-land, paradise, and fashion-centre all rolled into one. The land of *joie de vivre!* But instead of bumping into Hollywood stars at every corner and turn, as I had imagined, I ran into a gaggle of well-heeled Indian tourists, out 'doing' the Riviera.

A little pocket in the south of France, the region's been twice blessed by nature. You can explore a 116 kilometres coastline — a third of it long, pebbly or sandy beaches; visit the Iles de Lerins — Sainte Marguerite and Sainte Honorat; or the famous headlands of Cap Martin, Cap Ferrat, Cap d'Antibes, and the Pointe Croisette in Cannes. Or just 'star-gaze'. Yes, do just that if stars are around.

Harmony with nature compliments the Riviera's larger-than-life image. Azur Green unfolds with open hills, dense forests, and leisurely walks along fragrant hill trails; Azur White includes skiing in the mountains; Azur Rose includes Roman ruins, little hilltop villages, and picturesque markets, and Azur Blue comprises the sea, sky, lakes, sailing and swimming.

Beautiful lakes at Allos — Lac Nègre and Lac Vert; deep, dark, and majestic forests at Boreon and Turini; some 150 historical villages, and over 300 annual sunny days, collectively make it nature's unquestioned paradise. And so came the world's rich and famous.

Nice! The name tastes like holidays, and why shouldn't it? Morning time, and the sunshine was a golden blessing, lighting up the snowy Alpine peaks at one end of the town, and the deep blue Mediterranean at the other. Legend has it that the Côte d'Azur's capital emerged from the mists of time, with the Greeks being the first settlers to appreciate the region and establish a trading centre known as the Nikaia. They were followed by the Romans, who built Cemenelum, a rival to Nikaia.

Though buffeted by a turbulent history, the town grew in harmony with its beautiful surroundings and became the rendezvous of celebrities from all over France and also from England, Belgium, Italy, Russia, and Spain, all of who savoured its 'sweet way of life'.

I had managed the impossible. I had shaken Pierre off for a couple of hours and was determined to make the most of it. I set out to do what everyone does here. Something that's almost mandatory. Take a celebrated stroll along the Promenade des Anglais, the most famous sea-face boulevard in the world. Flanked on either side by the sea and opulent buildings, the garden-like promenade in high season reflects more glamour and glitter than all of Hollywood. You pass hotel after hotel gleaming in the sunlight, their white façades and golden balconies now part of local legend and folklore, symbols of a city forever basking in glory.

For me, the shining symbol is the Negresco, among the most celebrated of the Riviera's exalted hotels, shining like a glittering palace amidst the promenade's bright lights and festivities. A classified historical monument internationally renowned, the Negresco is a hotel that conjures up the style and luxury of the *Belle Epoque*, and of the elegant *savoir-vivre* that reflects the best of French courtesy.

My time alone was up and Pierre was waiting for me at our designated meeting point at the edge of the Promenade des Anglais. "You managed alone, I see," he said rather thoughtfully without wiping his moustache. I told him I had just about managed without his expert guidance, and off we went.

A less glitzy but enormously charming world unfolds in the Old Town, with its own rhythm and atmosphere. You can spend days soaking up the charms of the Cours Saleya which refuses to change with the times, and has clung on to its Greek character. Flower, fruit, and vegetable markets proliferate, lending the air a strong, sweet fragrance. Time means nothing as you walk along the narrow streets, buy souvenirs, sample food, and guzzle wine at little taverns whose tables spill out on to the pavements. "It's Nice too," Pierre tells me softly as we perch ourselves on the roof of a building for a panoramic view of the area.

Entertainment and elegance! That's Nice for you. With its colour, fun and pageantry, floats which are local symbols of pride and joy, and its inimitable flower battle which is the ultimate cultural extravaganza, the carnival is the highlight. But there is plenty else going on throughout the year, and you don't have to strain much to see it.

Come evening, and Nice glitters. This is when champagne corks hit the ceiling, and trays full of smoked salmon line elegant table corners. To imbibe the mood, stop by at any of the grand old hotels that have opulence etched across their interiors. The mood follows you to the famed Opera, or even to elegant coffee shops that await your late-night arrival.

Just get going! You can dance with the stars, be still and listen to the night breeze cleaving the palms, or take in a soul music session. There are nightclubs with a fairy tale setting, roulette and Baccarat at the casino, and horses to be backed at night at the hippodrome. And there's all that wonderful wine to be savoured.

31

From Nice to Cannes is a bit like leaving one oasis for another. Our half-hour drive took us past stretches of deep blue sea, low hills, and dozens of luxury villas with red tiled roofs and the proverbial swimming pools and striped deckchairs.

At first glance, Cannes resembles Nice, and though a bit smaller, radiates the same class. Dotting the harbour were hundreds of sailboats, their tall masts etched across the skyline. As I checked into the fabulous Hotel Martinez, the first people I met were part of a film crew. Well!

Glamour-wise, Cannes is globally unrivalled. In 1834, one Lord Brougham stumbled onto what was then a sleepy little Roman outpost, his brief halt starting a lifelong devotion to the lovely little coastal town that was to become the brightest, most photographed place in the world. A glittering parade of archdukes, princes, kings and consorts from all over Europe transformed the town into an enchanted domain studded with fabulous villas and palaces.

Those heady days! Princely palaces sprang up under the magical wand of architect Laurent Vianney; in the Villa Escarras, Baron Lycklama had his residence transformed into an Oriental palace for a single night's musical entertainment; the royal yacht *Britannia* often anchored in the bay; Jean-Gabriel Domergue painted Josephine Baker, and Bugattis and Rolls slid through dusk to the famous playgrounds of the night.

There were breathless times, like Rita Hayworth leaving Orson Welles and marrying Ali Khan because she 'couldn't live with a genius'. There were glittering times, with Grace Kelly and Cary Grant being on location with Alfred Hitchcock to shoot *To Catch a Thief*, and Elizabeth Taylor signing the visitor's book as Mrs Hilton, Mrs Todd, Mrs Eddie Fisher, and Mrs Burton. There were also tragic times, like Isadora Duncan, dancer of the veils, being tragically strangled to death by her own billowing scarf.

This legacy was the romantic pillar on which Cannes grew and glittered, and the legacy lives on.

'I'm in celebrity land,' I told myself as I took in the scene around me — from the myriad diamond necklaces and cufflinks that glinted in the lobby and restaurants of the fabulous Martinez Hotel, to the swanky boutiques with their top-end designer label merchandise, to the elegant cafés.

La Croisette is still one of the world's most famous promenades, and the old quarter of Le Sugvet still watches over the sun and star-struck city. Here, instead of the carnival, there's the annual, famous film festival that attracts literally the whole world of films.

I am in celebrity land!

Having dug my heels in rather easily in the glamorous whirlpools of Nice and Cannes, I suppose I had been lulled into believing that everyone and everything in the Cote d'Azur was larger than life. So it came as a bit of a surprise to learn that there are places here where the pace of life can be as slow as you want it to be.

The charming little town of Grasse showed me a different face of the Riviera. Another short drive, this time taking us away from the sea and into wooded hills, and we hit town. Grasse doesn't have the exalted credentials of Cannes or Nice, but it is the world headquarters of the multi-million-dollar perfume industry, and the home of the famous perfume house, Fragonard.

Established in 1783, Fragonard is among France's leading perfume manufacturers and raw materials suppliers. A conducted tour of the establishment gave me an insight into the intricacies of this carefully tended business. In the in-house museum, you see famous perfume bottles and boxes that tell the story of this trade. And the in-house boutique sells assorted perfumes at ex-factory prices. You can also take tips on aroma therapy, thanks to a special course whereby clients are provided some eight different fragrances with expert advice on the aromas best suited for their health and disposition.

Grasse lives, breathes and thrives on perfumes and their exotic accessories, attracting tourists and shoppers to its peaceful environment, soft landscape, and mellow climate. A whiff, and it was time to leave.

Our next stop was snootily fashionable even by the Riviera's standards. And believe me, that's saying a lot. Graham Greene described it as "the only town on the Riviera to have so well preserved its soul".

Blending the colours and accent of Provence with the extravagance of the French Riviera, the two-faceted Antibes Juan-les-Pins offers more diversity and contrast in appeal than any other town in the world. The result! A double bonus with each day seemingly twice as long.

The hills and the sea hem it in. Its sea face is a bit like Miami's, but smaller, and the town itself is trendy, chic, and full of tourists the year round. There are sumptuous English-style parks and shimmering beaches. Some of the greatest artists have chosen to live here; the oldest European jazz festival originated here, and the town's ancient walls echo with the finest voices, past and present. It is a town for sailors and gardeners, devotees of Mozart and Ray Charles, connoisseurs of art and nightclubs, those who love the patina of old stones, and those who marvel at the antics of dolphins.

I unearthed several reasons to be charmed by the town. Flowers and gardens; strolls through narrow streets brimming with flowers; theme restaurants; ambience; fragrances of the markets; splendid museums; azure skies and endless nights that are an invitation to prolong the daytime fun. In summer, the streets are on show until the wee hours of the morning, and the shops seem to be kept by night owls.

Juan-les-Pins has one of France's longest coastlines — altogether 25 kilometres of coast with a series of beaches and five harbours: Port Gallice, Port du Crouton, Port de l'Olivette, Port de la Salis, and Port Vauban — the world's second largest and Europe's largest yachting harbour.

From the billionaires' wharf in Port Vauban, the world's finest luxury vessels contemplate the 'bevelled austerity' of Fort Carré. In front of the harbour, where Guy de Maupassant often dropped anchor on his *Bel Ami*, stands the prestigious Chantier Naval Opera.

We drove around. And each passing second convinced me that this was arguably the most upscale part of this most upscale region.

Accelerated insouciance — this is Juan-les-Pins' characteristic trait of life, its cosmopolitan clientele drawn by a unique atmosphere that has no equivalent in the world.

Concealed in greenery, Port Gallice, Antibes' second port, embraces the Bay of Juan-les-Pins, whose exciting nightlife and luxury hotels have given the resort a worldwide reputation as the international capital of a certain 'fury of living'. Overlooking the harbour, Château de Juan-les-Pins was the Riviera home of Rudolf Valentino, the world's Latin lover. Villa La Vigie, the 'Art Deco' style Le Provençal — one of Europe's most elegant hotels — and Le Juana, which greeted among other celebrities, Ella Fitzgerald, remain flagship hotels. I couldn't see them all, and maybe that was a blessing in disguise.

Right next to the centuries-old pine trees in La Pinède, the legendary beaches stretch their hot sand along the Bay of Juan-les-Pins. This is where water-skiing was born. For those who enjoy dallying with lady luck, the Eden Beach Casino provides tempting pleasures at an hour when evening dresses and tuxedos are *de rigueur*... .

Cap d'Antibes! What can I say! Starting from the little harbour of La Salis, the Calvary Trail leads to La Garoupe sanctuary that has attracted pilgrims since time immemorial. Close by, the little shrine of Notre-Dame des Amoureux offers its protection to lovers. La Garoupe lighthouse is one of the region's most powerful, its 103 marble steps to the top paving the way to one of the world's most beautiful 360° panoramas.

At the foot of the hill, the Bay of La Garoupe with its beautiful beaches stretches nonchalantly. The beach leads on to the privileged area known as the Billionaires Bay, with its sumptuous villas with their luxuriant gardens. A park with Mediterranean trees surrounds Tour du Graillon which houses the Musée Napoléonien, the last trace of a military battery built by the young General Bonaparte.

Celebrities like Charles de Gaulle, Ernest Hemingway, Anatole France, Camille Flammarion, Douglas Fairbanks, Mary Pickford, Rita Hayworth, and Marlene Dietrich have been hosted by Hôtel du Cap-Eden Roc, among the world's most luxurious.

A 'mood' resort, I told myself as we were leaving.

Shortly thereafter, I said goodbye to Pierre and went forth on my own.

My last Riviera stopover was a real delight. On the boundary of the French Riviera and the Ligurian Alps, the Seigniory of Menton first appeared in the 13th century. Purchased by Charles Grimaldi, Lord of Monaco, in 1346, the city chose to become French in 1860.

"Welcome to the hidden Riviera, or secret Riviera, if you like," Michel Imbert, my scholarly local guide, declared grandly. "Plants and fruit have made Menton internationally famous. We're truly blessed." His enthusiasm was explained by the fact that he had a special passion for botany.

From the sweetness of an orange to the sourness of a lemon, this is clearly citrus fruit country. Legend has it that Eve chose this site to plant a lemon stolen from the Garden of Eden.

The city has warded off winter forever, boasting 316 annual cloudless days and a microclimate that has spawned and sustained gardens that preserve such rare trees as the legendary Sophora Toromiro from Easter Island, and some 40 other unique species not found elsewhere. The climate is one major reason for the town's fame, the others being its quietness and quality of lemons. "Yes, lemons," Michel declared with schoolboyish fervour.

Everywhere, gardens pay their court to the town. From the Val Rahmeh botanical garden of exotic plants, founded in 1905 by Lord Radcliffe — now part of the National Museum of Natural History — we got what are arguably the best views in the Riviera. As Michel diligently explained the salient features of each fig, leaf and root, it became obvious how generous the local climate had been to vegetation here, particularly of the citrus variety.

The Villa Maria Serena with its Napoleon II architecture and tropical plants turned out to be another delight, and I let Michel do his explaining and head-nodding. At Les Colombières, Mediterranean trees fill the air with their fragrance among statues and arrangements created by Ferdinand Bac. At Fontana Rosa, Blasco Ibanez's home, plants and the writer's busts recount the breadth of his imagination. At Parc du Pian, terraces and olive trees personify the nearby hinterland's permanence of landscape. And La Serre de la Madone, a listed historic building, offers a garden-museum with terraces, pergolas, grottoes and ponds imagined by Lawrence Johnston. Michel's joy seemed well founded. I had been blown off my feet by nature's gentlest facets.

Firmly ensconced among France's 120 Cities of Art and History, thanks to its rich heritage, Menton bears the stamp of prestigious builders: Tersling, Charles Garnier, Abel Glena, Alfred Marsang, Adrien Rey, Rives. It is quite a list. The memory of great names in history and literature — Katherine Mansfield, Robert Louis Stevenson, Guy de Maupassant, Gustave Flaubert, Queen Victoria, and Blasco Ibanez — still dwells in the fragrances from the gardens and the intimacy of the stones of fine homes and hotels that make Menton the showcase for the various architectural styles that fashioned the secret Riviera.

Sporting houses painted in pastel shades, narrow streets that look down on the Mediterranean, giving way to the sea face with boats lining the quays — the Old Quarter turned out to be a real delight. Just beyond lies Italy. We strolled through history, past little houses and glazed tile-covered church towers, designed by Stephen Liegeard who invented the very concept of the French Riviera. A brief stop at the Saint-Michel Church — the square offers a remarkable example of Baroque art — another at the Palais Carnoles, a listed historic building now housing a museum, and we ended up at the sea face with its famous landmark — the former bastion (1636), today a museum dedicated to Captain Jacques-Yves Cousteau and his marine exploits.

"People who come here are those who want quality of life. Millionaires seeking quiet and privacy. Things here are solid. People find things to see and do," Luc Lanlo, the town's suave deputy mayor said to us over lunch. He then personally led us to the Marriage Room, a town feature. Everything shown was painted — murals on the ceiling and walls, and all scenes with a theme. "Only marriages held here for Menton residents are recognised by government," Lanlo declared seriously. Fair enough.

A bit like at Nice, the beach here is pebbly, and has a sharp crescent shape with smart shops, boutiques, and restaurants lining the road. That evening, the wind turned icy, but normally the climate ensures that restaurants spill their tables out onto the boulevard even in winter. We settled down at l'Exocet, just one of the restaurants serving up the wonders of the sea that day.

Amidst nature and serenity, Menton has a packed and lively festive calendar. February–March features the Lemon Festival, with floats covered with hundreds of tons of citrus fruit brightening up the city. June is the month of gardens, and also features the Mediterranean Championship of purebred Arabian horses that brings together the elite of this aristocratic breed. July sees the streets come alive as theatres on Place des Fours and the musical evenings at L'Annonciade await their audiences. August features the Music Festival. September sees the city paying tribute to its plant heritage through the Mediterranean Garden Festival. October is devoted to a truly unique event: the Political and Historical Book Fair, followed in November by a meeting about the Encounter of Man's Origin. December sees the local French Chamber Opera offering original creations. The year's timetable ends with Christmas events that provide a fortnight's chance to admire giant flower patterns.

There are also water sports like diving, water skiing, windsurfing, and sailing. And the nearby mountains create a situation whereby you can enjoy the pleasures of the sea and the joys of Alpine sports like downhill racing, paragliding, mountain biking, and hiking on the same day.

If all this is too much, just walk to the cicada's song among fragrant eucalyptus trees, like I did.

The hidden Riviera! You have got to figure this one out for yourself.

Now that I had seen and done it all, it becomes crystal clear to me why the French Riviera is the world's foremost holiday playground. The fact is that everything here is hyped up, toned up, and with a larger-than-life quality and glitzy image. Trendy Nice and Cannes with their glittering hotels; Monte Carlo with its upscale casinos; ultra-fashionable Juan-les-Pins, and quietly charming Grasse are all internationally famous resorts that have combined to make the area hallowed turf.

Assets abound. The seaports, docks and beaches make it a mariner's paradise with some 27 ports, 24 yachting and boating clubs, over 50,000 boats, and 14,000 berths. While older ports like Cannes, Monaco and Menton exude old-world charm, ports like Antibes are ultra-modern and famous for pleasure-yachting.

Cannes, Nice, and Monaco offer numerous theatres, operas, ballets, dozens of museums, hundreds of artistic extravaganzas, and the costliest and snootiest casinos in Europe. The Fine Arts Museum in Nice exhibits the works of Jules Cheret, creator of modern poster art, besides paintings by Hubert Robert, Vanloo, and Fragonard. The Acropolis in Nice is a state-of-the-art tourism, art and convention centre that hosts some 300,000 convention days annually, with a capacity for over 4,500 delegates.

Gastronomy has been stretched to its finest limits. Nice has the maximum 3-Star restaurants per square kilometre in Europe. Some local recipes like Wild Beet Tart; Pissaladière (an hors d'oeuvre); Pan Bagnat; Ratatouille; Secca, and Tripes are world-famous, and along with Fish Soup, Ravioli, Dumplings, and Stuffed Vegetables, ensure hearty dining. Of the large variety of wines, Ballet's are the region's toast, having been classified as guaranteed vintage in 1941.

'Chic' is the only word to describe the Riviera's shopping outlets. Shining symbols of haute couture are abundant in Nice, Cannes, and Monaco, with top labels like Pierre Cardin, Lanvin, Chanel, Hermès, and Yves Saint-Laurent, radiating from famous boulevards and promenades like La Croisette and Promenade des Anglais. The other end of the spectrum is the little corner-shop and the popular fresh produce and flower markets.

The French Riviera has a larger-than-life image. Yet amidst all the razzle-dazzle of celebrities, the region is in harmony with nature.

'Folly, mystery, wonder, fascination.' Why is there a familiar ring to these words…?

# Lost in Africa

Remember the Africa of the great safari era, when blazing sunsets melted into lantern-lit romance, and service was an effortless whisper?

I do. I remember it all very well and would love to tell you why. And to motivate you to see for yourself what it is all about. And to tell you that in case you haven't done it yet, the time to do it is now!

Southern African safaris provide an experience to be cherished. And we were in the thick of it all. All the magic of the Great African Bush comes alive in Eastern Transvaal, recognised as prime game country with some of the greatest diversities of wildlife in Africa. And we had started at the right place. Kruger National Park, South Africa's flagship conservation area and among the world's best game parks, offers exceptional game-viewing, with exotic celebrities — both animals and human.

"For them sort of creature comforts, you should've stayed back with the softies in Joberg," Sam, the 'son of the bush' allowed himself a rare smile as we scampered back into our four-wheel drive. In these parts, what Sam said, you did. Simple!

It is a scene firmly etched in my mind. The sun was a huge orange ball, sinking slowly, turning the bush a soft golden brown, then changing its shades literally by the minute. Slowly, almost reluctantly, darkness set in. With the fading sunlight, the jungle comes dramatically alive, for this is when the predators hunt, the big cats stalk their prey, and scavengers skulk up to fresh kills. The daily drama of the jungle had begun. And another chapter added to a great African legend.

We had watched all this from our four-wheel drive, deep in the heart of Kruger National Park. The tone had been set earlier when we were just short of Paul Kruger Gate, one of seven gates leading into the park, on the first leg of our Southern African safari.

We had watched the terrain change from flatland to low hills, then to steadily thickening bush. Afternoon had come and gone. Excitement ran high! We were running late, resigned to the fact that we had violated park regulations that stated that one be back in camp by 6 p.m. But the sunset had disoriented us, and it was way past the hour when we arrived at Skukuza Camp where we had bedded down. The sprawling, self-contained camp features shops, restaurants, bars, and museums.

The mission of the national parks is to "establish a system representative of the country's important and unique features, and to conserve and manage them so that they will be preserved for all time in their natural state for the benefit and inspiration of the present and future generations of South Africans, and the sustainable economic benefits of the region and its people."

Kruger fulfils this principle to the hilt, and also provides a rare wildlife experience to tourists from the world over. Established in 1889 to protect the wildlife of the South African Lowveld, the park is unrivalled in the density of its life forms, and a world-leader in advanced environment management techniques and policies. It is also among South Africa's most popular tourist centres.

20,00,000 hectares of surface area means we are talking big. Really big! There comes a time when statistics mean nothing. You have to be there to realise what 'big' really means. A drive along all the designated roads and tracks covers some 10,000 kilometres, with a headcount of 100,000 animals, making it amongst the world's most densely populated wildlife sanctuaries. The vivid beauty and fury of nature are on display through the year. The park is home to a mind-boggling number and variety of species that include some 49 different types of fish, 34 species of amphibians, 114 types of reptiles, 507 bird species, and 147 mammal types that include the highly sought-after 'Big 5'. And there are some 336 different types of trees.

The next day, excitement found us at the camp itself, right at our doorstep, with the early morning stillness dramatically shattered by the roar of lions that had camped literally at the fence. A day before, they had decided to move in our direction. This unexpected bonus of seven magnificent cats — lions are highly territorial and don't move around too much — brought the smiles out and meant it was one very happy bunch of tourists that converged for breakfast that morning. After all, this was a wake-up call not encountered every day. I have never stopped wondering at the amazing effect animal sightings and bush environment can have on humans. There were smiles all around, more small talk, even some back-slapping.

We set out again, this time headed in a different direction. An hour's drive and we were on a different terrain — thick bush giving way to sparse vegetation with open flatlands. "Cheetah country! It's still too early in the day for them, but they'll be prowling around a bit later. They are the first cats to hunt in the evenings cause their eyesight isn't good," Sam chipped in. The sun had taken over, but the bush was alive. Dispersing a herd of zebra, we headed north, to "see if we can quietly hone in on them lions".

'Lions to the left of us, lions to the right of us... .' Well, not quite. But we did hone in on the magnificent cats. And on a herd of not-so-friendly elephants at a waterhole. And on several indifferent herds of impala. It was an embarrassment of riches, in wildlife terms.

The game drives were everything they were meant to be. The country was diverse and beautiful in its starkness, and we slowly began to see and understand the immensity of nature and wildlife. There was this leopard saga, elephant saga, and a few others worth remembering.

As we drove north, the terrain gradually changed. Thick bush predominantly acacia, gave way to sparser vegetation with open flatlands dotted with large patches of grass. Once again we were in cheetah country but the elusive cat remained just that. Elusive!

Anything but elusive, however, was a herd of elephants that we literally stumbled upon. There they were, magnificent specimens crossing the road, blocking the traffic, and making cameras click as if there were no tomorrow. We were late back in camp again, but with a different excuse this time.

Kruger belongs to the very top drawer of nature experiences. The park provides a wide variety of thrills and visual delights. The natural beauty of the terrain and the abundance of wildlife combine to give it its cutting edge. Herds of impala, sometimes a hundred strong, grazing along the roads are most commonly sighted, along with smaller herds of kudu, wildebeest and springbok. Normally away from the roads, one sees elephants feeding. In the mopane grass lurk lions and cheetahs, often a swishing tail being their only giveaway.

Enhancing the experience is the park's status as an important nature reserve, and a classic example of 'total conservation'. It shows to good effect, man's interaction with the Lowveld environment over many centuries — from bushman rock paintings to majestic archeological sites like Masorini and Thulamela. These treasures represent the persons, cultures, and events that shaped the history of the park, and are conserved along with other natural assets. The extensive wildlife one sees today is a tribute to total conservation.

Traversing large tracts of this outstanding wilderness area brought home the stark beauty of nature. You encounter innumerable vivid, famed images associated with the bush, which stay etched in your mind on visiting this outstanding game reserve. Among them, an African sunset stands out as an experience not easily forgotten.

Kruger done, we embarked on the second leg of our safari. For luxury in the bush, Mala Mala and Sabi Sabi, arguably the world's two most celebrated private game reserves, are quite unrivalled. The fact is that they are quite exceptional. Bordering on Kruger, in fact feeding off it, the reserves indulge and pamper guests, who include international celebrities, all here to savour a deluxe African bush experience.

A quick check-in (interrupted only by Sam meeting up with his cronies), and we were 'ready to roll' again. It's that sort of drill at the camp.

Take game viewing of some 200 animal species including the 'Big 5' — elephant, Cape buffalo, black rhino, lion and leopard — throw in luxury lodging, and champagne welcomes, and you have the ultimate top-end game lodge experience, real jungle chic. It is about safaris in four-wheel drives with trained rangers, sundowners in the bush, and seven-course meals with specialities of the African kitchen — Venison Steaks to name just one.

Dinners are *boma* style so it's meals under the stars. This is the African Bush at its most luxurious, and we were fortunate enough to share in its bounties.

You are in the hands of rangers who host you in camp and entertain you in the bush with their knowledge of the wild. With the famed Shangaan trackers in tow, they accompany the game drives in open Range Rovers custom-made for such reserves with split-level seating for clear views, rambling on about the myriad delights of the African bush. They also double up as 'bush barmen'.

Just a few hours back, Mala Mala was just an exotic name. Owned by the Rattray family for over 40 years, it is part of the Rattray Reserves. Straddling one side of the giant Kruger National Park, Mala Mala Game Reserve offers rare moments of nature and fine game viewing. Also straddling the innocuous looking but perennial Sand River, the 18,000-hectare reserve comprises a variety of habitat types like dense riverine forest, acacia-combretum bushveld, open grassland, and rocky outcrop, each supporting different plant and animal communities. Throw in upscale facilities and dining, and you have the ultimate game lodge. That's Mala Mala for you.

The game drive organised for us turned out to be as exciting as it could get. Ten minutes can be a long time if you are following a leopard with a spotlight, but she had ignored us, intent only on her hunt. With a young cub to tend to, she was desperately hungry, and had spotted a herd of impala right there in front of her. For a moment, she disappeared, then, in a flash she sprang up and brought down a small impala, its neck held in a vice-like grip. The stricken animal kicked about frantically, then feebly, until finally, there was just the occasional twitch. The law of the jungle had prevailed.

Seeing a leopard make a kill from just 15 metres away isn't your common game-drive experience and all of us knew we had shared in a rare moment of nature — the sort that comes once in a lifetime if you are lucky! It was cruel and so desperately one-sided, but that's nature for you and nature dictates its own terms.

"Everyone goes on and on about nature's bounties. I find that irritating. The fact is that nature offers bounties, but with several pre-conditions. Nature offers a way of life, and it's nothing at all like what we want it to be. It wasn't meant to be." Coming from Sam, this was almost like a jungle sermon, but he obviously knew what he was talking about.

Our three-hour drive had yielded other dividends. We had seen several elephants, hundreds of impala, and a couple of lions nearly making a meal out of an errant buck that had almost walked right into them. And all this amidst foliage that ranged from barren to lush.

With so many animal species, the game viewing is superb, the elusive cheetah, wild dog, and an abundance of antelope being added assets. Unlike most private game parks, here there's no fencing, with the 'openness' concept successfully revolving around shared borders with Kruger National Park. The animals roam freely from park to park, from waterhole to waterhole.

Set in an enclosed area, the main camp is the last word in jungle luxury, and considered the world's best-organised and best laid-out safari lodge. The ochre complex offers deluxe accommodation with air-conditioning, closets, tiled bathrooms, and 'bush furniture'. Embellishing the main lounge are all the trappings of the African bush.

"This is where we all meet after drives and have a few drinks and tell a few lies," Chris, the lodge's ranger told us.

The *boma* dinner, a tradition here for 70 years, was everything one could desire. We sat around the log fire under a canopy of stars, mulled over colourful cocktails, talked and laughed, and savoured the African kitchen's fabled delights. With its choice of venison dishes, impala steaks, and warthog kebabs, the dinner was as special an affair as it was meant to be.

Mala Mala has had no dearth of publicity, but perhaps nothing showcases the reserve's beauty better than the National Geographic production, *Beauty and the Beast — A Leopard's Story*, completed after three years of location shooting here, with scenes like a leopard drinking out of a swimming pool, that have now become legendary.

Another day, another delight!

"Hello there. I'm Becker, yes Becker as of 'Boris fame' and I'm going to take you in hand while you're here. There are three ground rules. Please don't feed the monkeys, don't wander around on your own beyond the compound, and last but certainly not the least, have fun!"

All this had come with a deadpan expression on Becker's face as we had arrived at the camp, the short journey across the bushveld in the customs-made Land Rover having given us a 'feel' of the place. We were in Sabi Sabi Game Reserve that nestles on the fringes of Kruger National Park, lying within the renowned 60,000-hectare Sabi Sand Wildtuin.

A quick check-in and visit to our chalet, and we were out on our first game-drive.

"It's best to get out there before the sun takes over," Becker had said, with his customary deadpan expression. Our drive was taking us to the very heart of this wilderness area that has found fame and recognition among the world's wildlife enthusiasts fraternity. The sun had taken over, but the bush was alive. Dispersing two herds of impala, we headed south, to "sort of creep up on this pride of lions that's made this area their home". So for the second time in three days, we got up-close and personal with lions.

In fact, we drove straight into them, a staggering 13 cats together. Becker crept up to within 15 metres of them, turned the vehicle around, and killed the ignition. "Just in case we need to exit in a hurry," he said reassuringly. They saw us but didn't stare. We did. As always — well, it has happened so often to me in different locales around the world — I found myself in the rather peculiar situation of being seated closest to them, right there in the back of the vehicle. And I wasn't too excited about the fact that a big male had got up and was slowly flanking us. 'Lions to the left of us, lions to the right of us... .' I tried my brave, funny bit, then frantically tried to get Becker's attention. Instead, I got the lion's. He stopped in mid-step and stared balefully at me. Suddenly it wasn't that funny or exotic any more, and I can swear it must have been pure sixth sense that made Becker suddenly start the engine and slowly, ever so slowly, drive away. The big male followed us for a while and then lost interest. No one else seemed unduly alarmed, but then they weren't in the firing line.

I'll never really know if this was part of the script or we'd had a lucky escape, but it had been a real and telling bush experience. In comparison, the rest of the game drive was a summer picnic. Scattering more impala herds — we'd had plenty of practice, remember — we arrived at the serene and beautiful but deadly Sabi River, home to crocodiles and hippos.

Two more hours in the bush and several sightings later, we arrived at the lodge for that most important of all wilderness activities: eating. The buffet-style lunch was announced by the blaring of a kudu horn, and it was all one could desire, with the salads fresh, the jacket potatoes 'hot' as hell, and the meats soft and succulent. Dessert was plum pudding, washed down with filter coffee from 'somewhere in Africa'.

Our morning encounter with the lion fresh on our minds, we sat back to enjoy the afternoon game drive. This was all about breathtaking landscapes, numerous animal sightings, and sundowners in the bush. Back at the lodge it was customary barbecue time. And tomorrow was another day.

Early morning! We woke to the smell of freshly brewed coffee. Now we were seasoned safari travellers, and the day promised much excitement. All this justified a huge breakfast crammed in, and we were back on the game drive on another dusty track. The sun rose from behind giant acacia and the forest came to life. The sightings were exceptional. And the stop for a quick coffee had been a pleasantly rejuvenating experience.

Out there in the African bush, it's the good life and no mistake. As dawn lightens the horizon, a knock on your door awakens you to a new bushveld day. After coffee and snacks on the safari patio, your personal ranger escorts you on a game drive in a four-wheel drive open Land Rover. Evening drives feature the luxury of enjoying a sundowner while watching the sun sink below the horizon. The safari now continues into the night, the tracker's spotlight scanning the bush.

True to form, Sabi Sabi presents so many images — the clear light of dawn, late afternoon's subtle pastel colours, fiery sunsets, the eerie laugh of the hyena in the dead of night. Every sound becomes relevant, every movement captures your full attention.

Our good ranger alighted, scouted around near the bank, and then drove on for a bit before stopping on a spur that gave us a good view of the river and its banks. Two dark spots bobbed in the water, then three, and then six! For their size and bulk, hippos can be amazingly quick and graceful when they choose to. And they look much bigger out of the water. "Folks get surprised when I tell them this, but the fact is that generally speaking, hippos don't mean any harm. The trick is not to come between them and water." Pearls of wisdom I filed away for future reference and display of my bush knowledge. Though Sabi Sabi prides itself on showing visitors the 'Big 5', we had seen just 'Big 1'. But then we had seen hippos, several wild boars, several zebras, and innumerable impalas.

A few hours later we were back in the wilds, this time describing a semi-circle not far from camp. More impalas, more wild boars, and then we literally stumbled onto a black rhino grazing in the mopane grass. Our, or rather my lion experience fresh in mind, Boris parked at a relatively safe 50 metres away from the brute, for that's what it was — a mass of hide and muscle weighing a tonne. "Mind you, if he really wants to shake us up, he can," our good ranger told us obligingly, with a pointed look at me.

But the rhino didn't 'shake us up' and the next two hours were among the most pleasant I can remember as we skirted the river, joked about who among us would "dive in to count the crocodiles", and drove slowly through ever-changing landscapes. The serene looking but deadly Sabi River teems with resident crocodiles and hippos that don't like human intrusion — which is precisely why humans love to hang around.

Back at camp, it was all bonhomie, with our group members actually smiling at one another, once again bringing home to me the amazing effect animal sightings and the bush environment can have on humans.

In between game drives, you can admire the varied bird life from hides overlooking waterholes or built into tall sycamore fig trees along the river's banks. The more energetic can opt for a walking trail.

When it was time to leave, I delved into reflection. It had been a week of jungle bliss. The real thing! We had seen it all. A cheetah making a futile chase, the big cats hunting deer, elephants closing flanks to protect their young, and as for your's truly, even been sort of charged by a lion. Everywhere, as always, the law of the jungle had prevailed. As it should!

Here, in the thick of the African bush, far from our familiar bearings, it became crystal clear to me why wildlife viewing and the jungle experience is such a big deal in Southern Africa.

It's a sublime experience. Any takers?

# Waltzing Through Salzburg

The hills are no longer alive with the 'sound of music', but things are buzzing all right!

Not that you notice it right away. At first glance, everything looks the way you would have imagined it here — quiet, relaxed, tranquil, almost sleepy in a dignified sort of way.

Quiet it certainly is, but there's a carnival-like atmosphere present, a legacy of the rich culture that's been the foundation on which the city has existed. Everything's been kind to the city, and it shows. Often called 'the heart in the heart of Europe', Salzburg's cultural richness includes being the birthplace of Mozart. All this apart, it is also a fine bit of urbanity set in a beautiful stretch of country.

There is history to the city, whose origins go back to AD 696, when Bishop Rupert of Worms received the desolate Roman city Juvavum as a gift from the Bavarian Duke Theodo. Progress and prosperity followed from the revenues from the Reichenhall salt mines, courtesy the Bavarian dukes. The money came in and the city grew in stature. Its wealth apart, Salzburg also owes its name to the salt revenues. The wealth enabled the Prince Archbishops to shape the city after their dreams, and it was quite a city the spiritual leaders created. So if you end up liking it, you know who deserves the credit.

Hemmed in on three sides by wooded hills, Salzburg's houses aren't aligned in straight rows, but ramble along the Salzach River in a disorderly fashion. Quaint narrow lanes curving around stately sacred buildings, flow into spacious squares, and then squeeze again between century-old burgher mansions. Apparently this is the kind of landscape artists craved for. Well, they got it, and it served the purpose.

Ask the 150,000-odd inhabitants who welcome some 20 million annual visitors who descend here to soak up the local culture and enjoy the superb scenery. Local festive celebrations include the famous Salzburg Festival that celebrates Mozart's works; the Summer Festival; Mozart Week; Salzburg Culture Days; the Easter Festival; Advent Singing; Pentecost Concerts; the Palace Concerts, and the Szene, a fine example of the traditional and modern co-existing in harmony. A theatre-dance festival, the Szene provides a dramatic counterpoint to the Salzburg Festival.

Culture, culture, culture! It doesn't take long to see that they really mean business. And why shouldn't they? There has been enough encouragement. Tina Turner used the whole city as a stage, and the Bee Gees and Herbert Gronemeyer turned the city into a natural backdrop for their open-air concerts. Mozart's city was animated enough to start with, but then came added and somewhat unexpected publicity, courtesy the highly acclaimed Oscar-winning *Sound of Music*, which was filmed here. The film's legacy lives on in the city, and they are keen to ensure you don't miss out on this great local asset. Special *Sound of Music* tours whisk you around to sites that featured in the film. If you want to do it all on your own, you just have to set out and you'll stumble upon some of the sites.

In the Mirabell Gardens, you find statue groups depicting Greek mythology, marble vases designed by Fischer von Erlach, a hedge theatre, a Baroque dwarf garden on the bastions, and a Baroque museum. It was at the fountains here that Maria sang "Confidence is me"!

With its Baroque monumental stairways with pictures by G.R. Donner, and large airy rooms, Mirabell Palace is a structure as grand as they come. The Marble Hall here is a popular concert and wedding venue and home of the mayor. Close by is Hotel Bristol where Christopher Plummer stayed for months during the film's shooting. The first few times around, I stayed at different hotels, but then found myself bedding down at the grand old hotel. It was worth the wait. Average in comfort levels, it makes up with its unique ambience.

All the recent good living and even better eating weighing on my mind, I was keen to stretch my legs. Braving a light but annoying drizzle, I ventured out to the 'fortress' to imbibe some invigorating fresh air.

For almost a thousand years Salzburg has nestled snugly in the shadow of the 11th-century Hohensalzburg Fortress, the largest completely preserved fortress in Central Europe. With its late Gothic Church of St George, castle courtyard, and museum, the hill-perched fortress dominates the region's skyline and offers excellent views. And Maria stayed at the monastery here!

The foray up the hill done and behind me, I settled down to mundane city sightseeing, of which there's more on offer than you would imagine at first glance. For a city this small, it packs in a sizeable collection of historic and interesting sites. Like the cathedral. Considered the most impressive Baroque building north of the Alps, the cathedral is a major city landmark, with a magnificent marble façade and two cathedral museums.

Charm and poise define the Old City, which is almost always crawling with tourists. Here, you walk and talk to old-timers, and stop by at little cafés for steaming coffee. You linger on Getreidegasse, the most famous street, and admire the wrought iron and gilded shop and firm signs with medieval graphics, and discover lovely inner courtyards and lanes. Soon you end up at No. 9, Mozart's birthplace, and family residence, a typical old Salzburg burgher's house with an in-built museum stocked with portraits, letters, and music of the famous composer.

With such high-flung sightseeing under my belt, it was appropriate to stop by at a local icon for a much-needed cup of coffee. Entering Hotel Sacher, I was immediately taken in by the simple elegance and distinct mood that have become hallmarks of the hotel and the city itself. A small reception foyer leads to a richly appointed, inviting lobby with thick carpeting and classy period furniture, which in turn leads to a dining area with a superb view of the Salzach River. With work matters weighing heavily on my shoulders, I couldn't afford the luxury of tasting their much-vaunted cuisine, but did find time to admire the lavish interiors and overall ambience of the establishment. And I also saw some of their guest rooms. Each room sports a different décor and colours, and each is a statement in style.

I have never been a good shopper, and never taken it too seriously either, which is precisely why I know so much about good shopping. And there's good shopping here. Unless you have sworn not to shop at all, you'll find yourself giving in. You'll be drawn to the glittering jewellers' shops and smart boutiques that stock traditional local costumes side-by-side with eccentric creations from several of Europe's fashion capitals. Tempting visitors are over 400 speciality shops on both sides of the Salzach, but if you are looking for something typical, buy some scented nosegays of dried flowers and spices. The fact that I bought two is a very positive sign. The fact that I haven't found a lady to give them to, is rather less so.

Salzburger nockerl anyone? Take my advice. Go for it. This fluffy souflette omelette is the type of food item just about anyone would like, so don't hold back. It occupies pride of place on the celebrated list of local delicacies that also includes the ever-popular Bauerng rostel; Wiener schnitzel; and palatschicken. These are the city's pride, along with the Salzburg Mozartkugel sweets that melt rather quickly in the mouth. Quick on the uptake, I attributed all these culinary delights as the reason for the city being home to the world-famous Salzburg Catering Institute.

While harping on this business of catering and cuisine, I would like to mention that nothing mirrors the local upscale cuisine heritage better than St Peter Stiftskeller, the oldest restaurant in Europe, churning out good food since AD 803, they tell me. My first visit happened to be in mid-morning, which meant they hadn't opened for the day. No guests around and total silence, but I did get to tour the premises, admire the interior furnishings, and learn about the venerated establishment's history. Owned and rented out by Benedict monks, the restaurant serves wine from their own vineyards. Mozart's favourite haunt, Stiftskeller stages Mozart dinner concerts that bring culture right up to your table.

Salzburg stands amidst those select few European destinations that offer visitors a bit of everything, throughout the year, and this explains its enduring popularity. Nature lovers have to journey out a mere ten minutes to be 'out there' in open grasslands, meadows and low hills. As for culture buffs, well, it is not just an important site but an essential stopover.

On my last day in the city, I was let in on a secret that I would love to have known on arrival. "Salzburg has its own special brand of pork sausages," my gracious lady guide in the long coat and short hair told me with a seriousness befitting a State function. "People don't really know this, but these sausages are quite different to those you get in other parts of Austria. They are fresh, tangy, and very tasty. Perhaps you'd like to try them," Serious-Face added.

Perhaps I would. In fact I did. I liked them a lot. Leaning over the little counter of a roadside snack-bar I had passed every day, I got to relish at least one of Salzburg's secrets. And its taste and tanginess have never left my memories.

# Ireland Rambling

"Life is too important to be taken seriously."

Only an Irishman (in this case it happens to be none less than the redoubtable Oscar Wilde) could have said this. And that's because the Irish like to live life the way it should be lived. With fun and laughter, and a few drinks tucked away on the side. They seem to appreciate the joy of living in the moment, and that's how it should be.

As for their country, well, no matter how you look at things, there's something 'different' about Ireland. Different in a very pleasant and refreshing sort of way, I may add. That's about it.

Be forewarned. If you are visiting, imagine the hardships you might face. It could be imbibing the taste of wild salmon and creamy Guinness at a seaside restaurant as the sun sets the bay alight, or glimpsing ancient round towers and crosses in the early morning light, or spending an evening of fun and frolic to the infectious rhythm of traditional music in a village pub?

My sojourn started off on a Saturday morning with a leisurely walk with Maeve Bracken from Bord Bia. We started off from Brooks Hotel in Drury Street, whose location just a couple of minutes walk from Grafton Street made it an ideal Dublin base.

A minute's walk got us into the elegant confines of Dunnes Stores at St Stephen's Green Shopping Centre, the flagship of the Irish-owned retail store chain whose slogan is 'Dunnes Stores' Better Value Beats Them All'. The huge store has an atrium-style glass ceiling and is strong on fashion, household goods and food items.

With its designer-label boutiques, cafés and pubs, Grafton Street is very much the centre of top-end shopping. Maeve took me into Sheridans' Cheesemongers, a traditional cheese, meat and wine outlet that has stuck to its roots. Butlers' Chocolate Café beckoned, but we skipped it. The ultra-exclusive Brown Thomas also beckoned. "It's Ireland's most exclusive chain. For real value, Avoca is the place," Maeve told me.

The weekly Temple Bar Farmers' Market brings the finest of Irish organic produce to Meeting House Square every Saturday — fresh Atlantic oysters, vegetables and fruit, crêpes, delicious farmhouse cheeses, chutneys and homemade breads, cakes and pastries as well as handmade chocolates. There was chicken and brie quiche for €6, and there were quality olives at the very well-known The Real Olive Co. It was an open-air gourmet's paradise!

Our walk in the Temple Bar area took us past several notable pubs like The Auld Dubliner and Oliver St John Gogarty. We walked along O'connell Street, past The Spire which is, well, unusual, and toured the Dublin Writers' Museum, before reaching Trinity College.

Trinity College, Ireland's oldest university, was founded in 1592 by Queen Elizabeth I on the site of an Augustinian monastery. Originally a Protestant college, it was not until the 1970s that Catholics joined in too. Among the many famous students to attend the college were playwrights

Oliver Goldsmith and Samuel Beckett, and political writer Edmund Burke. The major attractions are the Old Library and the *Book of Kells*, housed in the treasury. The *Book of Kells* is an ornately illustrated manuscript produced by Celtic monks around AD 800. It is one of the most lavishly illuminated books to survive from the Middle Ages and has been described as the zenith of Western calligraphy. It contains the four gospels of the Bible in Latin, decorated with numerous colourful illustrations.

Rewards for our walk included a delicious lunch at Cookes whose tables spilled over onto the pavement.

Sunday morning saw me on the highway with chauffeur Barry Hogan, on a four-day jaunt across Southeast Ireland. Exiting Dublin, we took the N7 for some good views of the countryside and meadows, entered County Kildare, home of horses, saw Curragh Race Course, 'Ireland's home of the classics', a sprawling mass of green, and stopped at Irish National Stud, a big stud farm and horse museum.

A short, pleasant stop at E.J. Morrissey, a classic pub, for a glass of Smithwicks, a dark-coloured local beer, and we drove on into County Kilkennery, and then into County Tipperary.

The Rock of Cashel loomed on the horizon. A spectacular group of medieval buildings set on an outcrop of limestone in Ireland's Golden Vale (an area so called because of its rich pastures and profitable dairy farming enterprises), the Rock of Cashel includes a 12th-century round tower, High Cross and Romanesque Chapel, a 13th-century Gothic cathedral; a 15th-century castle and the restored Hall of the Vicars Choral. Built with blocks of grey stone, the hill-perched site commands beautiful, panoramic views of the surrounding countryside.

Just as we were about to go exploring the site, of course, it started to rain and so we went for lunch instead and tucked in at Baileys of Cashel.

After this, we entered County Cork, the largest in Ireland, and eased ourselves into the truly wonderful delights of Ballymaloe House, Ireland's most famous country house hotel. Among the first country houses to open its doors to guests in 1964, Ballymaloe House squats gracefully on a 400-acre farm and its owner, Myrtle Allen, is internationally acclaimed for her culinary expertise.

Taking me on a personal, conducted tour of the premises, Myrtle told me about the establishment's history and of their desire to make their guests feel totally at home, and showed me some of the 32 guest rooms that sport different interior themes. The place is a dream. Festooned with creepers, the main building's façade — it was a former Norman castle — is impressive. The lobby is small but functional; the drawing room is elegance personified with a fireplace and period furniture; and the dining room is a fine mix of opulence and simplicity. In case you are shy, or crave privacy, they seat you in other, smaller rooms. There is also a 9-hole golf course, a swimming pool, and the Ballymaloe Shop that is tastefully stocked with Irish design, crafts, and kitchenware. It also has a café.

A night of silence, I woke up to the sight of ducks pecking away in the garden just outside my window, and it was time for the famed Irish artisan breakfast. And it was, quite simply, special. There was fruit salad (prunes, apricots, banana and reisens); Ballymaloe muesli; porridge made from Macroom stone-ground oatmeal; rashers; sausages; mushrooms and tomatoes; black and white pudding; eggs — boiled, poached, scrambled or fried, and fresh fish (pan-fried turbot).

Needless to say, Barry and I were both in good humour as we left the beautiful confines of Ballymaloe House to 'push on for work', which just happened to be a visit to Jameson's Old Midleton Whiskey Distillery. The Jameson Experience which includes exploring the Jameson Heritage Centre in Midleton, takes you back through time as you discover the history, and the magical taste of Irish Whiskey — Uisce Beatha (The Water of Life), the mystical spirit perfected by Irish monks in the 6th century AD.

The tour starts off with a film on John Jameson, then a walk through various parts of the old distillery including the courtyard; the grannary; the mill building; the water wheel; the steam engine; the mashing centre; the distillation centre which houses the world's largest copper still; the condenser; the cooperage; the warehouse where they store the whiskey; the whiskey-tasting area; and the shop which stocks everything an Irish whiskey drinker could possibly desire.

"Right, I need four volunteers," Karen, the tour guide informed our group of some 80-odd. "Who's ready for some whiskey? How about you, Sir?" she asked an elderly gentleman who instantly agreed. The group selected, we assembled in the café, and she sought me out. "You were always going to be part of the group," she told me with a huge smile as she ushered me to the selected table and seated me down. Each of us five 'tasters' had five small glasses of whiskey laid out before us — Jameson, Paddy, Power's Gold Label, Scotch, and American Whiskey. "Compare, smell and sip," said our good guide, and we did just that. In the interest of research, I finished it all to the last drop.

With all that whiskey in me, I could be forgiven a certain amount of light-headed humour as we left the distillery and drove to Cobh, headed for the Cobh Heritage Centre.

Situated on Ireland's southern shore, Cobh (or Queenstown as it was formerly known) is one of the world's finest natural harbours. Between 1848 and 1950, over 6 million adults and children emigrated from Ireland — over 2.5 million from Cobh, making it the single most important port of emigration in the country. Cobh was the last port of call for the ill-fated *Titanic*. Later, steamers and ocean liners continued carrying the Irish to new lives and new lands. Another ship, the *Lusitania*, sank off the coast in 1915 after being torpedoed by a German submarine.

Housed in a heritage building that was a former rail station, the Cobh Heritage Centre tells the story of Irish emigrants to the United States in search of a better life. And of the *Titanic*.

To get some 'blessings' before we left town, Barry took us to St Colman's Cathedral, a highly impressive structure with beautiful stained glass windows framing a giant organ.

Spiritually reassured, we stopped for a quick, business-like lunch at The Cornstore Wine Bar & Grill whose menu said they were 'Cooking up a storm 7 days a week'. And then we dropped in at Blarney Woollen Mills, which turned out to be quite a place. A big, bustling shopping centre complete with a café, it had the crowds out in force.

From here, it was a short drive to Cork, Ireland's second city with some 300,000 inhabitants.

The next morning presented a treat in the form of the English Market, Cork's famed food shopping area, which traces its origins back to England's King James I in 1610, hence its name. Among Cork's greatest assets, the market features an array of butchers selling traditional meats; organic fruit and vegetable shops selling at discounted prices; fishmongers; cheese mongers selling Irish, Italian and French cheeses; fresh bread stands; jams, marmalades; bakers and confectioners, and pots and pans. The market has some food products uniquely associated with Cork, such as drisheen (a pudding made from sheep's blood) and pig's crubeens (feet).

My companion for this unique site was food historian, writer, broadcaster and cook, Regina Sexton, and she really 'went to town' explaining the finer points of Irish food, and the special attributes of food shopping at the market.

We left Cork and backtracked to Ballymaloe Cookery School in Kinoith, Shanagarry, where I met its founder, Darina Allen, daughter-in-law of Myrtle Allen. Darina is Ireland's best-known cook. In addition to running the internationally renowned cookery school, organic farm and herb gardens, she's written a series of cookery books and presented televised cookery programmes in Ireland, Britain and North America My guided tour of the premises — kitchens; storerooms; demonstration halls; dining room; gardens, and greenhouses done, it was time to 'walk the talk' if you see what I mean.

"You're invited for lunch. Do join my table," Darina told us graciously, and so Barry and I found ourselves enjoying the day's cooking with the lady herself. With 58 cooks (the current number of resident students) out to do their best, the quality of the food was what you would expect in a top-end cookery school. "Delicious," we said in a chorus as we plied through the food, listening to Darina as she filled me in on the finer details of the 'grub'.

Come afternoon, and we left the cookery school, hit the road once again, and drove along the seaface to Youghal, where Sir Walter Raleigh introduced the potato to Ireland, and where much of *Moby Dick* was filmed.

We left County Cork and entered County Waterford, where our first stop happened to be another food outlet. Barron's Bakery in Cappoquin is a wonderful old-world bakery where the bread is traditionally baked each morning, since 1887. Esther Barron and her husband, Joe Prendergast, run the establishment which provides a 'real Irish bakery experience'. Today, the Barrons still use the same Scotch brick ovens to bake their bread and they are probably the last bakery in Ireland using these ovens which gives their bread its unique taste, flavour and crust. Joe showed me the original old ovens and told me the bread is proved slowly and naturally and the loaves are shaped by hand. It is a nice little café with tempting pastries lining the counter. You can also enjoy homemade meals, soup, sandwiches and local produce. We did. And left.

The evening shadows were lengthening when we checked in at the Tannery Restaurant & Townhouse Boutique Hotel in Dungarvan, and straight into the culinary world of Chef Paul Flynn. Discerning diners from all over Ireland (and beyond) make a beeline for Paul and Maire Flynn's stylish contemporary restaurant, which is in an old leather warehouse — the tannery theme is imaginatively echoed throughout the light, clean-lined interior, creating a sense of history that adds greatly to the atmosphere. While inspired to some extent by global trends and regional cooking, particularly the Mediterranean countries, menus are based mainly on local ingredients which Paul supports avidly and sources with care. The Tannery was voted Restaurant of the Year in 2004, and Paul has attained national fame.

I got the chance to interview Paul, learnt about his preference for "slow cooking which leads to good flavouring", and relished his culinary skills, thanks to the meal which he personally prepared for me.

It was early morning when we left Dungarvan and arrived at Waterford Glass Factory — home of Waterford crystal, in Kilbarry, Waterford, to see the world's finest crystal with exquisite craftsmanship. Each year, more than 350,000 visitors witness the creation of masterpieces and view the spectacular display, including their classic collections such as Seahorse, Lismore, Colleen and Dolmen. The Waterford crystal experience is unique in that you are visiting a real working, living, breathing factory, and get to discover the magic and spirit that lies behind the legendary crystal. It is a journey that reflects 200 years of glass-making history.

Having worked for the company for some 40 years, Louis Flynn knew his way about and took me on a personal guided tour of the entire establishment, and even invited me to 'blow glass' which I did!

We hopped into our van and drove away to Dublin, a three-hour relaxed journey. Awaiting me at the Ely Wine Bar was Sinead MacAodha, Director of Ireland Literature Exchange, and our pleasant lunch meeting was duly punctuated with suitable literary talk.

Ireland Literature Exchange is the national organisation for the international promotion of Irish literature in English and Irish, and Sinead is working hard at giving it sharper focus in India through Irish literary showcases.

And now the doors were open for me to swing by Guinness Storehouse to discover the world of this famed Irish drink. Well, it is something!

Located in the heart of the St James's Gate Brewery, Guinness Storehouse® is an enthralling place and Ireland's top international visitor attraction. The building dates back to 1904 and is built in the style of the Chicago School of Architecture, making it special for those interested in everything from Guinness to Irish culture and heritage. The Guinness tour brings alive a real segment of Irish history. A new brewing experience features a virtual Master Brewer, Fergal Murray, who guides visitors step-by-step through the brewing process. And you can sample 'the real thing' in the famous Gravity Bar on the top floor.

My Irish experience was rounded off with a dinner with Maeve Bracken and Gillian Swaine of Bord Bia. "We wanted to say goodbye and ensure you were all right," the two charming ladies told me.

Was I "all right"? Good question! I was about as fine as one could be after a week of sheer bliss in a beautiful country, amidst genuinely friendly people. I was smitten by what I call the 'special Irish charm.'

"Thanks, I'm fine. I'm all right," I told my gracious hostesses. And that, as they say, was *'that'*!

# Cast Away in Hawke's Bay

"Kia ora, Kia ora, Kia ora."

The early morning stillness hung over us like a shroud as we milled around our host, Tom Mulligan, Chairperson of Te Taiwhenua o Heretaunga, braving the wind that seemed to have come straight from a giant refrigerator. We were at the entrance of the Mihiroa Marea in Pakipaki, Hawke's Bay, being welcomed in the traditional Maori way.

It was all very ceremonial but simplistic, and in a way that sums up the Maoris themselves. As per custom, ladies go in first, men follow! "I'll tell you why, later," Tom whispered in my ear, but never got around to doing so. We stopped just outside the meeting house to 'reflect and think of loved ones gone'. Then, shoes off, we entered the plain-looking enclosure with its plain-looking interior, 'into the bosom of ancestors and their Lord'.

"Welcome to our Marea. You honour us," the local Maori leader said to us in a tone that sounded rather hushed to me. Politely, we heard him through. Tom said a short prayer, we all greeted one another by rubbing noses, and quietly left the Marea.

Though moved by the episode's simple intensity, I hadn't quite realised just how fortunate I was to be amidst the Maori at this particular time. For this was the Matariki Festival. The festival for the Maori! A very special time, with a special significance for a race of simple people.

And Hawke's Bay is an excellent place to enjoy Matariki, among other things. The next three days were a blur of activities that saw me pitch-forked headlong into generous doses of unique Maori culture, my stint including everything from hot-air ballooning to traditional feasting.

By given standards, Hawke's Bay is a region of wide-open spaces, but no one's really interested in its size. Food, wine, lifestyle! These are the local buzzwords, amidst a lifestyle that sets it apart for envy and praise. And it took me just a couple of days to see that the hype is justified and that Hawke's Bay has lapped it all up rather well.

Famed as one of New Zealand's three major wine-making regions, Hawke's Bay flaunts its internationally acclaimed wines, fresh local produce and a lively arts scene. And for those who like the outdoors, the entire region's a perfect playground.

For the purist, the region's got it all, and in just the right proportions, it seems. A Mediterranean climate they are passionate about as it underpins the very essence of life in the region; varied landscapes ranging from dramatic sea cliffs to fertile plains and clear rivers that meander down to the Pacific Ocean; and an interesting and highly diverse mix of population.

They like to say the sun shines here forever, and all arguments to the contrary fade before the statistic that the region boasts an average of 2,245 sunshine hours a year, which combined with the blue skies, are rather conducive to alfresco living. It has obviously rubbed off on the locals who come across as easy-going and uncomplicated.

Any time is a good time to shake a leg. What you can do in Hawke's Bay depends on your energy levels. You can swim with dolphins or see the world's largest mainland Gannet colony; jet-board; go hot-air ballooning at sunrise; surf in Mahia; paraglide off Te Mata Peak; sail and windsurf; hunt in the ranges; fish for brown and rainbow trout; cycle between wineries; go for long walks; play golf at one of the 20 courses around; or just sedate yourself and enjoy the sun and golden sand beaches.

Midway between Hastings and Napier is the Nga Tukemata O Kahungunu Waka, a 4-tonne, 18-metre-long carved canoe that takes visitors paddling on the Clive River for a true waka experience.

Brace yourself and get into discover mode. The dramatic coastline and marine reserves demand beach activity. The wilderness of Te Urewera National Park evokes a sense of inner calm. The dominant Art Deco and Spanish Mission architecture symbolises the region's strength of character and resilience to adversity.

I had been told all this before I arrived. And I managed to experience some of it first hand. But in the end, what charmed me about the place was its simplistic laid-back ambience. The emphasis is on being close to nature, helped along by fertile plains, high country pasture, and an abundant coastline and rivers — perfect conditions for the production of assorted produce and foods.

While on the subject of food, let me say it didn't disappoint. It never does in New Zealand. I am ready to stick my neck out for that. Here, food is celebrated every Sunday morning at the Farmers' Market held at the Hawke's Bay Showground in Hastings and every Saturday morning in Napier on Tennyson Street. The markets provide an interactive setting and hark back to bygone days when you could buy food the old-fashioned way.

If time allows, it is always a good idea to take the Wine Country Food Trail, a collection of farm gate, artisan food producers and food destination outlets extending from Mahia to Norsewood. The food trail features over 70 stops and provides a complete gourmet experience with everything from speciality meats to game, fresh produce, olive products, verjuice, honey, eggs, cheese and chocolate.

Food may be one of my passions, but this is essentially wine turf. Home to New Zealand's oldest operational winery, winemaker and first winery museum, the region's 40-odd wineries makes it the country's leading producer of the finest quality red wines with over 70 per cent of national plantings of Merlot and Cabernet Sauvignon grapes. The warm maritime climate and varying landscape also produces the richest and most complex Chardonnays. To experience Hawke's Bay wines you can self-drive with a designated guide or take a professional wine tour with guides or operators. Many wineries also operate lunch restaurants, serving local produce dishes to match their wines. Harvest Hawke's Bay in February; the Hawke's Bay Winemakers, Charity Wine Auction in June; and the Hawke's Bay A & P Mercedes Benz Wine Awards in October are major wine-related events that you can join in on.

Over the years I have seen that it doesn't take me long to become a wine lover, even wine expert. The conditions here were near-ideal. My local wine initiation came courtesy Rosemary and John O'Connor whose Matariki Vineyards account for some of the best local produce. The fact that both like and relish their wines and like to share their tastes with others, helped. While they talked, we drank. A win-win situation if ever there was one.

I didn't get around to telling you about the blessed stones? Rosemary and John like to talk about some stones from their vineyard which were blessed and specially marked by their local holy man and returned to them to bring good fortune and a bountiful season. The enterprising couple buried these stones on their land, and swear they are showing extraordinary characteristics — the patch with the buried stones is the only one to survive frost. So make what you like of this.

A vibrant arts scene compliments the great food and wine. You can explore home studios and galleries and meet the artists in their creative environment. The influence of the local Maori culture is evident from Nuhaka in the north to the longest place name in the world, located in the south — Taumata whakatangi hangakoauau o tamatea turi pukakapiki maunga horo nuku pokai whenua kitanatahu! If you are fit enough to say this, the world's longest place name with its 85 letters, and walk to the hilltop which takes its name, you'll discover spectacular views, feel you are in a special, spiritual place and also learn a little of New Zealand's cultural history.

The name was given by the local Maori, Ngati Kere, to a hill to venerate the eponymous ancestor Tamatea Pokai Whenua, and the Taumata walk is near Porangahau, Central Hawke's Bay. The 250-hectare farm is still owned by Tamatea's descendants, the Scott family, and paying them a visit is well worth the effort.

Art Deco and heritage predominates in the region, with buildings having become an attraction in their own right. Ever since the twin cities of Napier and Hastings were decimated by an earthquake in 1931, and subsequently rebuilt, they have been renowned for their distinct architecture. Napier features one of the world's highest concentrations of Art Deco architecture. Hastings has its own unique concentration of Spanish Mission and Art Deco design.

There are daily guided walks operated by the Art Deco Trust, and the region has some 17 heritage trails. Escorted by David Low of the Trust, I took a blissful morning, one-hour guided walk that started at Napier Visitors Centre and took me to several notable landmarks. Low gave us the lowdown and showed us a slide presentation on Art Deco's birth and evolution.

As towns go, Napier isn't large, but holds immense charm. Compact and made for walking, the town basks in the glory of the sea and fine beaches. Marina Parade provides a superb opportunity to walk along the sea face and do bits of shopping as well.

Hawke's Bay is home to the internationally renowned Kahurangi Dance Theatre, overseen by the legendary Te Rangi Huata, fondly described as a 'living treasure of Hawke's Bay'. As the mainstay of the Public Dreams Trust, Te is the creative energy behind Matariki, and not only spearheads the month-long celebrations — now a regular annual feature providing visitors a variety of experiences through diverse activities — but is its designated spokesperson. He's also soft-spoken and gentlemanly.

My main reason for being here at this particular time being Matariki, I deemed it wise to learn a bit about the festival. Matariki is a small cluster of tiny stars, also known as Pleiades. To the Maori, it is as important as life itself, a time to look forward, rejuvenate, and celebrate the reawakening of the rhythm of life. Matariki is so integral to this rhythm that it is closely studied as a foretell of the coming harvest. If each star stands out distinctly, a promising season will ensue with the promise that the earth will once again release her prosperous bounty.

In autumn, as the crops are gathered and preserved and the daylight hours shorten, Matariki disappears from the heavens.

Now it is time to stop, reflect and celebrate the year that's passed and enjoy earth's bounties, and wait for Matariki to reappear in the heavens and continue nature's rhythms. It is also time to garner food resources, bid the past goodbye, welcome the new growing season, make plans for the land and for the new spring garden, and plant new trees and bushes. Birds and fish are its harvests. It is a continuation of the life-process itself.

Matariki appears in the Eastern sky around the shortest day, usually around mid-June, the first Maori month. As the stars rise on the northeastern horizon, it signals the beginning of the Maori or lunar New Year referred to as Matariki. New Year celebrations were traditionally held on the sighting of the next new moon. In traditional Maori society, communities still sit up to watch out for Matariki.

Come evening and it was time for the Mahinarangi — moon beams. We drove out to an open area used for hosting outdoor events. For the first time since arriving in the region, I found myself in a swirl of people. It seemed half of Hawke's Bay was there, braving the cold, thronging around the stage that featured live music, dances — including, hold your breath, the Punjabi *Bhangra* — and the local Tina Turner who cavorted on stage with her two grandsons.

It was fun and fiesta. Five-metre fire wheels twirled and sparked, lanterns glowed, hot air balloons ten-storeys high stood ready to take flight, and fireworks lit up the night sky. The fireworks and balloons symbolised the kites that were flown by Maoris from hilltops as part of their traditional celebrations of the Maori New Year.

Fireworks are Huata's passion, and he likens them to looking at Christmas tree lights. "They engender a feeling of warmth, and are like light banishing dark, good triumphing over evil, an adventure in the celestial realm. They lift people's spirits unconsciously," Te says in his simple style.

Food time! Showing rare enthusiasm, I joined the queue. "Sorry, we've just run out," the lady at the hot-chocolate counter told me apologetically. "But they're selling hot tomato soup," she said, pointing south. They were indeed, and we got some, and ventured further afield, doing full justice to the offerings, including the traditional Maori Hangi (food cooked in the ground).

The grand finale of the Matariki Festival was the Matariki Kahungunu Winter Ball, a traditional but elegant affair featuring a Kahungunu cuisine chef leading Marae cooks in preparing a three-course indigenous foods dinner. Table settings by Maori artisans, entertainment by the Aotearoa Big Band, performances by the Kahurangi Maori Dance Theatre, and leading musicians! It was crayfish for starters, followed by mussels, vegetables and baked fish. Celebration in a true blue old-fashioned way!

A new day! We beat the sun and reached Matariki Vineyard in the dark for 'The Great Matariki Vintage Car Balloon Chase'. That's just what it was. You had a choice of either ballooning off and soaring across the country, or hopping into vintage cars chasing them in hot pursuit, in a wacky treasure hunt across the region. Needless to say, the daredevil in me saw me opt for the balloon ride, and with some unexpected, unwelcome results, as it turned out!

Those magnificent men in their flying machines! Well, almost. Some of them did look quite grand in their flying livery. It takes an hour to inflate a hot-air balloon and make it airworthy. In the meantime, the sun had come up, giving the balloons a touch of gold. I was approached by a lady dressed in 'flier's finery' with a lovely peaked hat. "You're welcome to come ride with us," she told me graciously. Politely declining her offer and explaining I had to "stick by my group" I offered to have a coffee with her 'later'.

And of course, never got around to having it.

We boarded and took off. And we immediately felt the silence. All quiet on all fronts. We kept low, skimming the vineyards, scattering sheep, watching the mosaic patchwork slip by below. It was all bliss except for the last bit. We crash-landed in a ditch. There was probably only one four-foot-wide ditch in the Hawke's Bay area if not in the whole of New Zealand, and we found it. A painful elbow, clothes soaked right up to my waist, and lots of 'oohs and aahs' and we returned to our hotel.

This famous little misadventure apart, the ride had been fun, even though half of New Zealand had heard about our 'mishap' within the hour, and several people politely asked me later if I had enjoyed my 'fishing'.

# Heidelberg Highs

Remember that adage, "If you have a good reason for doing something, just do it." Well, what if you have six?

I can think of at least six good reasons to visit Heidelberg. Its stunningly pretty, friendly, traditional, easily accessible, easy to discover, and most significantly, literally oozes old-world charm and atmosphere.

It was while boarding my train for Heidelberg at Frankfurt Main Station that I realised just how heavy my suitcase was. A minor struggle, and I was safely ensconced in my seat. But not for long, as I had to change trains at Mannheim. The ICE Express ate up the distance, and 28 minutes later, I found myself at Mannheim Station lugging my bags to another platform to catch the train to Heidelberg. A slower train this time. Within an hour of leaving Frankfurt, I was at Heidelberg Station (yes, still struggling with the suitcase).

It was still early enough in the morning for the sunshine to be the way I like it most — pale golden and balmy — when I hit town and checked in at Hotel Europa, a delight that merits special mention. An epitome of old-world charm and good service, Hotel Europa does credit to the hospitality industry. I have rarely seen such friendly and obliging staff.

My room was spacious, and awaiting me was the proverbial fruit basket.

I had barely opened my suitcase when the manager phoned to ask if I was comfortable and if I would care to join the owner for a coffee. While chatting, Ernst-Friedrich Von Kretschmann filled me in on the hotel's finer points, and on his long association with Heidelberg. He told me about the mix of guests that grace the hotel — tourists, business visitors, and conference delegates — all of who come to the city for leisure or business, and all of who get the same courteous treatment. He suggested the sauna to get over my travel fatigue. A terrific idea, as it turned out.

Armed with my new-found energy, I ventured out in a discovery mode, determined to make the most of my stay here. Heidelberg's reputation had preceded it. I had heard so much about the city's charms and now was my chance to find things out for myself and have a good time while doing it.

I started off by taking the celebrated stroll along the river to end up at the vantage point in the city — the castle, the world-famous local showpiece. I had done well. From the castle, the city appeared a tangled mix of rows of houses, large courtyards, and gabled streets, neatly dissected by the Neckar River. A few degrees up, the frame was filled by thickly wooded hills that formed a patchwork of green. Still further up, it was all blue skies and fleecy clouds. A stunningly beautiful backdrop if ever there was one.

My generous sweep had taken in hills, rivers and bridges. This is one of the two celebrated viewing points in town, the other being the historic Old Bridge, which also provides a stunning view of the city and the valley beyond.

Later, having 'done' both these vantage points, it had become abundantly clear to me why poets and writers were ensnared and charmed by the city.

But I also discovered a third vantage point — the large windows of the Heidelberg Convention & Visitors' Bureau. Their office is housed in an impressive old building located just 30 metres from the river, the same distance from the Old Bridge, and a mere five to ten minutes walk from anywhere in the Old Town. From here, I got a wonderful view. The castle squats on its famous perch just across the river, 500 metres away, and the Church of the Holy Ghost is a two-minute walk across the bridge and through the Bridge Gate.

"It's an old yet young city, small, cosmopolitan and cozy. Its main asset is that it offers the best of German qualities — tradition, a scholastic and university atmosphere, and commonality of language. It is a good representation of Germany's historical and contemporary life, offering visitors a stress-free stay with no danger of getting lost."

Nils Kroesen, the then Director of the Heidelberg Convention & Visitors' Bureau, knew what he was talking about. He had been talking this language for quite a while now, and 3,500,000 annual visitors will readily vouch for his words. Vera Cornelius, his charming successor agreed. "The fact is that this is a rather special city. Thanks to its history and literary legacy, it has so much to offer visitors. On our part, we try to make them feel at home, enjoy themselves, and ensure they get the best out of their visit."

A past of literary brilliance, refined passion, and a host of love songs combine to make Heidelberg the gateway to Romantic Germany, and a premier tourist destination. The fact that it is also a major medical research and educational centre with a strong university flavour just adds value.

The seduction's easily explained. Heidelberg is a mix of castles, rivers, and ancient structures set amidst mountains, forests, and vineyards. Intact for nearly three centuries, Old Heidelberg reflects the three-fold harmony so beloved of the

Romanticists and poets and writers of the Romantic Movement who found unbounded inspiration here — Old Town tapering down to a river, imposing castle walls towering above it, with a background of rising wooded hills — as if someone had painted a masterpiece and left it behind for posterity.

It was here that Brentano and Arnim published their collection of folk songs — "Des Knaben Wundhorn", and here that Eichendorff found his inspiration and celebrated works like Matthisson's "Elegy", and Holderlin's "Ode to Heidelberg" paid due tribute. Paul Richter, Victor Hugo, and Mark Twain — who came for a day but ended up spending the entire summer here — all succumbed to the town's myriad charms. Goethe, a regular visitor, lost his heart here to the beautiful Marianne von Willener.

All this was yesterday. Today the world descends here to imbibe as much as possible of the much-vaunted local charm. And there's plenty of it about.

The town was made for strolling, and this got a further boost with the centre of the Old Town being converted into a 'pedestrian only' precinct in 1978. Essentially you have two choices. You can either follow designated tourist circuits and take in the sites, or just strike out in any direction. If you have forgotten to pick up a local map from your hotel, just head for the river. The Neckar River is as intrinsic to the town as any landmark monument. And along with its banks, it is a beautiful sight in its own right. You can't go wrong.

Half a dozen walks on two days, and I felt I had done justice to the famed local landmarks. I had walked on both sides of the river, covered the Hauptstrasse, and ended up at the historic students' cafés and taverns, Sepp l and Roter Ochsen. They were exactly as described to me. Low-ceilinged, noisy, cozy affairs, strong on charm and atmosphere.

For a city as small as this, attractions come thick and fast. The Church of the Holy Ghost, which served as a burial place for the Electors; the Palais Morass; the University Library with its famed collection of medieval poetry — it's really worth spending time here, if only to browse through some priceless manuscripts; the Palatinate Museum, a typical 18th-century mansion with a grand staircase, banquet hall and adjoining salons; and the often-renovated and expanded Town Hall.

The Town Hall's worth seeing, and if you are lucky you might even get to meet Dr Eckart Wuerzner, the highly energetic and dynamic Mayor of the City of Heidelberg. Dr Wuerzner has a vision for his beautiful city and wants to reach out to the world and forge partnerships in various fields, like science, for instance. "Heidelberg has a lot to offer to the world and we're keen to exploit this asset for overall benefit and progress," the good mayor declares.

Downtown Heidelberg? It's a treat. There is a distinct character to the place, and it's bigger than you would have imagined. The buzz is at Hauptstrasse that stretches arrow-straight for some two kilometres and ends up at the foot of Castle Hill. This pedestrian zone's all about trendy boutiques, department stores, bakers, confectioners and chic little cafés and bistros whose tables spill out onto the pavements when the weather is kind. Café Extrablatt Heidelberg is always packed, and the Darjeeling tea I ordered along with a tart took some time coming. They also do good breakfast and brunch buffets that are very popular with locals and tourists alike.

It is always worth stopping by at Café Knosel located just by the Church of the Holy Ghost. This is the home of the world-famous Heidelberg Student's Kiss, which (in case you are getting excited) is a pastry comprising two tender wafers filled with chocolate nougat and praline bits, coated with a satiny bitter-sweet chocolate. It has been around for ages and remains as popular as ever. The café has got three sitting areas with 100-odd covers, a cake counter and cabinets with chocolates, and dozens of paintings and portraits on the walls.

It is only a matter of time before everyone ends up at University Square with its stately buildings and Crowned Lion, so who was I to miss out. You might say this is the 'heart of the heart of the city'. The new university building has taken over from the old one that's now used as a festival hall cum museum. A fabulous décor with wooden walls, flooring and a ceiling sporting grand paintings, make the Aula (festival hall) a special place. Just behind it is the Students' Prison, a town landmark, where students were locked up for their misdeeds. It is like any other prison except the walls are completely covered with scribbles and paintings, and its 'studio' atmosphere.

Mid-morning, day two! For the second day running, I found myself standing once again in the shadow of Heidelberg's grand icon, its *pièce de resistance*, so lovingly featured on all its tourist brochures. Rising majestically above the narrow lanes and picturesque maze of roofs of the Old Town, the castle dominates the landscape in dramatic fashion. If Germany has a more impressive castle than this one, I have missed it. For five centuries a centre of royal pomp and glory and the grand, glittering residence of the powerful Palatinate Prince Electors, the castle was built on the foundations of history, and enjoyed enormous stature and fame that made it the rendezvous of poets and artists, and a shining symbol of German romance. And of course, there are those stunning views for which I can personally vouch.

A short tour's enough to explain why the castle's so special to the city. Be it High Renaissance, Gothic, or Surrealist, every part of the formidable structure's art forms reflects the history of the times. The Kaisersaal (Imperial Hall) features rotating art exhibits; the Konigsaal (Royal Hall) was used for ceremonies and coronations; and the Friedrichsbaukepell is where many couples took their marriage vows. If you are fortunate enough to visit in July and August, you can see festivals that relive the glory and echo the merriment of bygone days. Picture the splendour of courtly life; hunting horns blaring, followed by hearty feasting, with fireworks brightening the castle's walls. Those were Romantic Germany's golden days, with the castle its centre point.

Albrecht Kossel for medicine, Georg Wilting for chemistry, and Philipp Lenard for physics were some of the celebrated Nobel laureates and scholars who owe allegiance to Heidelberg. It figures! Housing Germany's oldest and most famous university founded in 1386 by Ruprecht I of the Palatinate — whose history reflects the intellectual and political evolution of the country through 600 eventful years — lends Heidelberg with a distinct university faculty atmosphere and scholarly charm. Catering to over 30,000 international students — which counts to one out of every five residents — are different-coloured fraternity houses and a host of bookshops.

It was late evening and Hotel Europa was a beehive of activity as was the city itself. It seems just about everyone walks around the Hauptstrasse, and along the river's banks.

When it was time to leave, I was left carrying the special mood of the city on my shoulders. From my perch at the Bridge Tower, I stared down at the Neckar one last time. It was as still as ever. Things looked as quiet as ever. Only, I knew better.

Of all the tributes showered on the city, perhaps none sums it up better than an old song that still echoes across Germany: "I left my heart behind in Heidelberg..."

Of course!

Having told you about my favourite German city, it is time to shed some light on my favourite pastime in this country. Yes, you guessed it. It's eating and drinking. Naturally!

The Germans call it 'Rauchbier'. It is Bamberg's very own speciality, and one of its many claims to fame. Nothing complex or intricate, just 'smoked beer', and it has been around for nearly 400 years, drunk heartily by 'initiated' beer-lovers with an 'acquired, refined' taste.

The name that instantly springs to mind is Schlenkerla, the most astounding, most visited, most original, and most savoury smoked beer fountain in town. Nestled in the shadow of the mighty cathedral in the middle of the Old Town, it is a half-timbered house in which geraniums glow in summer, and eager diners converge day and night to savour choice offerings as traditional as anything else.

"Even if the brew tastes somewhat strange at the first sip, don't stop, because soon you'll realise that your thirst will not decrease and your pleasure will increase!" So proclaim the coasters, and very few disagree. I certainly didn't.

Though a magic word for a long time, not many know what 'Schlenkerla' means. Its roots lie in the vernacular 'Schlenkern', an old German expression for 'walking with a drunken lurch.' Allegedly a former brewer had a funny way of walking owing to an accident (or was it the beer?), and so the brewery he established in 1678 was called Schlenkerla. The ending 'la' is very typical of the Franconian dialect. The name remained unchanged, even though it is now the sixth generation of brewers tapping the beer. Today, the name covers the smoked beer, the tavern and the brewery.

It has become quite a brand name. Schlenkerla smoked beer is an original amongst beers, even amongst Bavarian beers. It is a dark, aromatic, bottom-fermented beer with 13.5 per cent original extract, equivalent to an alcohol content of 4.8 per cent. No doubt there's stronger beer going, but all the same, one shouldn't underestimate it, as old-timers point out. It can make you 'dangle' quite a bit.

Apparently, getting the smoky flavour is no mean achievement. The process involves exposing the malt to the harsh, aromatic smoke of burning beach-wood logs. After mixing it with high-class hops in the brew, it matures in a cold cellar deep down in the Bamberg Hills, into a mellow, tasty beer, best drunk directly in the Schlenkerla. There's variety for imbibing the famous drink. You can drink it in the Altes Lokal at white, scrubbed wooden tables — covering them with a tablecloth would be a sin — or underneath an old ceiling even darker than the beer. You can also drink it in the Klause, a former monastery built in AD 1310, or in the inner court next to a 500-litre wooden keg. So much for the legend called Schlenkerla.

Talk about savouring the good things in life. Connoisseurs drink it slowly and steadily and with relish, knowing that the second 'Seidla' (half-litre) tastes better than the first, and the third even better. They drink during the 'morning pint' and the afternoon break, in the evenings, alone, and with company, especially with company, as the beer makes one talkative and exuberant. It connects locals with strangers, which works out just fine, as it is common practice in Franconia to share your table with others.

I did my bit. Started slowly and faithfully drank my way through a litre and a half of the famous beer while listening to the energetic owner of Schlenkerla who explained what exactly producing and selling smoked beer is all about.

So much for the drinking. Now let's come to the eating bit.

How can I forget to mention Regensberg's Historische Wurstkuche (Historical Sausage Kitchen)? It is the place, and the meal that stick in my mind.

"Are you very hungry or just hungry"?

Before I could proclaim my trademark 'very hungry' bit, our good guide had ordered for us, because the 'guide always knows best'. Meanwhile, we had settled down with a light local beer, with the Danube flowing swiftly by and the air thick with barbeque smoke. It was all a bit sublime.

The wind wasn't friendly, but the sun shone generously as if in agreement with the general mood around. And some 300 enthusiasts just 'sat in' on the seduction provided by the Historische Wurstkuche, Germany's original, world-famous sausage kitchen. All roads lead to the Historische Wurstkuche. The river flows swiftly through the arches of the Old Stone Bridge, creating whirlpools and eddies. The restaurant is 850 years old, as old as the Stone Bridge itself, or as a local saying has it, "as old as all that's good in eating", our good guide informed us. The fixed menu of sausage, sauerkraut, and potato soup, applies to breakfast, lunch, and dinner, and its tables by the river are never empty, "Unless the weather's so bad that only the devil would venture outdoors."

Summer sees the restaurant's tables spill outdoors by the river in the shadow of the Old Stone Bridge. The furniture, linen and crockery are basic, the tables could well have come from a factory shed, but the food and atmosphere take some beating.

The sausage is king. There's grilled sausage, served with sauerkraut and sliced potatoes, and boiled sausage, served in a light, syrupy sauce. I asked the owners, Mr and Mrs Meier, the reason for their phenomenal popularity, and they just smiled.

Duly fed, I was ready for the city. Hugging the swiftly flowing Danube, Regensburg — Germany's only surviving medieval city — reflects a millennium of history and offers a special urban experience, with two outstanding eateries.

From picturesque old alleys, you step out into wide streets and squares flanked by patrician palaces and splendid castles that are witness to a thousand years of history.

A few short steps through a narrow alley studded with chic boutiques, brought me to Dampfnudel-Uli Café, the other celebrated local eatery. It is small — with a mere dozen-odd covers — compact, and comprises one room that serves as the café, display counter, and entertainment section.

So, what's the big deal? Quite simple. Dampfnudel-Uli Café is world-famous for its steamed pastry served with vanilla sauce. Basically, it is a pastry with multiple layers, strong on apple and liquorice, literally drowned in vanilla sauce. It goes best with an espresso or latté. Depending on your epicurean levels, it can be a snack or a meal in itself.

The café is also renowned for its typical Bavarian cuisine, which starts with dumpling of pork liver soup, with a main dish of sauerkraut, potato dumplings, roasted pork, green salad, and potato salad. With the famed pastry as a dessert fit for kings!

A sausage and a pastry in a kitchen and a café. Sounds a bit weird but believe me it isn't. It's gospel for gourmets.

I came away duly seduced.

# Istanbul: A Tale of Two Continents

There was this breeze that came and went, kissing my face and turban, plucking at my shirt collars, almost giving me a gentle massage. It was there, it was very noticeable but not intrusive.

Just like the city itself.

Reclining on the western shore of the Bosphorus, with one arm reaching out to Asia and the other to Europe, it is a city that has embraced and absorbed the world's most ancient civilisations.

The former capital of three successive empires: Roman, Byzantine and Ottoman, to say that Istanbul's crammed with history is to state the obvious. Nevertheless, I will say it. History shrouds the city and yet it appears refreshingly young. While preserving the legacy of its past, it has a certain freshness that seems inclined more towards the present and future. Which becomes just the right kind of tonic for visitors who are keen to explore the city.

If there is one thing all my travels have taught me, it is to have an open mind. I had arrived with just that. And it helped! Making it much easier for me to understand the riddle and absorb the layers upon layers of history and heritage that come through in the museums, churches, grand mosques, palaces and bazaars of this vast, throbbing metropolis of 12 million.

It is an action city with its own blend of action. It is different, but it is definitely there. Tucked away in the city's folds, there's not only plenty to see, but plenty to do. In my opinion, the greatest local asset is the subtle East-West blend that gives everything a romantic edge. There's something undefined, almost furtive about the place and it makes it all charming.

At the risk of sounding prosaic, I advise caution while out sightseeing. Not from a law-and-order point of view as the city's safe enough, but because of the sheer burden of history entombed in magnificent monuments that dot the urban landscape. It is that kind of place, and you need that kind of planned itinerary to do justice. I don't mind sticking my neck out to say that most visitors don't actually do justice to everything that's on offer. But that's contemporary life and contemporary travel for you!

The morning sun was still a pale gold when we arrived at one of the conventional city's must-sees. On a finger of land at the confluence of the Bosphorus, the Golden Horn and the Sea of Marmara, the Topkapi Palace is a maze of buildings that was the heart of the Ottoman Empire between the 15th and 19th centuries. It was from these opulent surroundings that the Sultans and their courts functioned and governed.

The palace is everything it is made out to be, and demands full attention.

The next couple of hours were a journey into the fabulous world of the Ottoman Sultans. Providing a regal sense of space is a magnificent garden that fills the outer court, while the second court houses the palace kitchens — now serving as galleries exhibiting the imperial collections of crystal, silver and Chinese porcelain. To the left is the Harem. The third court holds the Hall of Audience, the Library of Ahmed III, an exhibition of imperial costumes, the jewels of the treasury and a priceless collection of miniatures from medieval manuscripts. In the centre of this innermost sanctuary, the relics of Prophet Mohammed lie enshrined in the Pavilion of the Holy Mantle.

A fierce drizzle welcomed us when we re-emerged into the open, and kept us company all the way to Sultan Ahmed Square. With the Blue Mosque squatting majestically on one side and Hagia Sophia on the other, this is Turkey's most famous site and I must confess feeling dwarfed by the magnificent monuments here that have been national showpieces for centuries. Historically this is ground zero. Just standing here and making a full circle gives you a visual taste of the best of Turkey's architectural forte.

The Basilica of Hagia Sophia (Holy Wisdom), now called the Ayasofya Museum, is without question one of the finest buildings of all time. Its exterior is grand but plain, but inside, it is a world in itself. Breathtaking! Built by Constantine the Great and reconstructed by Justinian in the 6th century, its immense dome rises 55 metres high and its diameter spans 31 metres. Byzantine mosaics embellish the vast and stunning interiors.

Once again we came out into the drizzle for the short walk across the square. Across from Hagia Sophia stands the supremely majestic, six-minareted imperial Sultan Ahmed Mosque, known as the Blue Mosque because of its interior panelling of blue and white Iznik tiles. Set in spacious gardens, the mosque sports a stunning façade that's as intrinsic to

Istanbul's skyline as the Eiffel Tower is to Paris'. Summer months feature an evening sound-and-light show. But it is a tourist hangout throughout the year.

Let me mention the Istanbul Dubb Restaurant, one of only two really famous Indian eateries in the city. Those who know me may not believe this, but my lunch stopover there was really in the interest of research. I had heard about the views from the top-floor balcony, which embraced the area's historical jewels. And well, there was the lunch too, of course, and the meal was everything an Indian could desire: *naan* (bread); *kachumbar* (shredded vegetables) salad; *samosa* (savoury); chicken curry; *millijuli subzi* (mixed vegetables); *pulaoo* (pilaf); and *phirney* for dessert. I could well have been in downtown Delhi with my hungry belly!

Energised, we set out on our path of discovery again, arriving at another city landmark. Built by Mehmet the Conqueror in 1452 prior to his capture of Istanbul, Rumeli Hisari (European Fortress) is among the world's most beautiful works of military architecture. In the castle is the open-air museum amphitheatre that stages events of the Istanbul Music Festival.

Our next stop was equally noteworthy. Its walls decorated with superb mosaics, the Kariye Museum, the 11th-century church of St Savior in the Chora complex is the most important Byzantine monument in Istanbul after Hagia Sophia. Illustrating scenes from the life of Christ and Virgin Mary, the brilliantly coloured mosaics embody the vigour of Byzantine art at its very best.

After-dark Istanbul! Now this is a tough one. Not that there's anything difficult about finding nightlife in this huge city. It is quite the opposite, in fact. If you are a night bird, the thing to do here is to just take it easy. Unlike Paris or New York, you don't have to seek out night action. It comes to you. Literally. The belly dancers weave their way sinuously to your table, flirt with you, get photographed with you (you can buy your photo), and lead you on-stage if you dare. There are plenty of classy night clubs around but I would put my money on Kapvansaray Restaurant & Night Club that features a superb dinner; cultural and belly-dancing show; live band, and just the right kind of ambience.

A real, and I mean real treat awaits you when you visit one of the famed local *hammams* as the Turkish baths are known. I was fortunate enough to get my first-hand experience at one that's among the city's most original and authentic.

Tucked away in the folds of the city, Cagaloglu Hammam is a 300-year-old traditional Turkish bath that has fiercely clung on to its proud lineage. Step back in time, and get a dose of wellness that's been around for centuries, slipping into a delightful world of steam, spray and incense. Awaiting you is a large, square room with a high, domed ceiling with a single suspended chandelier and a single fountain in the centre, posters on the walls, cabins alongside (including a barber counter), and The Old Marble Café & Restaurant that has fed generations of visitors over the years.

The heart of the establishment is the hararet, a grand circular enclosure with a central dome, marble pillars, and Byzantine design. Along the walls are enclosures for visitors. They lie here, get doused with hot water, and then get massaged. Or wash themselves if they have opted for the self-service facility. You have a choice of traditional body massages, full-body massages, and foam massages. In between steaming, you can have your body scrubbed briskly with a coarse, soapy mitt *(kese)*. There's also the exfoliating body scrub. And in case you are worried about privacy, most have separate sections for men and women.

Over the years, this bathing temple has welcomed the likes of Kaiser Wilhelm, Franz Liszt, Florence Nightingale, Tony Curtis, Rudolf Nureyev, David Brown, and Cameron Diaz. Needless to say, I felt privileged with the experience.

Exploring historical monuments is just one part of the Istanbul experience. Don't even think of missing out on the much-hyped boat cruises on the Strait of Bosphorus, that winding strip of sea that separates Europe and Asia. They are everything they are made out to be, and they serve up a cup of decent coffee or apple tea which goes down rather well against the normally cold, scalpel-like wind that keeps you company.

Our 90-minute cruise matched the hype! The shores offer a delightful mixture of the past and present, grand splendour and simple beauty. Modern hotels stand next to *yalis* (shorefront wooden villas); marble palaces abut rustic stone fortresses, and elegant compounds neighbour small fishing villages.

One by one, several local landmarks slipped by — Dolmabahce Palace that houses the world's largest chandelier (four tonnes), Galatasaray University that looks like a hotel, then the imperial pavilions of the Yildiz Palace. Ciragan Palace — refurbished in 1874 by Sultan Abdulaziz, and now restored as a grand hotel — came into view, its ornate marble façades reflecting in the water for 300 metres along the Bosphorus.

Overshadowing the city's traditional architecture is the Bosphorus Bridge, a song the world's largest suspension bridges, linking Europe and Asia. The beautiful Beylerbeyi Palace lies just past the bridge on the Asian side, and behind it rises Camlica Hill, Istanbul's highest point. We rounded off our trip passing the fortresses of Rumeli Hisari and Ananolu Hisari, facing each other across the straits like sentries. Back on the European side, at Tarabya Bay, yachts seemed to dance at their moorings.

You know that saying "There's always time for shopping"! Well, disregard it and just get down to business. I must confess to a rare enthusiasm when confronted with the riches so generously on offer in the city's markets. Istanbul shopping is like the city itself: highly contrasted, yet subtly fused. It is easy to lose your head wading through gold jewellery, Turkish crafts, hand-painted ceramics, copperware, brassware, meerschaum pipes, leather and suede goods, and world-renowned carpets. They know how to sell their wares here. And they know a thing or two about bargaining.

For the real thing, stop by at the Kapali Carsi (covered bazaar) in the old city. A labyrinth of streets and passages that houses over 4,000 shops and features some good, old-fashioned bargaining, it is always worth the effort. While on the subject of bargaining, let me say that while everyone talks about the Arabs' frenzy for bargaining, well, the Turks aren't too far behind. If you come away thinking you have had the better part of the deal, you may quickly come down to earth and find out you haven't.

The names recall days when each trade had its own quarter: the goldsmiths' street; the carpet-sellers' street; the skullcap-makers' street. With enticing aromas of cinnamon, caraway, saffron, mint and thyme, the Misir Carsisi (spice bazaar) next to Yeni Mosque at Eminonu, transports you back to fantasies of the mythical East.

At the other end of the spectrum are the sophisticated shops of the Taksim-Nisantasi-Sisli districts that contrast with the chaos of the bazaars. On Cumhuriyet Avenue, Rumeli Avenue, and Istiklal Avenue, you can browse in the most fashionable outlets strong on elegant fashions in Turkish textiles, exquisite jewellery and fashionable handbags. The Atakoy Galleria Mall, the Akmerkez Mall in Etiler, the Carousel Mall, Atlas Passage in Beyoglu and Capital Mall on the Asian side are other notable outlets.

Depending on your outlook, Istanbul can be heady or staid. But whatever your levels of pursuit, the city leaves its stamp on your memory. You don't just come away and forget it. You just don't.

After all, two continents can be quite a handful.

# Piemonte Week

They have clung to their traditions. And no one's complaining.

There is of course, Torino, the regional capital, the cultural and culinary stronghold, and the city of some flair. What can I say, except that only Italy could have done this to a region and its culture. I mean this positively, of course. The place is a pure delight.

From a Roman and Medieval culture to a Baroque capital, from a coffee-and-chocolate culture to global tastes, from its royal residences, magnificent church domes, stately mansions and 18 kilometres of arcades, to grand theme museums, Torino's strong on charm. And from the Café Storicis (historical cafés) with their robust ambience, to ethnic outlets like Gattodolcione, the city wears its 'sweet-tooth' tag with a rakish elegance that's teasingly pleasant.

Things go back well into the past. Torino was Italy's first capital in 1861, and having hosted great architects like Guarino Guarini, Filippo Juvarra and Ascanio Vitozzi, its impressive architecture that spans several generations comes as no surprise.

For once, I wasn't hurried, and it is only now that I realise just how important it is in Italy to take things easy and be laid back. Bit by bit, I explored the city and its mysteries. The Piemontese Baroque style Carignano Palace is a compulsory stopover, as is the hall of the first sub-alpine parliament. Across the square lies the famous Ristorante del Cambio where Camillo Benso, the Count of Cavour, dined in between meetings. And dined well too.

Agnolotti, bolliti and bonet! Eat heartily. Have an aperitif (a Tourinese invention) or a glass of wine or some vermouth (invented by Benedetto Carpano in 1786). The place to imbibe these and some real atmosphere is Quadrilatero Romano. Try a Marocchino, a hot chocolate or coffee cup. And the famed Bicerin — a typical Torino coffee, chocolate and cream-based beverage, drunk hot and steaming, considered by Alexander Dumas as being "among the good and pleasant things of the city".

Choose a typical, famed trattoria, or try renowned restaurants like Ristorante Sotto la Mole, and Arcadia. Torino is chocolate turf, inventing the famous Giandujotti, that's become the symbol of this sweet-toothed city. Enjoy home-made pralines, creams, truffles, alpines, marrons glaces and 'tourinots' (nut chocolate mignon shapes that weigh only 2 gms). You have my personal assurance you won't regret it.

Happily, Torino is also the Italian wine capital, offering rich and full-bodied reds, and sparkling, full-flavoured whites. One can sample the best Piemontese labels, accompanied with 'grissini' (bread sticks) with cheese.

Home to studios of well-known designers like Bertone, Giugiaro and Pininfarina, local shopping is typically thematic and elegant, especially in Via Roma; Via Garibaldi; Radadan 'n Piassa in Moncalieri; the Mercantico in Carmagnola, and the Belle Epoque in Venaria.

Torino apart, the Piemonte region was one big charming blur, a weeklong odyssey of fine wining and dining and a close look at prime local products that just happened to be chocolates, cheeses and wines. And with an expert like Silvia Bruschieri of the Italian Institute of Foreign Trade, I remember telling myself this was a slice of the good life. Elegantly dressed, soft spoken, and constantly sporting a half smile that lay hidden on her lips, Silvia turned out to be wonderful company.

Our first foray was to the little town of Pinerolo. I had never heard of it, but then as I said, it was a little town. Here, tucked away in a side street is Dolce Idea, a company engaged in the sweet business of producing chocolates dressed to look like cheese, sausages, and ornaments. Apron-clad Signor di Rosetto Franco, the amiable owner showed me how little chocolate chips taste heavenly with a sip of Grapa, which is best matched with chocolates, as are cognac and brandy. "Just my kind of work," I told myself as I partook of the offerings. Having gone through the gamut of tasting six different types of chocolates with equal helpings of Grapa, it was one happy journalist who left Signor Franco's lovely little shop tucked away in a quiet side street.

The next day was all about travelling around eating and drinking things in the 'interest of research'. If you just put your cynicism aside for a moment, you'll believe me when I say that eating and drinking can be serious business. We hit the highway and headed south to Novi Ligure, the Alps looking down on us, a little snow still clinging on to rocky escarpments. For the rest, it was flat, green country. We arrived just in time for some sweet delights at Novi, a company manufacturing some 10,000 tonnes each of chocolate and candy annually, under the brand name Elap. The next hour was spent doing things I don't normally do — seeing piles of chocolates moving on an assembly line, reaching out to pick up a few, and then seeing them getting wrapped.

"I like them too," Silvia told me softly as I devoured my fourth piece of chocolate, deftly scooped off the assembly line. "Especially the soft ones with the raw nuts," she added as a sort of encouragement. Taking my cue, I helped myself to another piece.

It was time to move on to other things (read 'wine'). Things started off with 'hospitality at a historical house', courtesy Tenuta La Marchesa, a famed wine company whose owner, Signor Dott Vittorio Giulini — a man with typical Italian flair — showed us around the estate, chateau, guesthouse, vineyards and cellars, and told us his produce blends different types of grapes and is 'really high quality'. The place is charming. We tasted wine indoors, and out in the mellow sunshine.

Lunch at the restaurant Locanda dell'Olmo in the village of Boscomarengo (the wine's excellent, by the way, but they don't stock beer) and we wound up our day-long tour with a short visit to Giraudi, a chocolate shop in the little town of Castellazzo Bormida. In this neat little shop of sweet things, we tasted cookies, chocolate bars, cakes, and bagettes. The two 'trays-full' they had set out for us lasted all of two minutes, but stocks were quickly replenished, and all was well. We then got back into our van with 'somewhat more energy', completely ignored the pretty countryside, and after an hour's drive, were deposited back in Torino.

Another day, and more stories to tell. Our morning outing brought a pleasant surprise. What was portrayed as a mere rice factory turned out to be a real charmer. Principato di Lucedio is a world in itself, sheer movie stuff. A former nunnery and abbey founded in AD 1123 by Cistercian monks,

101

its large brick buildings straddle a giant courtyard, watched over by a 1,100-years-old chapel. In the distance, the Alps formed a cup on the horizon and framed us in. We were stretching our legs and sort of getting used to this strange place when we met our hostess.

My first impression of Countess Rosetta Clara Cavalli d'Olivola was that she was a lady who had seen and lived a lot of life, and lived it well. She just had that aura about her. All grace and elegance, she welcomed us with a firm handshake, asked if we had enjoyed our trip so far, escorted us around the 'premises', gave us a rundown on the place and its activities, and over coffee in the shadow of the cloisters, told us the story of her life, her passion for history and culture, her love for golf, and her house in Sardenia.

Then came the wine tasting, courtesy Agricola Marrone, a local wine company that had heard of our visit and decided it was good advertising opportunity. For the second time in two days, I drank loads of excellent wine in 'the interest of research'. The location and setting were different, but the basic aim was similar. Well, that's my theory anyway, and I'll stick to it.

"There's no money in agriculture. This is just my passion," Countess d'Olivola told us over lunch — salad, risotto, and ice cream of rice with giant strawberries — in the spacious hall, under a sloped roof. Keen to develop her property, the Countess has clear-cut plans. A guesthouse is to be started, offering guests a package of history, tours, and sheer relaxation. "One has to move with the times. It's time to change things around," the good countess said in her soft voice.

We said our goodbyes and left. Later, we stopped at Caseificio Rosso in Biella, met Signor Enrico Rosso, gentleman cheese-maker, and saw the mechanics of a mid-sized cheese factory that produces 10,000 pieces monthly, all from cow milk purchased from some 50 dairies.

Winding up our day tour was a stopover at Enoteca della Serra and Ristorante Castello di Ropollo in the little village of Ropollo, a 1000-year-old restaurant of sheer class and character. With the owner in tow, we toured the premises which feature stately banquet dining areas, period furniture, well-stocked cellars and views to die for.

The next day! The sun shone brightly and our driver seemed to feel it would be pleasant weather all through. His spirits seemed greatly lifted, to the point that he actually smiled at everyone! Another drive through rolling countryside, and we were in the heart of Italian wine country. Snuggled in a valley, two hour's drive from Torino, watched over faithfully by vineyards all around, Canelli is a small town with a big wine history.

Moscato, Barbera, Dolcetto, Cortese and Chardonnay are the main varieties of grape grown here, while the foremost wines produced are Asti Spumante (sparkling) and Moscato d'Asti (still), both from Moscato grapes. Other brands are Barbera d'Asti, Dolcetto d'Asti, Cortese Alto Monferrato, and Freisa d'Asti.

The town's uniqueness is its least visible characteristic: a wide network of underground cellars — 'cathedrals' built underground. Controlled temperature and humidity conditions and protection from the sun's rays make these unusual 'aisles' the place to refine 'still' and 'sparkling' wines. I had never seen such huge cellars, but then I had never done such serious wine research before.

Welcoming us in the Town Hall were none other than Signor Oscar Bielli and Signor Sergio Bobbio, the town's Mayor and senior citizen, both affable men with a fondness for their town and its delectable wines, who didn't mind sharing their enthusiasm with visitors. Signor Bobbio struck the right chord by asking us to shed our inhibitions in the interest of wine tasting. Fair enough!

"Welcome to Canelli, my friends. We have plenty of wine for you," he said grandly, to generous applause all around. He allowed time for his statement to sink in and then strode off purposefully, our group in tow, to the Cantine Contratto, a famous wine producer whose cellars can only be described as gigantic. "200,000 bottles, more or less" was what I was told when I inquired how many were stored in the giant cellars on that particular day.

An hour later, the good Mayor and his colleague strode off once again, this time to lunch, which he hosted in the Enoteca Regionale di Canelli, a cellar restaurant of some pedigree. "Sorry, the band isn't playing right now. I don't know why, but there must be a reason. But the food's good and the wine's local," our gracious hosts told us as we settled down at the main table dutifully reserved for us.

Our two-hour lunch over, we all got into our van and drove over a low hill to Barisel, a small local vineyard producing 30,000 bottles annually, which I was told is the bare minimum required for sustenance. In between all this, we had paid a brief visit to Fimer, a company that manufactures bottling equipment (yes, it is that wine connection all over again).

Our last day in the Piemonte region! We passed the region's famed 'sweet hills' and arrived at Enoteca Regionale Piemontese Cavour, a place I would definitely recommend to anyone who is in the vicinity. The establishment's charming wine cellar stocks not just wines, but also chocolates, candles and herbs, and for a cellar at least, has lots of light. Up the steps we went to the Masks Room; then to the 'Last Room' on top of the castle; saw a typical rural workshop, and savoured the atmosphere of old.

Now all had been said and done. Before I could say 'holy ravioli' it was time to leave. As always, time had passed by in a flash.

A week in Piemonte! I wish it were longer.

And of course, I am going to blame it on all those sweets, chocolates and wines.

# An Arabian Break

High up in the cloudless skies, the little bird flew in ever-widening concentric circles, soaring, diving, soaring, diving, the sunlight lighting up its feathers with a brilliant hue. Then, as if by a remote control signal, it plummeted at a blurring speed and perched itself on the broad shoulder of its master, an equally proud specimen.

Ali Hasan smiles a lot these days. Life is looking up. His falcon, a 'blond *Shahin*', among the strongest and speediest birds of prey, has done him proud. The last few hunts have been highly successful and his peers are happy. His prized bird has hunted with the stealth, speed and cunning all falconers dream of. He has become the toast of the desert. Hunters seeking the prized Houbara Bustard have approached him to help them bag the cursorial desert bird. "Soon I'll send him after deer," he says with unconcealed pride.

To understand his joy is to understand Arabia and the complex Arab psyche. In romantic terms at least, falconry means more to Arabs than worldly affairs like the discovery of oil, momentous as that is for the wealth of the region.

This is a land apart, a world where contemporary life meets the timeless desert. What you encounter is the mystique associated with the Arabia of old. Which makes it all a bit special.

Though Arab culture is among the world's oldest, the federation of the United Arab Emirates is still young, the seven trucial states joining only in 1971. When, after ruling these states, the British were pulling out, the rulers of the states realised that their geographical, historical and feudal differences were far outweighed by factors of commonality like language, history, traditions and culture that united them. Thus the Sheikhs of the Emirates, Abu Dhabi, Dubai, Sharjah, Ras Al Khaimah, Umn Al Quwain, Ajman and Fujairah united in a federation. It was a new beginning for an ancient land.

The country that emerged on the southeastern flank of the Arabian Peninsula was small but highly prosperous, culturally diverse, yet bonded by age-old traditions. The discovery of oil in the '60s has hugely boosted development and created a diversified industrial economy. The once trackless deserts today boasts highways; half a dozen modern, international airports, and several seaports that have bridged the gulf. The world descended here hoping to encash on the newfound 'boom'.

Small is beautiful. It fits the bill here. Sea; sun; sand; scenery dominated by a rugged landscape; a people full of pride and simplicity, and a lifestyle that refuses to buckle under modern-day stress. What more can one say.

I had walked from my room at the smallest Hilton hotel in the world to the beach that lapped its backyard, waded into the water, and flapped around for a bit. The water was tepid, and clear enough for me to see the seabed. There was no one about. Just the sea, the sky, and I! It was the quietest of initiations to a land as barren but historic as any to be found on this planet.

Tucked away on the southeastern corner of the Arabian Peninsula, the Emirate of Fujairah is one of the seven members of the United Arab Emirates. The number of people worldwide who haven't even heard of it, exceeds the number who have. I actually believe this to be true.

They knew what they were talking about when they called Fujairah the 'Arabian Jewel'. There's a sort of picture-postcard beauty to the landscape, and until recently it was a well-kept secret, well preserved in its own time-warp. Today the secret is out, but all the exoticism remains. Small in size, and relatively new in stature, it is, however, beautiful and interesting, and could easily be the mythological land that inspired visions of magic lanterns and flying carpets. You step back in time into a setting that's as romantic as it is remote, as quaint as it is offbeat. Quite simply, you are off the beaten track.

The solitude also helps. If ever there was a place that afforded secluded bliss, this is it. Expanses of golden sand and seagulls are often all you see for hours. As a romantic, honeymoon destination it is right up there in the very top drawer. And they mean it when they say visitors are "twice blessed and thrice welcome". So it is time to take some good advice and just land up.

Fujairah's strategic location close to international shipping routes is one aspect of its good fortune, the sea being another, with the Gulf of Oman being one of the world's last great untapped fishing zones, its bountiful catches feeding the people and making fishing a major industry and means of livelihood.

Fujairah has no large deserts and no oil. But what it does have are the country's best beaches — long, sandy stretches gently washed by the Indian Ocean — a coastal plain verdant with farms that feed much of the UAE, and the mountains. Much of the Emirates' 1,300 square kilometres is covered by the rugged, towering and jagged Hajar mountain range, criss-crossed by valleys that slope down to the sea. Though barren, uncultivable, and scarcely inhabitable, these awesomely beautiful mountains trap more rainfall than falls over the entire desert areas of the country, permitting selective agriculture in the mountain *wadis* (dry beds of streams that flow after winter rains from the Hajar mountains that comprise Dubai's backbone onto the desert) and along the coastal plain. This means that the land too has its uses, though paradoxically. Its stark mountains, hidden *wadis*, and shell-strewn beaches have given the East Coast a variety of sceneries unique to this part of the world. This sea and land combination is captivating, and is further enhanced in the form of picturesque farms, forts and castles, and the comparatively temperate climate that's an added bonus.

In the midst of this raw, beautiful swathe of nature, you see industrial dreams too, mainly centred around available raw materials like copper and cement, besides fishing, with the Fujairah Trade Centre being the focus and centre point of foreign trade.

Commerce is strongly visible, but commercial matters don't mean an end of traditions and passions in the Emirates. And it doesn't take long to find out that Fujairah's uniqueness stretches beyond its physical dimensions, stark and beautiful as they are.

Take its favourite sport, for instance. No, it isn't falconry, and it isn't camel racing. It's bullfighting! An ancient ritualistic contest that pits bull against bull, great pampered beasts weighing a tonne or more, carefully raised on a diet of milk, honey and even meat.

The bullfight I managed to see had all the trappings of a national event. It was one big crowd of excited locals who circled the arena, talking animatedly. The contest lasted a bare five minutes, but it was enough, and I can tell you, it isn't for the faint-hearted. Bullfights are normally straightforward contests of solid strength that gets the crowds cheering, shouting, cursing and cajoling the animals to slug it out. The contest normally ends with one bull, deciding he has had enough, making a dash for safety. That's it. It's all over. The crowd disperses.

Travelling around Fujairah, you get a sense of space, of tranquillity. But it wasn't always so peaceful here. The land has seen trouble and bloodshed. The great castles of Bithna and Fujairah, and the smaller forts and watchtowers that guard almost every village, testify to a turbulent past. But today there is peace, and where once battle-locked armies travelled the harsh terrain, you now find solitary camel caravans casting a lonely furrow on the sand.

Perhaps Fujairah's most unique and endearing feature is the fact that it has clung to its roots. Despite its apparent economic progress, it appears nothing has changed. The pace is slow, and the living good.

It was still too early in the day for the desert sand to get hot when we made the journey to Dubai that lies almost alongside.

Starlit dinners, endless shopping bargains, sea, sand, and not a cloud in sight. Can't ask for a better hand to be dealt. I know it all reads like tourism brochure copy, but believe me, it's all true enough.

Modern city meets timeless desert in the leisure, shopping and sporting capital of the Arabian Gulf. Uninterrupted sunshine and a superb climate make it easier for visitors to go about experiencing a unique blend of magnificent Arabian heritage and contemporary design extravaganzas; tradition and hospitality; discovery and adventure. And a superb infrastructure ensures stress-free stays for the well-heeled and the well-informed.

Gateway to the Gulf, the second largest Emirate, and the federation's commercial capital, Dubai is boom country with a capital 'B'. That's the only way I can describe the frenzied growth taking place right in front of your eyes. Hotels that arch up scores of storeys high; towers that pierce the skies; mega malls that want to test conventional architectural norms; even islands with modern housing, all find place in the current building boom.

But in spite of this frenetic urban boom that's almost a blur, the good news is that Dubai hasn't been totally taken over. Not just yet. Some of it still lives to its original beat. And still shows the mystique associated with the Arabia of old. It's just that the city's boom time which started two decades ago refuses to end.

Dubai's popularity isn't just by chance. From the rolling desert to the glittering waters of the Arabian Gulf, a wealth of evenly spread attractions offers ceaseless excitement. Unspoilt beaches and gentle seas offer every conceivable water sport. The Dubai Desert Classic and the famed Dubai World Cup crown the list of high-profile spectator sporting events held in the Middle East's premier golf and horse-racing destinations.

Dubai had been a thriving commercial centre long before the discovery of oil, with pearling and fishing giving it a 2000-year-old link with the sea. Oil, struck offshore in the '60s, and onshore two decades later, created a diversified industrial economy, symbolised by Jebel Ali, the world's largest man-made port. The Jebel Ali Free Zone has attracted many commercial houses keen to exploit the bureaucracy-free environment. Port Rashid is also a regional and international fishing centre, while Dubai International Airport is amongst West Asia's busiest.

Within an hour of arriving, I landed up at one of the age-old, romantic symbols of the Emirate. At the heart of Dubai is the saltwater inlet known as Khor Dubai or Dubai Creek. I don't mind admitting I was a bit surprised, even dismayed at how busy and crowded it was, but my first impression of the creek centred around its paradoxical nature, with tradition and modernity going hand-in-hand.

In days gone by, the creek was the hub of the old pearl-diving trade and provided a rare, sheltered anchorage in the southern coast of the gulf for dhows laden with spices, gold, sandalwood and other priceless cargo. It still harbours these sturdy vessels, along with oil tankers, while its quays are lined by sleek office and hotel buildings. While major international shipping has moved to the modern container terminals at Port Rashid and Jebel Ali Port, the old teak dhows, their sails replaced by motors — much to the dismay of diehard romantics like myself — still moor three abreast along the creek side, loading a bewildering assortment of cargoes. Remnants of old Dubai are found at the mouth of the creek, still home to several bazaars and souqs.

For more glimpses of the Arabia of old, stop by at areas like Shindaga and Bastakiya which still operate windmill towers despite the availability of modern air-conditioning systems.

I have often been asked what one can do here. My answer is quite simple, really. It all depends on you and your fitness levels. Mellowed down visitors can take city tours that include local sights and landmarks like the creek, the souqs, wind-tower houses, Dubai Museum, Dubai World Trade Centre, Jumeirah Mosque, the Sheikhs' palaces, and Emirates Golf Club.

But for the warm blooded, there's ample adventure lying in wait within and just outside the city. An endless list beckons those with a taste for something different. Immerse yourself in the tumbling waterfalls and gorge-like rocks at Hatta Pools, or seek out the hidden secrets of Sheba's Palace and Shimmel. Explore the dramatic shades of red, purple and green of the Hajar mountain range, beautifully offset at sunset. Venture out on desert safaris, try sand-skiing, dune-bashing, *wadi*-bashing, and enjoy the evening safaris by four-wheel drives into the desert that present glorious sunsets, and open-air Arabian and Bedouin barbecues under vast night skies.

Four-wheel drives are available for hire, and you can explore off the beaten track. An hour of rough driving will be rewarded with scenes of unexpected beauty. I can vouch for that. Thursdays and Fridays throughout the winter months feature camel racing, which while a serious sport with locals, also attracts tourists. And there's falconry, so beloved of the Arabs. But don't expect to find falconers at every turn. They are a special class of people and tend to hang out in select areas.

My excuse for not doing it was the one I use the most often. Lack of time! Too much work, too many interviews. But for once, I regretted having slimed out of what I later learnt was a sublime experience. But I'll do it next time I visit, I told myself. Scuba dive, I mean.

The fact is that Dubai's waters are a diver's paradise, with scuba divers guaranteed to get their fill. It is professionally run and you are in the hands of expert divers, so don't worry too much about it. Just take the plunge.

Sailing is also popular. A constant, predictable year-round wind, little current or tide, and warm weather make conditions near perfect. Lasers, toppers and catamarans are available for hire from the Dubai Offshore Sailing Club, Jebel Ali Sailing Club, and the hotel-linked marinas.

And then, of course, there's the shopping. Whether your designs are label-led, off the shelf, or even a little off-the-wall, every taste is catered to in this shrine to shopping, from grand and gigantic complexes to traditional market stalls crammed in noisy streets. And after the ultimate treasure hunt — striking gold at the famed Gold Souq, with its hundreds of tiny shops that gleam with bangles, chains, necklaces and pendants — celebrate your day's success with the plentiful post-shopping partying to be enjoyed in the welcoming Emirate. With the souqs being at one end of the spectrum, at the other end are huge plazas like the Al Ghurair and The Centre. This contrast of lifestyles is what gives Dubai its special charm.

You can do just about everything but walk. Simply because no one else does! This is limo-town, and the only real chance to stretch your legs comes in the souqs.

The morning sun hadn't quite settled down to its smoldering best when we journeyed to Sharjah. Moving on from one Emirate to another isn't dramatic. But you do notice some changes.

Lying midway between the group of seven Emirates, flanked by the Arabian Gulf to the west and the Gulf of Oman to the east, Sharjah, which literally means 'Rising from the East', is the third largest of the seven Emirates that combine to make up the UAE.

The cultural capital of the Gulf, Sharjah has emerged from a troubled past, surviving successive attempts of domination by various powers. Babylonians, Assyrians, Persians, Greeks, Phoenicians, and Romans, all descended here with their visions of conquests and domination. But despite repeated onslaughts, the region was never completely subjugated, which prevented any one distinct culture from predominating. This enhances its charm, as does the fact that it's a startling combination of originality and modernity, featuring ancient buildings nestling alongside gleaming modern structures.

"It's like no other" is how locals describe their port, which for long had been a landmark for the entire region. The two gulfs that straddle it made Sharjah a major seaport, trading centre and docking point for shuttle ships between India, the Far East, Europe and Africa. Today, the port's busier than ever, its size enhanced by two modern ports, the Khalid New Port and Khor-Ifakkan. But despite feverish modernity, you can glimpse the past in simple things like traditional dhows berthed alongside modern tankers.

Tradition also shines through prominent buildings. 220 spacious mosques, simple in colour but imposing in size, are the architectural mainstay. Also imposing are the souqs, magnificent buildings that offer tribute to modern architecture. The most prominent is the Central Souq, a huge, towering building with ornately decorated façades, blue-domed roofs, and high-wind towers.

The 18th and 19th centuries saw Sharjah at the height of its glory as a leading centre for Arabic languages and religious studies, and its status remains undiminished today. The cultural and artistic lineage here is drawn from classical Arabic traditions that cover a wide field, stretching from trading and farming, to everything from poetic verses, traditional dresses, community smoking, and day-to-day domestic lifestyles.

Name the tradition and chances are that Sharjah is its original source, as seen from colourful national dances like Alna Ashat, Al Ardah, and Al Liwa, and from institutions like the Old Al Bediyah Mosque, whose history has been traced back to the Hijr period of the Ottoman Empire.

Though visiting with a group, I did the smart thing. I broke away and went about discovering things on my own. A drive through the so-called downtown area took me past gleaming structures that must have put design and architecture professionals to test.

The Emirate's modern face is best seen in the Al Boorj Avenue, Sharjah's 'Wall Street' and financial and commercial hub, a world of high rise buildings with banking and commercial establishments. Turning the financial wheels here are the Sharjah Chamber of Commerce and the Local Economic Department.

For unadulterated luxury, try the Marbella Club, an Arab-Andalusian style village surrounded by exotic gardens and lapped by the waters of the Khalid Lagoon. Speciality tours, restaurants, bars, a discotheque, and plush villas combine to offer a package of first class hotel facilities in a discreetly luxurious style. The Al Jazira Park is another oasis, a natural playground of flowers, palms, lakes, and children's playing areas.

Plush, swanky, and thoroughly modern! But somehow, I didn't feel this to be the real thing. The place offers more, I told myself as I kept up my local sightseeing tour, in search of tradition and old-world charm.

I did find it and in plentiful supply, and believe me, it was worth the effort and wait. The spirit of Sharjah is best captured in select areas like the Al Rolla Square. The word 'rolla' originates from a famous old tree that grew in the heart of the Emirate. Historically, the area around the Al Rolla tree was the venue for social interaction, Muslim festivals, and commercial transactions. In early days, rulers sat under the tree, holding council and passing resolutions. It was here that the main souq originated, attracting buyers and sellers.

The old tree has now died, and with it some of its stories, and the area is now a public and leisure park. But the tree has been immortalised in a memorial, a reminder to the people of a symbol no one wants to forget. It wasn't that crowded when I happened to pass by, but I could sense just how important the place was for the locals.

For some real local flavour, drop in at the Popular Coffee Shop situated in the Khalid Lagoon area, where you can enjoy traditional preparations served in the same manner and utensils of the olden days. If it is atmosphere you are seeking, this is the place. And the coffee's not bad either.

This business of shopping in the UAE! It's a story by itself simply because everyone asks me about it and then before

I can answer, they volunteer their own opinion on it. The fact is that shopping here is something to talk about, and quite an experience. One of the fallouts of the Emirate's wealth is the quality and variety of goods available, with an endless array of international labels, all duty-free, and while Dubai is exceptional in its wealth of offerings, Sharjah doesn't lag far behind. You see this the moment you enter the giant souqs like New Central, Al Majarrah, and Khor Fakkan. With their buildings and façades considered architectural symbols of the Middle East, these establishments stock everything from designer clothing to period furniture and antiques.

Look for bargains in antique silver, handmade jewellery, and local artefacts, and buy your gold here at fixed, competitive prices. Al Oruba Street is a modern shopping area offering international brands of electronics and textiles, and there's good family shopping at Al Mahda Street that has several boutiques and restaurants. For local merchandise and local flavour, visit the Old Souq, the oldest market around, with shops selling antiques, herbs, and medicines. Your money will go quite a long way here.

Sharjah is on the move. And you can catch the pulse of locals and see for yourself that the land which 'Rose from the East' is still rising.

My jaunt across the Emirates was a lesson in history. The country is the heart of Arabia! One thing I saw with great clarity is that Arabs are proud, colourful people, conscious of their status and physical appearance, and they do like to cling on to their customs, which is precisely what makes them and their homes interesting. Men in traditional white *dishdasha* (dress) and white *kaffiyeh* (head cover) secured by black cords, and women in *abaya* (burqa) and veil, can be seen in a variety of places and in a variety of modes, from driving flashy cars to working on computers.

Nothing mirrors the Arabia of old better than two traditional sports that border on passion here. Falconry is an intrinsic part of the land and its people, with the hunting of small animals and birds being a means of livelihood for the original Gulf population. The Arabs perfected the art of falcon training and the bird's physical strength and speed make it a formidable hunter and bird of prey. Falconry as a sport is supported by the UAE authorities, and having one's own 'Shahin' or 'Baz' is a status symbol.

And then there's camel racing. For centuries the camel was a major means of livelihood in Arabia, being the sole means of transport and the main food and clothing source for Bedouins. It was with the camel's help that Arab culture and civilisation spread overland through trade routes. Today, the camel's status has changed, and it is featured in races, with much money and honour at stake.

If there's one place in the world where I would like to be hungry, it's Arabia. I mean it. The local dining experience leaves little to be desired, with all the bounties of Arab cooking on offer. You can enjoy genuine, traditional hospitality, and with a bit of luck and the right contacts, an invitation to a local home, which is always a special treat. If you are fortunate enough to partake of a domestic meal, you can expect a wholesome fare including famous regional dishes and local delicacies, notably *thareed, harees,* and *mohamma* — a fine mix of meat, fish, rice and vegetables. The sweet-tooth is catered to by succulent preparations like *ligeimat khabeeza, halwa* and *aseeda,* and everything is accompanied by a wide assortment of fruit, and washed down with light tea.

There's a wealth of other tasty dishes too. Like the famous *jos mahrouse* nut dip; spicy homemade sausages; baked fish in Tahini sauce, and the breads stuffed with minced lamb, tomatoes, onions and herbs. The *shish barak* (meat-filled dumplings cooked in yoghurt sauce) melt in the mouth.

118

Speciality Arab food apart, there is a huge range of cuisines from other regions. For a subtle change of taste, try the delectable Lebanese cuisine: richly flavoured, slow-cooked stews and varied hot and cold *meze* (the Middle Eastern equivalent of the Asian dim sum), *falafel* (fried chickpea balls) and lamb and chicken *shawarma* (meat slices from a spit) are specialities. Other specialities include *hummus* (chickpea spread), *baba ghanoush* (smoked and mashed eggplant), and the Lebanese cracked wheat-based salad *tabbouleh*. *Bossara* is a broad bean puree with fried onion, and *tamiya* fried cakes, also broad bean-based, are very Egyptian.

Try the Maghreb cuisine of Morocco, Algeria and Tunisia with its unique blend of African, Arabic and European influences. *Harira* is the traditional spicy Moroccan vegetable soup. There are also boureck pastries filled with lamb, dried figs and roasted almonds. Main dish specialities are the tagine clay pot stews and couscous.

Turkish delicacies include authentic *doner kebabs*, mint cigars, baked eggplant stuffed with minced lamb, vegetables and cheese, and the famously sweet baklava dessert.

Upscale eateries provide rich fare. It's all quite luxurious. Diners recline on silk cushions, and pass around the *'chichi'* (water pipe), while belly dancers weave their way sinuously between the tables. For some genuine flavour, visit one of the smoky taverns that are strong on simple food and gossip. Sip Bedouin coffee in tiny porcelain cups. Listen to the hubbub.

What can I really say about my Arabian break? There was no Aladdin's lamp, and there were no flying carpets.

But sometimes even these become redundant.

# Small is Beautiful

'Simple things are the best life has to offer.'

'Less is more.'

'Small is beautiful.'

'Look, honey, I shrunk the world.'

Most times I am a serious guy. Most times! That's a fact. But I have learnt to accept the non-serious part of life with a smile and a wink, if you see what I mean, and I am amazed at how often I would have to smile and wink if I kept up this attitude with any consistency. Anyway, let me tell you smiling and winking are harder to do than you would imagine. Especially when you travel to distant, foreign lands.

But I was fine for now. This was perfect turf for non-serious diversion and entertainment, and the fact had sunk in and I had sort of blended in. To be perfectly frank, I had no idea of what I was going to see and experience. How's that for pre-travel planning?

It took me just five short steps to cross two canals, two streets, and a park, and arrive at the city centre. On my right lay train tracks with a speeding locomotive, all of six feet long, and confronting me was a typical Dutch pasture with a foot-high windmills. You could say it was just another normal day in The Netherlands.

In fact, everything was completely normal except for the Lilliputian setting. And this wasn't Gulliver's Travels. Just mine!

Having seen the magnificent Peace Palace just an hour ago in The Hague, I couldn't help marvelling at the stunning accuracy of detail of its 18-inch-high replica that lay just in front of me at my feet.

Honestly, it's something only the Dutch could have thought of. Charming in its composition, skill, ingenuity, simplicity and ability to surprise, it tugs at your imagination, offering just that right kind of mental escape. Hundreds of tiny structures (miniaturised versions of famous sites and structures) are set out and displayed with precision, blending into the devised landscapes — buildings, public areas, houses, train stations, airports, and tiny models of buses, cars, people — all the physical ingredients found in cities or in the country.

For first-time visitors, the miniature city of Madurodam in The Hague comes as a complete and very pleasant surprise. At least that's how I felt. It's a theme park — actually a miniaturised capsule of the country — that focuses on several important national symbols, and provides an unusual and exciting experience and an escape from everyday life. Besides charming everyone, its fairy tale type of escape is also an educational exercise that highlights The Netherlands' industrial progress, skillfully woven into its colourful traditions and lifestyles.

Day after day, the year round, Madurodam tells the unique story of Dutch history, heritage and development through the medium of its miniaturised models. Built to the smallest detail on a scale of 1:25, and set in lawns and gardens — which add to the general landscaping — the replicas that are stunningly accurate in replicating the design and composition of their original models, mirror the country better than any tourist brochure. So vivid are the reproductions, and so illustratively complete, they are simply mersmerising.

It's obvious that a lot of thought and research has gone into the project and they have done a superb job of national representation. A lot of what's worth seeing in The Netherlands is on display. Name a notable feature of the country, and it is there, looking exactly like the original, only much, much smaller. There are replicas of the Palace on the Dam; the Peace Palace; the Alkmaar Cheese Market; dykes; bridges; the celebrated canalside houses and warehouses of Amsterdam and Delft, and that most famous and romantic of all national symbols — the windmill.

Featuring all the trimmings of an aviation hub, there's Madurodam Airport which shows all the activity of a normal, working day, with aircraft of some 30 airlines out on the tarmac, runways, terminal buildings, and parking lots. Superb replicas of national highways, complete with vehicular traffic, form a girdle. Amsterdam's Railway Station shows its customary flurry of activity. Rotterdam's world-famous harbour is its usual busy self. There are also churches, cathedrals, banks, and shopping malls, all of which show a high degree of ingenuity.

While most models are made of stone, metal and wood are used where required and the paintwork is similar to that of the original buildings. Everything's like the original. It's just as if someone waved a magic wand and shrunk everything to minuscule size.

Dwarfing everything in sight, tourists walk around the park with 'giant strides', marvelling at the precision and imagination of the miniature models. One gingerly steps over trains that criss-cross the city on 4.5 kilometres of tracks, and over flat-bottomed boats that tour the canals. One stops to gaze at and admire public buildings and windmill sails that turn cheerfully.

I don't know if it was just the models on display or the enthusiasm shown by everyone around, but the mood got me. And I am not really an amusement-park buff. Just a 'make the best of any given situation' kind of person. I had also been lucky with the weather, which isn't something to be taken for granted, by the way. Sunshine bathed everything in a golden hue when I was there. Visitors milled around the exhibits, chatting and laughing; adults gave serious educative lectures to kids who didn't seem to be listening. With all the movement taking place around the 'city', there was plenty of life all around and things were animated enough.

Also featured in the miniature city is 'Sand World', the world's only indoor sand sculpture show, which shows panoramas in sand that relate the historic tale of The Netherlands, and its struggle against the sea.

Adults join children in playing out their 'giant' fantasies, peering at the little displays, taking giant strides and stepping over tiny structures with an exaggerated sense of power. You could say it's a bit comic, but that's the whole point of the project.

What wine is to France, flowers must surely be to The Netherlands. They are always around everywhere. Depending on the season, the city is a sea of brilliantly coloured roses or tulips that form a delectable background.

As is often the case with me, I decided that all this wonderful walking around in such salubrious surroundings called for something nice to eat and drink. And I had a very good idea about what's good to eat in The Netherlands.

In case you are interested, the Dutch kitchen boasts specialities like 'zuurkool' (pickled cabbage); peasoup; pork with sauerkraut; and smoked eel, which don't just taste good but are also 'figure-friendly'. There's also the must-try 'rijsttafel' which can comprise up to 20 different dishes stretching from very spicy to sweet, and the omnipresent '*broodjes*' (bread rolls filled with ham, cheese, liver, shrimps, or steak tartare). And there are the pancake specialists, and of course, the famous Dutch herring. And there's Jenever (Dutch gin).

I guess I had over-estimated the catering establishments here, and eventually settled for chicken sandwiches and salad, but that was perfectly fine.

Comes nighttime, and another Madurodam emerges. The city is transformed into a totally different type of world with some 50,000 twinkling lamps giving it a fairy tale character that adds to its mystique and enhances its image.

My initial misgivings about the place notwithstanding, I stuck around and walked its length and breadth.

The afternoon had slipped by and before I knew it, it was time to leave. All too soon as far as I was concerned. And I did mention I am a serious sort of guy. A few hundred 'giant' strides and I had done justice to the place. A few more and I had exited.

Outside, it was the normal world, or the world as we know it. But in there, it was a world too. Just very different. And very charming.

# Muscat Musings

It could have been any old street back home!

It wasn't. It was an old street quite far away from home, but somehow I didn't feel that way.

Single-file, I followed Darwish, who for a man of his size moved with surprising agility. And some purpose! But then he was home turf. Insisting he wasn't trying to "shake me off", he strode past shop after shop, each overflowing with merchandise, some the size of a small lounge, others no bigger than a walk-in closet. Just when I thought walking right through the souq was the drill, the only drill, he stopped and pointed out a cluster of three shops with a flourish. "Buy your dates here when we return. The quality is good. Now let's carry on. I'll bring you back later."

All this wasn't much of an initiation really, but it did convey a vivid feel for the place. Our brief bazaar experience at the Muttrah souq had been an insight of sorts, making me feel a bit at home. Amazing what dingy streets, crowded shop-counters, a babble of voices, and heady fragrances can do for one's orientation.

But make no mistake, there's nothing dingy or noisy about the city as a whole. This was just one little pocket tucked away in the folds of tradition. The city itself is a product of thoughtful, careful planning and ranks among the world's cleanest, quietest, and least cluttered. I am ready to put my signature on that.

Once a thriving, strategically located port of the Arabian Peninsula, Muscat today presents a blend of the old and the new, the traditional and the modern. It is Oman's capital and hub of government machinery, a bustling commercial centre, and home to some 500,000 inhabitants. And for those who know where to find them, there are interesting old stories of former romantic times, still doing the rounds. I heard some, while sipping strong black coffee from tiny porcelain cups, seated amidst old locals who have had their brush with history and transition.

My impressions about the city had been formed even before we landed. From the air it had looked like a display model, all the structures appearing to be the same colour, same shape and almost same size. All square, all white, making the white shine out on the overall expanse of brown.

The city's first and most telling impression on the visitor is its physical composition, characterised by wide, open spaces, carefully planned buildings, and landscaped gardens that form a neat patchwork. Dominating the impressive cityscape of concrete and parks, are pale white structures that all seem to be freshly painted. The blend of these structures co-existing with traditional ones, hints at careful architectural planning and lends a distinct character and charm to things.

Having spent over 20 years with the Ministry of Information, Darwish knows how to sell his city. Ever the host and guide, he started off my 'touch & feel' city tour at its undisputed showpiece, the seaside palace of HM Sultan Qaboos bin Said. Nestled between steep rocky hills, the stately palace with its huge multi-coloured columns that

126

feature different architectural styles, presents a spectacular sight both from the sea and land. Featuring a high level of architectural skill and intricate workmanship, it's an opulent structure that befits royalty. Unfortunately, you can't just 'walk in' so we peered between the railings of the main gate and got our fill of the magnificent building.

The next couple of hours were spent driving around to see the local sights. And driving here is truly enjoyable for two reasons: the roads are superb and the traffic never dense. Parks, statues, and artefacts dotted the highways as we travelled around the city, passing white buildings — some Islamic in architecture — others sporting a somewhat standard, modern look. There are fairly long distances between different government offices, hotels and markets, but our tour did full justice and we got to see the impressive cityscape with its distinct white structures.

It wasn't really part of the script, but our next stop turned out to be the other local showpiece! The Al Bustan Palace Hotel goes beyond being a mere hotel to having become a symbol of national pride. It's got grace, style, and most significantly, it's got affluence written all over it.

Set against a dramatic mountain background on 200 acres of private beach and lush green gardens, the hotel enjoys spectacular views over the Gulf of Oman. The tone is set even before you enter the spacious gardens. Perched on the roundabout at the hotel's entrance is the Sohar, the ship that sailed to China years ago on the fabled Silk Route.

The huge, magnificent structure features fancy dining areas where waiters serve the choicest caviar and prawns; luxurious rooms overlooking the gardens and seafront, and a stunning, absolutely stunning lobby. Large enough to hold a Boeing 747 standing on its nose, the atrium lobby must rank as one the world's most ornate and opulent. 33 metres high and equal in total height to the jebel that was blasted away and occupied the area of the atrium, it dwarfs you not just because of its high-domed ceiling with its white, inlay rotunda, but also its overall impact.

Flat, giant mosaic-enriched pillars, each sporting one chandelier, spiral upwards with impunity and also hem the lounge in. Offering regal comfort are rich carpeting and leather and silk settees with accompanying side-tables showing fine-quality inlay work. A fountain in the centre breaks the monotony of the furnishings. A marbled corridor encircles the lobby, leading onto other areas.

"My kind of place," I told a smiling Darwish as we left.

Then came my exposure to genuine local flavour! True to his word, Darwish took me back to Muttrah, a busy commercial centre renowned for its corniche, girdle-shaped promenade, bay and harbour with romantic old dhows and visiting cruise ships and naval vessels, and the smells of the sea. Lining the promenade are offices, shops, cafés, trading houses — Silverworld and Mustafa Sultan Trading Co were names I noticed — and souqs, notably the Muttrah Souq.

The afternoon slipped by as I meandered through the complex maze of this market souq with its seemingly endless corridors of little and not-so-little shops. I waded through stalls of vegetables and dates, and saw the day's catch on display for sale in the busy fish souq. Incense fragrance was everywhere as I did the mandatory dates and dry fruit shopping. It was my first real taste of the famed Arab art of bargaining.

Haggle, bargain, enjoy yourself. Munching on ripe dates and sipping mildly spiced herbal tea, I listened to three shopkeepers talking to me simultaneously, and discovered why Arabian shopping can be delightful, exciting and tiring at the same time. Clocks, watches, electronics, a wealth of hand-crafted jewellery, antiques, and assorted foodstuffs from the world over, besides silver coffee pots, tribal rugs, and *khanjars* (curved ceremonial daggers), are just some items available in the souqs, which also offer a typical 'market-day' oriented atmosphere, with noise, robust bargaining and lots of head-shaking. But the best part of the deal is that they accept multiple currencies.

In Souq Al Juma, popularly known as Friday Market, you can pick up an assortment of items that range from furniture to cars. In Al Qurm, elegant shopping malls beckon visitors, and though the bargaining decreases, the atmosphere remains the same.

The sea has contributed generously to Oman's beauty, and several sports reflect the country's intrinsic relationship with the seas. The good news for visitors is that some of the country's best seaports are easily accessible.

It didn't take me long to exploit this fact. Afternoon saw us making tracks out of town, this time in a chauffeured limousine. The road sliced through the hills, a strip of black tarmac on a brown patchwork, as we headed for Bander Jussa, also known as Qantab Beach, a mere 15-minutes drive from downtown Muscat. People had recommended the place to me and one of the hotel managers had described the beach as 'beautiful'. Well, he had it spot on. In my opinion Qantab Beach must surely rank among the most beautiful in the entire Middle East.

A sheltered bay on the edge of the beach, this is a stunning, spectacularly beautiful area with a golden beach, and deep blue sea whose colour becomes more stark because of the contrasting golden sands and huge pale brown rock formations eerily jutting out of the water. Things were about as quiet as they could get. There were some boats bobbing on the water, a few people trudging along the beach, and a few seagulls flying about. That's about it in terms of activity. But it was beautiful.

An added asset to the beach area is the Oman Dive Centre rated among the world's best for snorkeling, diving and dolphin watching. Being a serious journalist trying to earn a decent living, I didn't have time for such trivial pursuits, but if you can find the time and energy, don't miss the chance. Take the plunge.

Marina Bander Al Rowdha offers scuba-diving lessons, chartered cruises and sailboats for hire, and the restaurant that overlooks the harbour serves arguably the Middle East's best fish curry. The main nerve-centre of the large-scale shipping activity is the state-of-the-art deep-water port, Mina Sultan Qaboos. At the Yacht Centre of the Marine Science and Fisheries Centre, you can see both the practical and leisurely side of marine life. But for me the best stopover was the small fishing village of Qantab that provides a great view of the sea, and a close look into the unique lifestyle of local fishermen.

Several other places beckon visitors. My favourite is the Bait Al Zubair Museum that serves as a valuable link between Oman's past, present and future and contains a fine and comprehensive collection of antiques that include traditional and historic Omani weaponry, jewellery, costumes, domestic utensils, as well as recreated urban and rural environments. Housed in a regal building, the museum's easy to reach, discover and appreciate.

Definitely meriting a visit is the Natural History Museum which is a 'shop window' through which you can see Oman's wealth of flora and fauna. Displayed are animals, shells, insects and photographs. A separate section — The Whale Hall — displays the skeleton of a huge sperm whale and smaller species. Also interesting is the Omani French Museum, and the Petroleum Development Exhibition Centre.

My two excursions out of the city proved well worth the effort. A three-hour drive through the rugged mountains got me to the Wahiba Sands region that seemed to step right out of the *Arabian Nights*. Sand dunes stand as silent sentinels guarding vast tracts of desert and scrubland, and there's not a soul in sight. I got out of the four-wheel drive, walked for half an hour up a sand dune that turned out to be higher, softer and more difficult to climb than imagined, collected a respectable amount of sand in my clothes, face and beard, and called it a day.

My other outing was to Quriyat, some 95 kilometres from Muscat. We left the capital's white buildings behind and hit the highway, and almost immediately, brown, jagged low hills closed in on us, before it all opened up into a flat valley, the hills becoming more distant, flanking us on our right and left. Ahead, the mountains lay bare, layer after layer. The closest, lowest were dark brown, fading into brownish grey as they progressed further afield. The last, the highest one seemed to touch the clouds.

10 kilometres short of Quriyat, we topped a ridge and literally 'ran' into a stunning view. The sea was a pale blue carpet in the distance, framed by jagged mountains, with the highway meandering through them like a black ribbon. 'Wilayat Quriyat Welcomes You' said a sign on the road. Nothing else and no one else.

The little town comprises single-storeyed houses, some lower than the palms — that jutted out into the skyline — hardy sentinels of the desert. We passed The Celebrations Square and reached the shoreline, with a few houses and the offices of the Ministry of Agriculture & Fisheries, located just by the sea. The town is separated from the beach by a headland and narrow lagoon. As for the beach itself, it was 'crowded' when we arrived. With flamingoes! Literally hundreds of them, and not a human in sight!

Modern and progressive it may be, but Oman remains distinctively and proudly Arab in outlook and attitude, and Muscat personifies this to the letter. The call of the muezzin summoning the faithful to prayer, souqs typically Arabian in atmosphere, and traditional styles of dressing — men in white *disdashas* and caps or turbans, women in long black silk robes — serve as constant reminders that you are in the heart of Arabia.

Dress codes are important and the *disdashas* are almost always spotlessly clean. You never see a crumpled or dirty *disdasha*. While most are white, some coloured ones are also seen. Men and women both seem to glide along in their graceful robes.

In true Arabian style, the city mirrors several different images, some journeying back to its founding 900 years ago: old shipyards that built the famous dhows that sailed the seas in those early days, and battle-scarred old structures, notably two old Portuguese forts, Jelali and Merani, that flank the rocky cove around which the city is built.

Oman is on the move and moving forward, as I saw through my meetings with their senior government personnel. Perhaps the best summing up of Muscat was done by Abdullah Bin Abbas Bin Ahmed, President, Muscat Municipality and Municipal Council, who stated that he found it difficult to describe any particular favourite areas, "because I love each and every aspect of the city."

According to Ali Mohamed Za'abnoot, Director General of Information, Ministry of Information, Oman combines heritage and culture, and at the same time is moving forward and transforming. And you get to experience this first-hand in Muscat.

As the setting sun painted the western edge of the city a pale gold, way out, the luxury yachts cut a swathe in the water, their bows shining against the spray. And the Al Bustan Palace Hotel shone like an emerald against the backdrop of the sea.

It was Arabia, served on a platter. Nice and easy!

# 'Mud-Slinging' For Health

I must confess I was a bit skeptical.

Hearing things and nodding wisely at cocktail parties is one thing, and actually trying them out is quite another matter altogether. But then what did I really have to lose, I told myself as I 'took the plunge'.

What happened next is an experience I'll long cherish simply because it was a one-off, something you can do only in one single place in the entire world. So it's all firmly etched in my memory as being amongst my most exhilarating experiences ever. I tend not to get excited about things, but I mean this.

I floated around like a weightless being, splashed and frolicked like a child, even tried to 'drown'. And couldn't. And so, the story goes on. The high salt content in the water keeps you afloat, and seeing all those excited folks out there in the water means it must be some kind of a big deal.

My dolphin-act done, I was ready for further action, namely, the famed mud packs. They cover you with their famous black mud, wrap you up like a mummy, massage your body and ego, and recommend what's good for you and what's not. And no one ever seems to complain. Even after paying the hefty bill. As for me, well, I'll tell you all about my massage experience later.

Legend has it that Cleopatra was among the first to exploit the therapeutic benefits of the Dead Sea mud. Talk about having a super model to promote your products! Archaeologists have actually uncovered what was an ancient cosmetics factory here, and evidence that it served the Egyptian queen whose beauty literally shook the world. The biblical kings, David and Solomon also frequented the local cure centres. With such a burden of history before me, I couldn't possibly stay behind and miss out.

At first glance, the place does seem dead, with overpowering silence, eerie salt pillars poking through the early morning fog, and the water completely still. But in fact, the Dead Sea region is actually full of life and it doesn't take long to see this. Graceful gazelles graze close to the saltiest water on earth. Minutes away are freshwater springs and nature reserves. And of course, how can I forget to mention the tourists. It seemed all the tourists in Israel were there when I checked in at the Nirvana Hotel and Spa.

Here, at the lowest point on earth — 400 metres below sea-level — at the world's saltiest and most mineral-rich expanse of water, are located the ultimate health and beauty resorts, thanks to the mineral-rich Dead Sea water and health-giving springs, the famous therapeutic mud, and the clear sun's rays that all combine to form an unbeatable wellness package.

Also known as the Salt Sea, the Dead Sea gets its name from the fact that nothing lives in it owing to its 30 per cent concentration of salts and minerals like potassium, magnesium, bromide and calcium, all important for cell metabolism. This makes it ten times more saline than other seas, and also accounts for the water's phenomenal buoyancy, which precludes swimming but keeps everything and everyone afloat.

From the Jordan River at its northern point, to Sodom at the southernmost tip, the Dead Sea coast harbours a variety of spas and nature-care centres, skilfully exploiting the region's extraordinarily rich mineral wealth and benefits of the soil. All the big hotels have spa pools filled with piped-in Dead Sea water, and offer mineral-rich mud pack treatments and underwater and normal massages. Pampering clients are a host of recreation therapy techniques that include everything from treatment concentrating on the application of the minerals, to peloid mud packs and wraps, bathing in mineral-rich water pools fed by sulphur springs, and programmed exposure to the sun. Floating in the sea itself is also beneficial as weightlessness relieves pressure on joints. At least that's what they'll have you believe.

Not surprisingly, the world converges here to look 'fresh and beautiful' by reaping the benefits of the rich minerals on offer. A million annual visitors, 70 per cent foreigners, bathe playfully in the sulphur springs and douse themselves in the famous black mud. Skin problems, joint ailments, arthritis, rheumatism, sports injuries! Any excuse will do.

Therapy apart, the other major industry here is the minerals themselves. The Dead Sea cosmetics and skin-care products business is booming, with over 30 companies busy exploiting the extraordinary local mineral wealth to make and market medicines and cosmetics. They are packaging Dead Sea mud and minerals, and refining a large range of products from the waters and elements from the desert vegetation, like bath salts, mud for facials, soaps, creams, and lotions. Dead Sea cosmetics today line the shelves of beauty shops and parlours around the world.

Talk about living off the land!

Though exports are major, a visit to the region is a visit to the source. And the local prices are unbeatable. Kibbutz

Nitzha Shalem produces the famous Ahava line of cosmetics and also houses a visitor centre that gets 100,000 annual visitors. Ahava, which by the way, means love, has some 60 per cent of the total Dead Sea market.

Health and wellness apart, historical treasures abound in the Dead Sea region, which mirrors the glories of the past and documents grand moments of history. It was where the Jordan River flows into the Dead Sea that Jesus was baptised. Today, the devout come here in large numbers to immerse themselves in the holy waters. A quick car ride took me to several important sites in the area. They are all ancient and historical. But the one I want to mention is Qumran, where the Essenes — closely associated with Jesus — lived their strict religious and disciplined lives, leaving behind the priceless heritage known as the Dead Sea Scrolls. Remains of their buildings have been excavated here, shedding light on their lives, and attracting tourists from the world over.

You can also take desert safaris to biblical spots like Mount Sodom, made entirely of salt, and try to figure out which among the salt pillars is Lot's wife.

'Fortress With a View!' I almost didn't go, the thought of trying out the hotel Dead Sea water pool again tugging at my fancy. But my sense of adventure prevailed. 'What the heck, I'm not going to be here forever,' I told myself and joined the group bound for the excursion. And what a delight it turned out to be.

I took the cable car up. I have taken several cable car rides around the world, in calm weather and rough, but this one was exceptional. And with good reason! The Fortress of Masada is among Israel's premier heritage spots, marking the site where zealots made their last, heroic stand, amidst much bloodshed.

Today the fortress stands brooding, telling the story of its past and providing a stunning view of the Dead Sea and its surroundings. We were in the midst of a geographical phenomenon, perched high above the water and yet barely at sea level. Descending to 'ground and water' level (which meant we were once again 400 metres below sea-level), I realised the sheer geographical and geological magnitude of this place. 'What a low,' I told myself, awed by everything around me.

This may or may not have had anything to do with my feeling a sudden pang of hunger, which actually pleased me because so far I hadn't done any sort of justice to Israeli cuisine. There's a lot to be said for it. Reflected on the table, are the various resident communities with their diverse geographical and cultural origins. The Israeli kitchen harbours a multitude of cuisines and recipes which have accompanied the Jewish people's return to the Promised Land. The local hospitality has its basis in Jewish antiquity. The Bible relates the story of the three angels who visited the tent of the patriarch Abraham and his wife Sarah, and were treated to a lavish meal.

There's richness in everything. It is said that when the settlers first beheld their land, they described it as one overflowing with milk and honey, lush, fertile, and bountiful, with fruits of enormous proportions. A famous image depicts a cluster of grapes so gigantic that it had to be carried by two ancient Israelites.

For snacks and light meals, local specialities are flat *pitta* bread with *hummus* (chickpea spread) and *tehina* (sesame seed spread), *falafel* (fried chickpea balls), and *shawarma* (slices of lamb from a spit), also eaten with *pitta* or with the larger *lafa* bread. High-quality citrus fruits are always part of a meal, be that in the main course or as desserts. Exotic fruits, fresh vegetables, olives and olive oil almost constitute an industry by themselves. Combined with a high quality range of dairy products and an inventive way with meat-substitutes, they cater to vegetarians in a society that generally likes its meat.

And there are all those wines! A discriminating palate rather than capacious thirst dictates the Israelis' drinking patterns. Wine has been produced here for thousands of years, with the country being an ideal grape-growing area thanks to the sandy, red soils of the coastal plain and the volcanic soils of the Golan Heights. The happy result is quality wines such as Cabernet, Sauvignon, Grenache, Merlot, Zinfandel, Chardonnay, Emerald Riesling and Semillon.

So much for food and wine. Back at the hotel, it was business as usual. Which meant sipping on endless fresh and tangy fruit juices; hanging about at the spas and pools; and in my case, a bout of unexpected, unsolicited adventure.

"You can't come all this way and leave without doing the, you know, 'health thing'," purred the lady behind the spa counter. She sounded serious, and that was good enough for me. And I was a long way from home. I signed up with a smile and a flourish that would have done credit to Broadway.

"Anything goes," I declared grandly. "I'll try anything once." The smile this evoked almost knocked me and the six other males present in the hotel lobby over. "It's settled then," she purred. "Just go through and register yourself, and oh by the way, I do recommend the mud pack."

I signed up for the 'bath' and 'mud-pack treatment'. They pipe in the famous Dead Sea water into large tanks and you float around in relative privacy. It was sheer ecstasy. As mentioned earlier, with 30 times the salt and mineral content of normal sea water, the Dead Sea's waters are not only highly therapeutic but also ensure that you can't 'sink'.

Floating on the surface, I felt on top of the world at the lowest point on earth.

Now it was time for the mud pack. I had heard about it of course. Led into another chamber, I was made to lie down, and without fuss or ceremony, three attendants — a male and two ladies — went to 'work' on me. They kept up a constant chatter. Where was I from? How long was I going to be in Israel? Was I enjoying the trip so far? Had I ever had a mud pack done on myself before?

I sensed her presence but did not see her. "Hi there," she chirped. "It's me again. How much mud would you like? You can choose the quantity, you know."

Apparently, they had different packages stretching from 3 kilos to anything like 10 kilos or more. "I think you should take 12 kilos," she declared with a deadpan expression without waiting for my reaction.

The attendants froze. There was this silence. I should have caught on something was amiss but my ego refused to let me appear fazed. "What's a measly 12 kilos of special mud for a seasoned travel-writer and traveller like myself," I declared softly to no one in particular. As if by remote-control, they all nodded in agreement.

So 12 kilos it was. With great love and care, they covered me with the finest quality Dead Sea mud, telling me all sorts of things that ranged from how 'good' the mud wrap was for me, what a good sport I was, and how mud just 'became' me.

Later, with the mud washed off me and my skin sort of glowing, I accosted her in the lobby. "Thanks for the health thing," I told her graciously. "You're welcome," she countered equally graciously. We chatted for a bit, exchanged pleasantries, and then I asked her if she was always so obliging and helpful to guests.

"Only when I meet men whose hair is longer than mine," she shot back. This time her smile could have knocked over the Fortress of Masada.

The Dead Sea continues to captivate one's imagination as it has done for over 2,000 years. Beautiful, peaceful, almost ghostly, it is a special place with a special history and geography. Every day and every night, it comes 'alive'.

Ask the beautiful people.

# Disney Dance

There isn't much to be said for late-night arrivals anywhere.

Through a haze of fatigue and jetlag, I lurched into my hotel room, weary in limb, grim in thought. "How about some service, for God's sake?" But the only bellboy on duty was off carting other guests' baggage to their rooms, so that, as the saying goes, was *that*.

Five hours' sleep under my belt and I was a new man. Breakfast was the other great boost, and eight o'clock found me full of vim and vinegar, ready for action, smile and humour firmly in place. Ed and Jerry, my local escorts, were faithfully waiting for me in the Dixie Landings' lobby, and polite talk and introductions done, off we went to our introductory briefing over my second breakfast of the day.

Driving around the neat little city (for city it is), Ed filled me in on the drill for the next week. "We're gonna have fun," he declared grandly. No one protested.

The breakfast-cum-briefing-cum-welcome was in what they call the Boardwalk, a stunningly elegant boulevard by the lake, which backs off from the lobby of the Grand Floridian Resort. Here were gathered the faithful from the world press, who had come from far and wide to savour the 'experience'.

Walt Disney World (WDW) provides a special experience. For one thing, it's far bigger than you would have imagined, its vastness making it a composite city in itself. For another thing, it offers a staggering variety of things to see and do. You can stay for a fortnight and still have places to visit and see.

"Magic and fantasy rule here, which means that when you visit this unique vacation destination you can leave your real world behind, become part of this special world created for you, and enjoy the 'Disney Magic' factor, which comes from years of tradition, making this a sort of heritage operation." One of WDW's Marketing and Communications Managers, Christopher Fruean had obviously rehearsed this slogan, but he sounded sincere and totally convinced, and that was good enough. As it happened, he was dead accurate.

"He's quite right, you know. I think you'll be pleased," Ed whispered in my ear. By now I had learnt that you couldn't leave Ed out of a conversation for too long. "Most of the folk who come here end up being pleased. I can tell from their smiles," he added for good measure.

It all falls into place. The aura of fun created to charm visitors, and the marketing of Disney World as 'Disney Magic', an umbrella that includes the branding — everything from magic, animals, and showbiz — all combine to provide the Disney experience. To its credit, it must be said that in spite of all the hype and in spite of a world-known brand name, the resort still manages to surprise visitors with the sheer size of its operations, its robust freshness, and its amazing collection of entertainment areas and programmes.

What you really get is a break away from the mundane, a holiday filled with everything from spinning, splashing, cavorting and feasting.

An almost 122-square kilometres recreation and entertainment centre, WDW has it all. Three water-adventure parks — Blizzard Beach, Typhoon Lagoon and River Country; four theme parks — Magic Kingdom, Epcot, Disney-MGM Studios, and Disney's Animal Kingdom; 27 resort hotels with some 25,000 rooms; The Disney Institute; Disney's Wide World of Sports Complex; Disney's Wedding Pavilion, and Downtown Disney, an entertainment-cum-shopping-cum-dining complex encompassing West Side, the Marketplace, and Pleasure Island.

There are thrilling rides at the Magic Kingdom; train rides to the 'African Bush' in Animal Kingdom; globe-trotting at Epcot; camera safaris at Animal Kingdom; and the lights-camera-action of show business at Disney-MGM Studios. There are 'Innovations, Spaceship Earth' and the Living Seas in Epcot's Future World and in the World Showcase Lagoon. There's The Liberty Square, Main Street, U.S.A., Fantasyland, and *The Lion King* in Magic Kingdom. And there are The Great Movie Ride; Star Tours; *The Indiana Jones* Epic Stunt Spectacular; Fantasmic; and *The Twilight Zone* Tower of Terror in Disney-MGM Studios. There are recreational adventures on scenic lakes, 99 holes of golf on six sylvan courses, or rooting for a favourite team at a state-of-the-game sports campus. There are also other recreation options like two full-service health spas, tennis, water-sports, horseback riding, and car racing. The resort is also included in vacation packages of Disney Cruise Line.

There are brightly lit nights of dancing and dining. Add to all this, wholesome shopping, vibrant nightlife, and award-winning dining, and some 55,000 staff known as 'cast members' to look after you, and we are talking big-time entertainment.

As the days passed, I tried it all — *Star Wars* type of stuff, movie rides, stunt shows, simulated spaceship rides, and terrifying rides. I walked around The Liberty Square, and Fantasyland, and saw *The Lion King*, and took a train ride into the African Bush in Animal Kingdom. "What the heck, it's the thing to do here and everyone's doing it," I told myself as I freewheeled from show to show.

"People visit to eat and drink and see Mickey while they're here," Franz Kranzfelder, WDW's Manager, Menu Development & Culinary Standards, told me with great earnestness. I couldn't help agree. The fact is there's great feasting in store for those who care. Some 507 food and beverage outlets and a 25,000-strong staff bear this out.

Whether it is *questo fundido* in the Mexican San Angel Inn, slow-roasted lamb in the Moroccon Tangierine Café, chicken-and-leek pie in the English Rose & Crown Pub, or *bouillabaisse* in a French setting, the dining is of an assured class. Over two dozen restaurants in Epcot present the food of 11 nations. Citricos in the Grand Floridian Resort & Spa; the innovative Pepper Market in Conardo Springs Resort; the outlandish Rainforest Café in Animal Kingdom, and the historic Brown's in Disney-MGM Studios, are just some of the exciting food outlets on the property that I happened to try. A breakfast in the Wilderness Lodge features Mickey and his friends in costume, and the Boardwalk provides fun and fiesta in the evenings.

Weight-watchers beware. The helpings range from 'large' to 'enormous', and they don't mind heaping extra potatoes and fries on your plate if you so much as look up between meals.

Nightlife is the good life at Downtown Disney, and once I discovered this, it was goodbye to the 'early to bed' routine. A district of shopping, dining and nightclub fun, plus Cirque du Soleil La Nouba, and Disney Quest family entertainment center which comprises 100,000 square feet of the latest high-tech interactive adventures, Downtown Disney swings with gay abandon. At Downtown Disney Pleasure Island, BET SoundStage Club and Wildhorse Saloon, they add urban and country-western to the music mix that includes everything from jazz to oldies to disco to contemporary pop and rock. Acts change nightly at House of Blues, located at Downtown Disney West Side, which also features the expanded AMC 24 Theatres and some really good eating at Wolfgang Puck Café and Bongos Cuban Café. Downtown Disney Marketplace offers the most expansive display of Disney character merchandise anywhere in the world.

At Disney's Boardwalk, you can stroll, pedal a cycle built for four, catch all the live sports action from around the world at the highly rated ESPN Club, or go dining and dancing. Or just hang loose and browse.

One of the things that impressed me was the fact that you can choose and match attractions and activities. There's something for everyone, from $80 to $1,000 per night. The Disney Travel Packages offer a universe of options that include some 17 resort hotels, award-winning dining, shopping, beauty and health spas, vibrant nightlife, and recreation options like golf, tennis, water sports, car racing, and horseback riding. There are 4, 5, and 6-day passes, and the 'Unlimited Magic Pass', among others.

Why vacations? What are people looking for? The folks at WDW will tell you that they always get the same answers. Escape from reality, escape from the ordinary, and a reaffirmation of family lifestyles. The park creates an environment where all family members can come together and enjoy the product.

Offering an environment of 'family togetherness' to enjoy the product, WDW fits the bill and provides a formula that's calming, relaxing for the mind and body, and stress-lowering. The congenial atmosphere, music and fun at every corner, vibrant colours, parades, charades, and general merriment make people relax and unwind. People tend to smile more, laugh more, and take more time out to be nice to one another.

The wide range of products offered apart, it's this 'wellness' factor that's fuelled the resort's phenomenal success.

The resort's vastness makes it a composite city in itself, with a staggering variety of things to see and do. Depending on the type of person you are, you can kid yourself into believing you are young, you can lose yourself in your own thoughts and dreams, and you can rid yourself of your hang-ups. You can stay for a fortnight and still have places to go to, as 45 million annual visitors will corroborate.

Entertainment and relaxation apart, you can also get married in a fairy-tale setting at Disney's Wedding Pavilion.

Well!

# Thailand's Northern Delight

Walking the main boulevard, I couldn't help thinking I had taken a gamble coming here.

The fact is that I could have gone elsewhere, spent less time and money. But I had opted for this place and here I was. It was as simple as that.

I must confess to being somewhat biased in the city's favour to start with. That's what advertising does for you. So I had been softly brainwashed into expecting to find something 'different'. Something nice! That I wasn't disappointed says it all. Really!

You know how it is. Sometimes you just tend to go with the swing. And allow yourself to be swallowed up by the experience at hand. That's how I felt here. It's hard to put a finger on it, but I did feel I was in a somewhat different sort of place. It's there in the atmosphere, a bit to do with the way the locals conduct themselves — never mind the shopkeepers — a bit to do with the surroundings, and more than a bit to do with the bounties on display. You find courtesy levels not encountered elsewhere in Thailand. And we all know that courtesy does matter.

Old timers say it emerged from the mists, a symbol of natural beauty and social graces. You can make what you like of this, but the fact is that Chiang Mai does have a paradise-like character that has endeared it in equal measure to tourists and to the Thais themselves. And you do come away with a sense of happiness. I just happened to become one more fan.

"You may or may not believe this, but this itinerary was prepared with you in mind. I just knew you would like this place. In fact, I was sure you would like it." Having worked for years for Thai International, and with innumerable trips to Thailand under his belt, K.B. Mathur knew his facts about the country about as well as he knew anything. In any case, this time he had put his finger right on the button because I ended up liking the city more than I have liked many cities around the world.

Chiang Mai's history is old, its past eventful, and its character colourful. Some five centuries back, it was the proud capital of Lan Na Thai, popularly known as the 'Kingdom of One Million Rice Fields', the first independent Thai kingdom in the fabled Golden Triangle. Prolonged prosperity elevated the city to great prominence in religion, culture, and trade, till its sacking and reduction to a vassal state by a Burmese invasion in AD 1556. After the Burmese were expelled in AD 1775, Lan Na Thai regained its premier status in Northern Thailand.

Thailand's second city after Bangkok is at heart a large village, famed not for its size or population, — which by the way are both increasing frenetically — but for its myriad attractive features like the 14th-century historical temples, misty mountainscapes, extensive fruit and flower cultivation, courteous people, and arguably Thailand's prettiest women. You don't have to look far beyond all this to see why this sprawling city at the foot of forested mountains is such a big deal for just about everyone, and such a big draw for international tourists.

Today, the city thrives on its elaborate handicrafts industry, superb natural surroundings, and fertile orchards. And of course, on the tourists who come to savour its unique atmosphere and enjoy all the bows and courtesies on display.

I found Northern Thailand as different from Bangkok as Paris is from New York, which makes Chiang Mai individualistic in character, best seen in the distinct local cuisine and eating habits, physical appearances, and mannerisms. The city's isolation from Bangkok till as recently as the late 1920s has spawned a distinct identity, with its own festivals and traditions, its own cuisine, and a separate lilting dialect.

Welcome to the land of pagodas. What else can I say? Some 300 temples await your presence. Some are small and basic, some grand and lofty. They have their own background, mythological guardians, dragons, griffins, serpents and *garuda*s — all works of art in their own right — and almost all the shrines have a faithful following.

From the first time I visited it, my favourite is Wat Phra That Doi Suthep. Majestically perched on a hilltop overlooking the city, this is not only the city's most important temple, with priceless Buddhist relics stored in its 16th-century golden pagoda, but also a vantage point for truly stunning views. Walking around the pagoda, I saw the country stretched out below me endlessly, and misty mountains forming a rim in the distance in all four directions. Up here, I truly felt in a different world.

Like the palaces, the temples show the unique architectural style called Lan Na Thai, a bold mixture of Lankan, Burmese, Mon and Lan Na Thai styles that makes liberal use of symbols and materials like gilded umbrellas, Naga staircases, woodcarvings, angel guardians, and gold filigreed pagodas.

There are so many of them and they are all priceless shrines. Wat Chedi Luang, with its massive pagoda; Wat Phra

Sing with its tastefully decorated Lai Kham Chapel which houses the holy Phra Sing Buddha image, and the beautiful Wat Chiang Man, the city's oldest temple, are just some of the noteworthy pagodas of the region you can visit with ease.

I believe all tourist cities around the world draw visitors because they have a specific purpose in mind about what to do and how to spend their time in a particular city. In the case of Chiang Mai, I am quite certain visitors come not for any one specific attraction, but to become part of the local experience, to slow down and just take it easy, which isn't too difficult to do. Sure, there's traffic, but it isn't annoying in its density. At least not yet! There are crowds, but they aren't overpowering. Put simply, the city is still within the limits of what we would term 'urban tolerable'.

Things may seem quiet, even a bit sleepy at times, but there's plenty to see and do, both within the city limits and beyond. The ornately beautiful pagodas apart, there's a lot more to keep you gainfully amused if you so desire. Local sight-seeing can include several other interesting and historical sites. Like the imposing, beautifully landscaped Phuphing Ratchaniwet — the Royal Winter Palace that straddles a mountain. If you manage to gain entry, you'll see some prized possessions of the royal family.

It's also worth dropping in at the Tribal Research Centre with its in-house museum and research facilities that show the lifestyles of several tribes of Tibeto-Burman origin. You get to see a fair bit of local art at the Chiang Mai National Museum with its superb collection of ancient weapons and valuable old Buddha statues.

You don't have to do it, but the very best way to get around and enjoy the city's varied attractions is to hop on to a 'tuk tuk', as their scooter rickshaws are known, with your map and just do the rounds.

I may or may not admit it to myself, but in reality I am a night bird. Came evening and the prowler in me took over. Chiang Mai after dark does swing, though not in the hurly-burly, raucous Bangkok style. You have to find the action, but once you do, it's heady enough. And it isn't hard to find. Night owls can unwind in discos, bars, cocktail lounges and nightclubs, and at quality restaurants that feature Thai classical dances. And yes, there are massage parlours around.

Though looking for a few beers rather than a massage, I teamed up with a couple of European tourists at our hotel and ended up parlour-crawling. At Blue Moon, they dish out everything from disco music to dancing, and ask you to peek through a glass panel to choose your masseur.

It's in the eating-out department that the city scores several brownie points. I find food all over Thailand to be not only fresh but immensely tasty, but Chiang Mai has the distinction of possessing its own unique cuisine. For general eating, you can indulge yourself with a variety of cuisines — Italian, American, French, and true Oriental.

But nothing, just nothing, comes close to the Khantoke meal, a local culinary highlight that's part of the region's tradition. Normally comprising five courses served in small bowls set on a low table, while you sit on the floor, a typical Khantoke meal includes meat; vegetables; curries with garlic; ginger and chillies; fish sauce; minced meat; onions; lime juice, and ground dried rice called *laah*, all eaten with sticky rice. Believe me, this is special stuff, a truly delicious meal that finds favour with most.

"Each time I visit, there are more restaurants around, and they seem to get better all the time," K.B. announced. "I suppose that's what makes the wheels of tourism roll," he added. Once again, I found myself marvelling at his ability to put his finger right on the button. The restaurants were excellent, and their main sustenance was from tourism.

If you have heard of Thailand's beautiful local festivals that are a treat for the eyes and senses, well, let me say they don't come any better than in Chiang Mai. Tradition has seen to that. The result is a wealth of festivities without letup.

While all festivals have their place in local folklore, none is more charming than Loi Krathong. Under the full moon, the devout descend on canals, rivers, and streams, and float banana leaf boats bearing a small coin; incense; a lit candle, and a flower, in a poignant ritual to honour water spirits and 'float' away the past year's sins. It's all quite simple and graceful, and quite poignant.

Also very important and very moving is Songkran that celebrates the traditional Thai New Year with a three-day carousel of pilgrimages, religious merrymaking, dancing, and beauty parades. It's a time to unwind and have fun and they do just that. If you are fortunate enough to be around in February, you'll get to see the Flower Carnival with its elaborate floral floats and parades, celebrating the blooming of temperate and tropical flowers.

Shopping is the real great local adventure, and with good reason, as I found out on all my trips. Thailand is an undisputed handicrafts centre; the city thrives on local cottage-industries whose mind-boggling range boasts skilled craftsmanship in woodcarving, fabrics, silks, antiques, silver jewellery and lacquerware, to name a few.

Little shops line noisy bazaars and feature robust bargaining. It's definitely worth stopping by at the renowned Bo Sang San Kamphaeng Road area where you can see artisans at work. The Night Bazaar is the place for anything from everyday clothes to fancy music systems, and you can, and will, pick up good stuff if you just show a little patience and do a little bargaining.

But what sticks in my mind about this market has nothing to do with shopping. I remember one night when it rained so heavily that most of the shop stalls had to be dismantled. There were no customers, and the shopkeepers just rolled up their trousers and sat on their wooden stalls, their legs dangling above the knee-high water. And they were laughing. No business, but life was still good for a laugh or two.

The great outdoors can't be ignored. Surrounded by hilly forests still worked by elephants, and landscapes studded with meadows, orchards, and silvery waterfalls, Chiang Mai lies smack in the midst of interesting excursion country. All you need is your energy. You can ride elephant back on hilly tracks, walk narrow trails, do organised jungle treks to remote hill settlements, or river-raft for fairly long distances. Seven major hill tribes with their own distinct courtship rituals, dances, and aesthetic values, reside in the region, share animistic beliefs, and honour forest and guardian spirits.

The city is ringed by popular resorts, but my pick would be the Mae Sa Valley, renowned for its exotic waterfalls, orchid nurseries, and elephant camps, all conveniently located near well-furnished resorts. My other favourite is Doi Inthanon National Park with its waterfalls and elephants, and the Karen and Meo tribe villages.

Whether it is the salubrious climate, hazy mountainscape, beautiful orchids, or the inimitable Khantoke table delights, Chiang Mai showcases the charms of ancient Siam to the hilt.

It is easy to visit, easy to do, and easy on the eye!

# Chopsticks & Computer Chips

It's a small place that lives large.

It's hard for me to put my finger on it, but I had taken a mild dislike to the city a long time before I actually saw it. Somehow, it got stuck in my mind as a huge mass of concrete with an unwelcome climate and intensely unfriendly people.

The first thing that struck me about the city was that it doesn't do things by halves. Maybe it doesn't have to. Maybe it never learnt how to. Anyway, it's too late to speculate on such things now.

The fact is that this is a city that can lay claim to being truly unique. Step on to any street and you'll be swept away in a wave of commotion, smells and clamour. But what's noticeable and noteworthy, at least to my mind, is the fact that amidst the whirl is a constant, almost frenetic effort at reinventing itself, balancing the old with the new, the brash with the traditional, the mainstream with the offbeat. The result can be a bit unusual, a bit amusing, but quite heady.

When people in Hong Kong want to hear what quiet sounds like, they take the ferry to Tap Mun, an island at the east end of a long, narrow New Territories waterway boasting pristine scenery. It's quite another world where civilisation hasn't quite arrived.

As for the rest of the city, well, civilisation arrived! With a bang! And stayed! Combining 150 years of colonial influence and 5,000 years of Chinese tradition, the sophisticated heart of Asia sports its own brand of mystique. And a terrific pace of life, with things moving at a fast clip. If there's urban chaos, you don't notice it.

It's worth looking at the city's vital statistics and history. Situated on China's southeastern coast, spread across 1,100 square kilometres, including over 260 outlying islands, Hong Kong's main areas are Hong Kong Island, Kowloon Peninsula, and the New Territories. A collection of fishing villages when it was claimed as a Crown colony by Britain in AD 1841, it was then described as a 'barren rock', much to the amusement of today's property barons. As the original British presence grew from Hong Kong Island to include Kowloon and the New Territories, it thrived as a trading port and gateway to Mainland China.

At the stroke of midnight on 1 July 1997, the world stopped to watch history being made when Hong Kong returned to Chinese sovereignty. It's now a Special Administrative Region of China and operates under a 'One Country, Two Systems' principle of government, with a high degree of autonomy, with its own legal, social and economic systems. As things stand, the formula seems to be working just fine.

Basically, Hong Kong is a city of stark contrasts. East doesn't simply meet West. The two collide head-on in a kaleidoscope of colours and cultures that invigorate the senses. Classic trams share the bustling streets with luxury limousines; executives in pinstriped suits rub shoulders with elderly men taking their songbirds for a walk; temples sit dwarfed in the shadow of glass-chrome skyscrapers; traditional Chinese junks bob in the wake of luxury cruise liners; elderly Chinese performing the ancient, graceful art of Tai Chi (Chinese shadow-boxing) share the city's parks with joggers and lovers strolling hand in hand; street-side food stalls crouch beside Chinese restaurants so big, the waitresses use walkie-talkies.

The fusion of Chinese traditions with Western customs creates its own themes. There are remnants of the colonial heritage, such as the Noon Day Gun, immortalised by Noel Coward in his song "Mad Dogs and Englishmen". It still fires at midday, as it has since the 1840s. There are barristers in wigs and gowns pleading their cases in Cantonese, and British royals' names still grace street signs. It's all one big medley in a city that is in a constant, frenetic rush.

Different people will describe Hong Kong in different ways, but for me, it's essentially a city with a modern face. A forest of skyscrapers crowds the harbour and rivals the island's mist-shrouded peak. Just behind the Star Ferry, Jardine House catches the eye with its hundreds of porthole windows reminding people of local maritime connections. Two monumental towers stand out: The Bank of China and the Hong Kong and Shanghai Bank. When it opened in 1985, Sir Norman Foster's bank was the most expensive building in the world, costing over US$1 billion. Using technology more common to bridges, Sir Norman created a structure whose floors are suspended from steel trusses attached to twin towers without interior supporting walls, its inner workings thus open for all to see. Just down the street, the world-renowned architect I.M. Pei encased his 72-storey Bank of China in a zigzagging sheath of blue glass and steel. Its central core pushes upwards as it disappears through low-scudding clouds into the lapis-lazuli sky. It's a definite statement if ever there was one.

All this is official and quite the norm, but beyond the city's intoxicating charms, classy restaurants and shopping malls, lies another, and if I may say so, quainter, Hong Kong waiting to be discovered. Here you find a world of traditional fishing villages built on stilts where time stands still and ancient customs live on. It's a world of rugged mountain trails where hikers may see wild monkeys. There are white sand beaches that form an idyllic backdrop to watch the sun sink majestically into the island-studded waters of the South China Sea, playground of Hong Kong's rare pink dolphins. In the New Territories, bird-watchers can view some of the world's rarest birds at the Mai Po wetlands.

All dressed up and everywhere to go! Well, what's stopping you? Just go. On the 'must-do' list is Victoria Peak, where you can grasp the city's diversity and scale. In eight minutes I was up in the clouds, thanks to the Peak Tram, a historic form of transport that must never be allowed to be phased out. Before and below me lay a panorama of modern skyscrapers and mountains. It was the picture-postcard scene I had seen a hundred times in advertisements, but seeing it in person was something else again.

They took me to Central, home to the business and financial world, with charming colonial buildings standing proudly among futuristic monoliths. I must confess I wasn't overly impressed. In fact, I wasn't impressed at all. But my mood thawed the moment I hopped onto the legendary *Star Ferry* that provides scenic boat trips across one of the world's most photographed harbours. This was an hour of bliss, never mind the pesky tourists. For the record, Central is a shopper's paradise too, and houses Lan Kwai Fong, the famous nightspot, and fashionable SoHo (South of Hollywood Road).

Wan Chai is another major attraction. Famous as the home of the fictional Suzie Wong, as portrayed in the 1957 movie, today's Wan Chai is notable for its dizzying array of small shops — from wet markets to quaint printers selling traditional red Chinese wedding invitations. At its core is the nightlife scene, with new trendy bars complimenting the older traditional establishments. The 78-storey Central Plaza is Hong Kong's tallest building, its rooftop neon lights changing colour each quarter hour after 6 p.m. to signal the time of day. Another definitive statement!

It doesn't take long for one to descend on Causeway Bay and Happy Valley, which are very popular for shopping and entertainment — Causeway Bay's Japanese department stores are among the town's biggest — and the area also has one of the world's greatest horse-racing venues at the magnificent Happy Valley track. But get off the beaten track and seek out some authentic local atmosphere in the local teahouses offering unique Hong Kong milk tea and snacks. Days and nights are frantic, but a crack-of-dawn stroll through Victoria Park is peaceful and you can watch locals achieve inner peace by practising Tai Chi.

Step out of the hustle and bustle into a slower pace of life in South Side. Aberdeen Harbour may be ringed by high-rise housing estates, but fisherfolk still live on high-stern, varnished-wood junks. At night, the Jumbo Floating Restaurant — which I honestly feel must be the largest and brightest in the world — moored in Aberdeen Harbour comes into focus. It's worth boarding, and signing on for lunch.

Nearby is Ocean Park, an amusement oasis perched atop a mountain, with the world's largest reef aquarium; hair-raising rides, and more sedate entertainment in the form of dolphin shows.

As if the locals aren't populous enough, there are thousands of tourists milling about, trying to make sense of the urban wonder in which they find themselves pitchforked. And trying to get the best out of their stay in a city whose reputation has preceded it.

Kowloon's Tsim Sha Tsui is the local tourist Mecca. A long boulevard of shops and tourist hotels running from the tip of the Kowloon Peninsula down Nathan Road, the 'Golden Mile' is Hong Kong's answer to Fifth Avenue and the Champs Elysées, and provides an unforgettable shopping experience. The evenings see thousands of locals and tourists sauntering around. It's a nice place. The only snag is that you need deep pockets here.

With the unending traffic, you would be tempted to avoid walking around all the time. But contrary to what you might think, the city's fairly receptive to walkers and walking provides a superb way of imbibing local atmosphere. In particular, it's worth traversing Yau Ma Tei (place of sesame plants), a maze of narrow, fascinating streets, and Mong Kok which is reputedly the world's most densely populated urban area. Bustling with fascinating markets, these neighbourhoods show the 'workingman's Hong Kong'. Yes, there is such a thing.

Obviously, the contrast is infectious and extends beyond the city. Sprawling between Kowloon Peninsula and Mainland China, the 794 square kilometres of the New Territories are a rich tapestry of scenic contrasts — hilly, rolling woodlands and buzzing 'new towns'; duck farms and wildlife reserves; sandy bays and ornate temples; bustling markets and isolated hamlets.

Chinese heritage permeates the city. Belief in lucky numbers and the ancient art of Feng Shui are alive and kicking. Literally 'wind and water', Feng Shui is the popular practice of positioning objects in harmony with nature to create good fortune, which also means good health, good business, good relationships… Locals take their luck anywhere they can get it. Fortune-telling thrives. Soothsayers reside at the north end of Temple Street Night Market. Resplendent in ornate robes, they look out of place and out of time, but for a small fee will read your palm. For a little more, they'll read your face too.

Most foreigners wouldn't have thought of associating the city with religion. But it's there. It exists. Once you begin to understand the city, you can see how everyday life is influenced by religion. Over 600 temples are devoted to three main religions — Buddhism, Taoism, and Confucianism. Arguably, when people wonder about their future, they might consult their broker. Actually they are more likely to ask the gods, and two in particular — Man and Mo — the Gods of Literature and War. Their's is the richest temple this side of heaven because the Chinese are always careful to share their good fortune with the gods.

Let's talk about food. There's plenty to talk about. Perched on the doorstep of Mainland China, Hong Kong features food from every mainland province. Regional styles include Cantonese, Chiu Chow, Shanghainese, Yunnan, Peking, and Szechuan.

The city's location at the crossroads of Asia means a lot of great chefs have passed through, and many stayed on to open restaurants. Culinary treats can be enjoyed in every corner of the city and especially in its six best-known dining districts like Causeway Bay, Kowloon City and Stanley, for instance. There's a captivating mix of laid-back and formal eateries that offer a smorgasbord of tastes at prices that vary from downright affordable to outrageous.

For a quintessential local experience that's never the same twice, try dim sum. The incredible variety of dumplings, buns, pastries, soups, and other tasty morsels served at dim sum means you are only limited by your appetite.

The refined pleasure of afternoon tea is still a fixture of local life, and there's no better place to experience it than the lobby of The Peninsula Hotel in Tsim Sha Tsui. Music from a classical string quintet wafts down as you nibble on cucumber sandwiches, or scones with clotted cream and jam.

Across the harbour, some 15 different types of tea are brewed at the Mandarin Oriental's 'high tea' in its Clipper Lounge. At the Island Shangri-La in Admiralty, bookworms cosy up for tea in the Library. Coffee seekers head to the Patisserie at Harbour City for *tiramisu* and Cuban coffee bean brews.

In between the hurly burly, do spare some time for local heritage. Hong Kong's museums and galleries showcase splendid collections of Chinese antiquities dating back thousands of years. The largest, the Hong Kong Museum of Art, features galleries filled with worldwide exhibits, as well as jade and ceramics from the Han to Ming and Qing dynasties. The University Museum and Art Gallery of the University of Hong Kong boast the world's largest collection of bronze artefacts from the Yuan dynasty. In Tsim Sha Tsui, you can visit museums devoted to space, science and history.

Let the show go on! The largest of its kind in the world, combining traditional instruments and Western orchestrations, the Hong Kong Chinese Orchestra deserves your presence. The internationally recognised Hong Kong Philharmonic Orchestra is in residence from September through July. Dance is represented by the Hong Kong Ballet; the City Contemporary Dance Company, and the Hong Kong Dance Company. And there is Chinese opera. And there's more to it than you think.

If you are visiting in January, you'll step into the City Festival that attracts artists from the world of music, dance, drama, and art. The Hong Kong Arts Festival in February-March, showcases a potpourri of renowned artists from around the globe. The International Film Festival in April is a cross-section of international cinema. Other festivals are Le French May and the International Arts Carnival.

Night fever? It's fine! This is a late-night city. There are British pubs, American bars, high-tech karaoke clubs and all-night dance clubs. A great place to start is Lan Kwai Fong, the city's premier nighttime entertainment area, with dozens of bars and restaurants crammed into a three-block radius. A short walk brings you to Hong Kong's version of SoHo, packed with upmarket eateries and watering holes. If you are the sort who gets into the mood rather late in the night, Wan Chai features bars and dance clubs that are still humming as the sun comes up.

From early in the morning till late night, there's a shop waiting for you — in glitzy designer boutiques or open-air markets. And if you time it right — from July through September and December through February — it is sales time, which means discounts. The Hong Kong VIP Card offers good savings. From jewellery to fashion, electronic goods to tailor-made clothes, the card can be used at hundreds of participating stores for discounts through the year. Hollywood Road and its offshoots in Central are the best areas for antiques and old memorabilia. Silk carpets, Neolithic pots, Ming dynasty horsemen and Mao souvenirs compete for space with ornate Qing cloisonne and Chinese wedding cabinets.

The city's a hub for all things Asian: Korean cabinets, Thai Buddhas, Indian brassware, and Indonesian batiks. 'Cat Street' or Upper Lascar Row (Chinese slang for sellers of odds and ends) is the place for antique lovers, but don't go unless you have mastered the fine art of hard bargaining.

For electronics and high tech, head for Tsim Sha Tsui and the shops along Nathan Road for a variety of the latest in camcorders, cameras and video disc players. Hong Kong being a free port, there is no tax.

Tailor-made is big-time business. You can't leave without having a suit stitched, and believe me, they stitch it quickly if you want them to. Barney Cheng's design team will create a gown that will turn heads. Kow Hoo Shoe Company in

Central has been cobbling for three generations with custom-made shoes that will have you walking on air.

All things retro are the rage. At Shanghai Tang, entrepreneur David Tang turns traditional Chinese style on its head with stunning cheong-sam dresses and Mandarin collar jackets in lime green and shocking pink. Alan Chan's shop on the Peak specialises in 'retro-chinois' T-shirts and tea boxes covered in 1940s designs.

Vivienne Tam and Barney Cheng made their mark here before hitting the big time. Local style queen Joyce Ma stocks international designer labels at her upscale stores. And there are dozens of unsung designers who can whip up trendy dresses without too much fuss or ceremony. For cutting-edge fashion, head for the Beverly Commercial Centre in Tsim Sha Tsui or Island Beverly in Causeway Bay.

Chop sticks to computer chips — it's a grand show in an immodest city that can afford to be immodest.

# A Boat to Catch

It was just another flight from Miami to San Juan!

Which meant lots of chatter that typically meant nothing. If it was supposed to set the tone for things, it probably did. But that's about it.

I have come to the conclusion that people tend to kid themselves into getting into what they consider to be suitable moods. So if they are about to go cruising, it's considered suitable and perfectly appropriate to laugh a lot, indulge in silly conversation, and down more drinks — alcoholic or otherwise — than normal.

This was exactly what I found here. Just that there were more people than anyone had bargained for. Certainly more than you would see in Scandinavia, for instance.

As always, it was carnival time at the boarding docks. The deal was a four-day cruise aboard Royal Caribbean's *Nordic Empress* that would start from San Juan, and sail the high seas of the U.S. Virgin Islands, docking each morning at world-renowned islands like St Thomas, St Martin, and St Croix, before returning to San Juan.

Now, how does one describe a Caribbean cruise? You tell me. How about 'dream stuff'? It may sound a bit prosaic but isn't far off the mark. All right, maybe I laid it on a bit too thick, but it *is* dream stuff. And you have got to live the experience to believe this.

A spirit of adventure has lured visitors to the Caribbean since the days of Columbus and the conquistadors. Modern-day explorers discover new experiences on nature walks through verdant rain forests, or on more vigorous hikes to the lush peaks of dormant volcanoes. Snorkelling excursions take you to iridescent coral reefs full of neon-coloured tropical fish, while challenging dives reveal the last secrets of stoned shipwrecks and get the adrenalin rushing. Skim across the waves on a wind-surfer; or ride the big rollers; bird-watch at nature reserves; sail to unspoiled coves; reel in a game fish. In the Caribbean, adventure beckons at every isle. It's all just a shout and a clap away.

The incessant beat of the calypso and the overpowering smell of the sea set the tone to enjoy beaches as pale, and climate as inviting as anywhere in the world. And all this comes with a richness of history, nature, culture and cosmopolitan entertainment. The result! Holidays the way holidays are meant to be. So get into your Bermuda shorts and grab those strong, tall icy rums.

My first glimpse of our 'floating home' was enough to get me into the mood and start the seduction. She stood there grandly, hugging the pier, a giant mass of steel gleaming with fresh paint, the evening sun softly etching her graceful outline and proudly protruding turrets. She was 48,000 tonnes of sheer elegance in design, 692-feet long, 100-feet wide, with a 25-feet draft. The *Nordic Empress* isn't the largest luxury ship in the world, but it must surely be among the sleekest and prettiest, and is certainly one of the flag-bearers of the Royal Caribbean fleet. I made up my mind that I was going to like my home on the high-seas, and I did.

Old San Juan is true Latino turf, with the 'spirit of the south' coming through in the music, sunshine, and rum-swigging parlours. Originally conceived as a military stronghold, this 485-year-old neighbourhood today welcomes thousands of daily cruise tourists to shop, dine, and laze around before boarding ship. I did just that.

With the streets paved with cobbles of adoquine and the buildings a happy jumble of old colonial styles nudging modern ones, a leisurely foot tour is not only a delight but also the best way of seeing the town. You get to see the houses and buildings, peer into little shops, smile at passing locals, and stop anywhere you like for a drink. Also worth the effort, is a harbour ferry cruise past landmarks like the Advana Federal, Casa Blanca, the City Hall, San Juan Gate, La Forteleza, and the El Morro Fortress.

Time is well spent! Fascinating shops, art galleries, and cafés grace the historic district where you can simultaneously admire Gothic cathedrals, towers, massive 16th-century forts, and lively casinos, concert halls, and acclaimed restaurants. There are modern designer boutiques, floorshows, and art galleries, and the 'must-see' restaurants of the Mesonos Gastronomicos programme, a Puerto Rico Tourism venture that identifies high quality in restaurants. The local project features a nightly Le Lo Lai cultural festival at various hotels, with a buffet of local delicacies and an evening's folklore ensemble.

Shoppers will find plenty of variety, and definitely worth trying is Calle del Cristo for gold, disco jewellery, and traditional crafts like carved *santos* (small wooden figures of saints, or religious scenes).

We sailed at sunset.

Ahead, the ocean was a pale grey, melting into black, while behind us the twinkling lights of San Juan faded into tiny specks. The party had begun.

For four days and four nights, the *Nordic Empress* was a floating circus of ceaseless cavorting, eating and drinking, with the occasional serious safety-drill. The night flew. Early morning saw us docked at our first stop. It was the real thing! The party continued.

Blackbeard once had his pirate lair here. Forty beautiful beaches, world-class dining, exciting nightlife, and some of the Caribbean's most spectacular views identify St Thomas as one of the world's foremost cruise stopovers. It doesn't take long to realise this. There were cruise liners all along the harbour.

With its lush green foliage, colourful flowers, and picturesque harbour, the island is natural beauty personified. And Magens Bay has been rated by National Geographic as being among the world's ten most beautiful beaches!

Little waterfront restaurants and quaint shopping arcades give downtown Charlotte Amalie high entertainment value. You find some of the best deals going in the Caribbean for leather goods, jewellery and cameras. While downtown, brush up on the island's history in the museum at Fort Christian, visit the synagogue, and then climb the 99 steps for a spectacular view of Charlotte Amalie Harbour, before taking the shaky drive to Mountain Top — birthplace of the world-famous banana daiquiri.

Up there on the mountain, I felt everything from the strong breeze to the electric atmosphere. For $10, you can get your photo taken with the birds, which is just what I did. The view was nothing short of spectacular — boats docked at the harbour; little houses hugging the green hills, and a tranquil blue sea.

Snorkel at Bolongo Beach or Magens Bay, or simply view the treasures of the deep aboard an Atlantis submarine. The more active can take guided kayak tours through the Marine Sanctuary and Mangrove Lagoon to see herons, egrets and rays.

The next morning presented another delight. Co-owned by The Netherlands and France, St Martin is a Franco-Dutch treat. While the French part offers great cuisine and trendy hotels with somewhat discreet entertainment, the Dutch side has casinos with a vibrant nightlife. But you'll find a degree of activity everywhere. There is calypso music everywhere. Welcoming tourists with fine shopping and bistros is Philipsburg, the small but stylish capital.

Relax! Let yourself go and unwind completely. With some 38 white sand beaches, coral reefs, small pearl-like islands, and multi-toned grapevines festooned over houses, nature has worked wonders on such a small territory.

On the island's Dutch side, follow steep Sucker Garden Road to Guana Bay Point or Dawn Beach for fabulous vistas. Snorkel at Little Bay Beach, or ride horseback along nearby Cole Bay Beach. At Simpson Bay, don custom-made deep-sea diving helmets for a sea floor walk. Go deep-sea fishing for dolphin, blue marlin, sailfish and wahoo. And pick up a sun tan for free while you are at it.

On the French side, climb to the top of 1,500-feet Fort St Louis for a dramatic harbour view, or climb the 1,391-feet-high Paradise Peak. On the island's west side, dive off Rouge Bay or surf Plum Bay. Go on snorkelling or shallow-diving expeditions to offshore Tintamare, Pinel and Prickly Pear Islands.

When he discovered it over 500 years ago, Columbus called St Croix a 'lush garden'. Crystal-blue waters, sugar-sand shores, and rolling green hillsides, provide clinching evidence of this claim.

The sea was a myriad shades of turquoise and purple in the largest of the more than 50 islands that comprise the U.S. Virgin Islands.

From the calm waters surrounding Buck Island Reef, to emerald-green golf courses overlooking the Caribbean; from famed dining in restaurants to late-night snacks at waterfront cafés, it's all on offer. Go sword-fishing or explore the island's turquoise waters by sailboat. Bike past historic great-houses, and stop for a refreshing drink at a beachside joint. Featuring distinct 18th-century architecture and sumptuous seafood are the island's two waterfront towns, Frederiksted and Christiansted.

Frederiksted's 'Harbour Night' held at various times yearly, and Christiansted's 'Jump Up' invite everyone to shop while local bands belt out their stuff and party-goers frolic in the streets alongside Mocko Jumbie stilt dancers as they 'dance away evil spirits.'

Dive or snorkel at breathtaking Buck Island Reef National Monument, an 800-acre undersea nature reserve. Explore the island on horseback, or hike through the Salt River National Park and Ecological Preserve, where Columbus is believed to have landed in AD 1493.

Is it all safe? Let's put it this way. If all those sloppy tourists in their sloppy shorts can do it, I can do it, and if I can do it, you can do it. So do it.

If the stopovers are exciting, the cruise itself is an adventure. Aboard ship, 'anything goes', and goes on throughout. The mood is deliberately easy. The operative word is 'casual'. Don't worry about business suits except for the stipulated 'formal nights' which require men to wear jackets and ties, and women, dresses and pantsuits. The rest of the time it's all 'smart casual', which means rubber-soled footwear, jeans, shorts, and T-shirts.

Did someone say entertainment? Just sit back and listen to live bands in the bar and club areas — there's recorded music in most public areas — join in at sophisticated lounge evenings, go wine and cheese tasting, or go star-gazing. It's all included in the prepaid package. Just in case all this isn't enough for you, there are staff talent shows with stage performances that would do credit to Broadway. The gamut can stretch from stage comedy to cancan, from performances by professionals to robust musicals! The shows go on and on, and audience participation is encouraged. There are also 'singles bingles' where singles could meet up in an intimate, relaxed setting (and of course, I had to meet two women who were both up to their heads in 'contented relationships'). To top things off, there are 'good spirit' events which in our case turned out to be the 'Mr. *Nordic Empress* Sexy Legs' contest, with men required to show off their legs to an all-women jury. Whew!

If the idea is to indulge and spoil passengers, the guys who run cruises do a good job. A quick look every morning at the 'Cruise Compass' reveals the day's programmes and venues, and all you have to do is be there. The centre of things is the Purser's Desk that functions round the clock and doubles up as a shore excursion handler, information centre, bank, post-office, and safe deposit trustee. On occasion, they have also been known to give useful tips on saving marriages and other such things!

Burn those newly acquired calories off! Get into shape in the gym with special 'shipshape' exercise programmes. There's also a beauty and hair salon, a children's section, and, you guessed it, the inevitable casino. Offering lower than shore-side rates are the duty-free shopping malls that literally overflow with perfumes, watches, designer garments, jewellery, everything worth retailing in alcohol, and general bric-à-brac.

Food is the first love! Maybe, a few centuries ago, Confucius had taken the same type of cruise I did. The fact is that the on-board dining experience is an adventure by itself — aimed not just for the stomach but for the heart too — delicately priming together delicacies from the world over. Lining the shelves are layer upon layer of steaming curries, piping hot breads, cold meats, and a mix of salads and cheeses. All meals include low fat 'shipshape' items, and just in case three meals aren't enough, there's a special 'midnight buffet'. As for the eating areas, well, they stretch from dining halls to corridors, and spill onto open decks.

The dinners were theme affairs. Your typical Italian dinner could start with buffalo *mozzare antipasto* as an appetizer; clear beef *consommé* with vermicelli as the soup; Caesar Salad, *pesta*, and grilled top sirloin *pizzaiola* for the main course; and an international selection of cheeses and *tiramisu* for dessert. To be rounded off with strong coffee or the inevitable cappuccino.

Talking of eating and drinking, we were privileged to be invited to the captain's table that hosted some dozen-odd important guests. "Listen up, folks. You're here to enjoy yourselves, don't worry too much about a little over-eating and drinking," the good man declared. Well, he was the captain and this was his ship, so who were we to disagree.

The days had gone in a flash. Before I was quite ready for it, we had re-berthed at San Juan, heavier in body but lighter in mind (and pocket), a memorable vacation behind me. Disembarking, I rubbed shoulders with excited crowds about to start their cruise. Hitting me was babble and chatter that typically meant nothing!

Now where had I heard this one before?!

# Tokyo: Modern Eldorado

Forget the comparisons!

"They don't exist. Don't prejudge. You'll go off-track. And don't rush it. It just doesn't work here. It isn't the way to do things. Ease yourself in and you'll blend in better. You might even get to understand the city. Not everyone does, you know."

Ever the local girl, Ria allowed herself the luxury of a smile. But in fact, I wasn't comparing or prejudging, and for one very good reason. I hadn't really got a chance, having been pitchforked head-first into the giant urban circus that's the city.

As first impressions go, it was a bit of a dampener. On a rainy day, the throbbing metropolis looked a grey blob of glass, steel, and concrete, less than impressive, even less inspiring, leaving me wondering about all the fuss and hoopla.

But that was just my own, personal damp start to a city sojourn that spawned a thousand memories. The fact is that Tokyo shrugs pre-judgments off! All the enigma and charm of Marco Polo's supposed 'golden palaces' is visible in Japan's political, commercial and cultural hub. And though it may stagger first-timers, it's actually an easy city to discover. But then that's Japan for you.

There couldn't be a statement more truthful than Tokyo is a mega metropolis. Within a 45-kilometre radius of the Imperial Palace live some 30 million people — the same as in California. Poor and wealthy; dreamers and achievers; blue, beige and white-collar workers, all converged here to Japan's 'Big Apple', in something like a final quest for over-achievers in a country where over-achieving is a mania. The result — throbbing commercial activity and a globally unmatched lifestyle in a giant city that has raised the bar in urban existence.

It's hard to imagine it today, but Tokyo was once a mere fishing hamlet. That is till Ieyesu Tokugawa, founder of the Tokugawa Shogunate, moved here with his retinue to establish Japan's new centre in AD 1590. Then called Edo, the city grew and developed fast. Though featuring a centuries-old history, little remains from the Shoguns' era because of fire and earthquakes that took their deadly toll. Twice in the 20th century, first by the 1923 Great Tokyo Earthquake, and then by a blazing fire during the 1945 air raids, Tokyo was almost completely destroyed. The city of today has been rebuilt from ashes.

Today's Tokyo throbs with activity and opulence! Whether it's attending a tea ceremony, watching Sumo wrestling or a Kabuki performance, travelling the world's fastest trains, riding the world's fastest lift up 100 floors, or gambling at astronomically high stakes, you can't help notice the buzz. If cities have a heartbeat, Tokyo is on full acceleration all the time.

But the pace doesn't take anything away from enjoying oneself. The ruthless urban grind that has seen historic sites and ancient buildings crowded out by modern structures notwithstanding, exploring a city that reflects the traditions and aspirations of an ancient race of people is not only educative but highly enjoyable, almost fascinating. Amidst the hurly burly, there are still little things that fascinate with their simplicity. While it may not be obvious at first glance, traditionalism has survived and still exists in surprising forms.

Look for the little things — like a Sumo wrestler in a kimono and topknot, at a phone booth, or a narrow path lined by bobbing paper lanterns, or a finely pruned pine tree gracefully draped over a stonewall.

Passing under a gateway formed by 1,700 year-old cypress trees, I entered the very heart of Japanese tradition. The Imperial Palace — the Emperor's official residence — is an elaborate and interesting complex of guard towers and gateways and popular spots like East Garden, Plaza, and the Nijubashi Bridge. Like the Meiji shrine dedicated to the Emperor Meiji and Empress Shoken, the palace is open to the public on the Emperor's birthday. Two things struck me instantly. The palace's total calm and serenity, and the fact that just across the street lay the hustle of fashionable Harajuku. Further contrast of this nature was provided by a short walk to the huge open space of the Plaza, a favourite lunchtime rendezvous for office-goers of the Marunouchi business district.

Fashionable downtown Tokyo is a city by itself. Harajuku and Shibuya are designer-label territory. A wide boulevard fringed by restaurants, coffee shops, and boutiques, Harajuku swings with great vigour. So does Shibuya with its elegant shopping and dining outlets. Life moves fast here, even on Sundays, when hundreds of dancing teenagers dressed in '50s' styles, jam the streets in a festive mood. Offering entertainment and shopping in the shadow of the huge Olympic stadium and the Meiji shrine, Shibuya takes off from where Harajuku ends. For some real action, drop in at Koen-Dorji Street.

With its remnants of Old Tokyo, the Ueno area is traditional and lively at the same time, with Ueno Zoo offering a good outing. Walk around, stroll past the station, savour the atmosphere. Then move on and climb up to the viewing centre of the Tokyo Tower for an unforgettable view of the city and beyond. On three sides, glass and concrete structures reach for the sky. On the fourth, there's a green break with a patch of blue water, making it hard to believe they are part of the same city. But that's Tokyo for you!

If you feel doing justice to a city means seeing its museums, or at least one museum, I would put my money on the Tokyo National Museum of Modern Art. Using the latest technology to good advantage, the museum showcases a superb collection of national art through the last two centuries.

The Japanese love greenery and gardening, and they don't let big-city blues come in the way of pursuing their passion. In a burst of colour, the Shinjuku Gyoen National Garden spills over with chrysanthemums and cherry blossoms; the Hibiya Park is a welcome patch of green, a famous nature study centre in its own right, and a paradise for birds and butterflies, and the Rikygien Garden features traditional Japanese landscapes of stone, water, plants and ferns, which makes it a lush oasis in the middle of an urban world of concrete and steel!

If daytime is given over to a sort of hurly-burly urban regimen, dusk is the city's finest hour, best enjoyed in places like The Ginza, which, contrary to popular perception, is a whole district rather than a street, with several lanes and boulevards heading off from Chuo Dori (Main Street). Distinguished by day as Japan's luxury goods and high-fashion hub with the greatest concentration of art galleries, and by night for the world's most expensive nightlife, The Ginza isn't just one of the best addresses in town, but quite simply, a special place, internationally renowned and thoroughly cosmopolitan. Tokyo's economic fame is reflected here through chic shopping, trendy restaurants, nightclubs, *Sushi* bars, big bars, small bars, dimly lit bars, and 'family-type' bars.

Famous stores edge side streets fringed by restaurants, bars, cafés, nightclubs, and speciality shops. This is where you rub shoulders with distinguished old rich and flashy newer rich. Though class-consciousness is discreet in Japan, aristocrats and tycoons are still on the scene and The Ginza is where you are most likely to find them. For the city's rich, The Ginza is simply 'it'.

From my vantage point in the shadow of the Sony Building, the view of the district was about as good as it gets. Early evening bears a fashion-parade look as regally attired hostesses, many in kimonos, make their way daintily to work. Millions of office-goers pour out of buildings, on to the streets, and into thousands of bars. It's an entertainment rush of unparalleled proportions. And then, the *mamasans* escort men to the waiting taxis. And all this while, the famous neon lights flash their commercial messages.

Being here for just one night of fun and glory, I felt I could afford to splurge and enjoy. Yes I will 'enjoy', I told myself reassuringly as I walked past the Sony Building, which I was told also housed the famous Maxim's de Paris restaurant, and was great competition for Mullion, which houses the giant Seibu and Hankyu Department Stores and five movie theatres. My quest for 'enjoyment' took me past giant architectural wonders, street corners, and beautifully decorated shop windows.

I joined the crowds.

The first person I encountered was an old Japanese gentleman with an expensive suit and expansive smile. "I'm Nakimoto, but my friends call me Moto," he said pleasantly. I bowed and introduced myself, not letting on that my friends, given a choice, didn't call me at all.

"Your first time in Tokyo?" "Yes" I said, trying to be heard above the din. No, I wasn't a golfer; no, I wasn't attending the international convention on keyhole surgery; no, I wasn't attending the convention of the Asian forum of political analysts; no, I wasn't in town to negotiate with Japanese car manufacturers. I was a travel journalist writing on Japan.

Moto declared he had worked for three different Japanese companies for ten years in India, his 'second home'. I politely told him I had worked for myself for 25 years in India, my 'first and only' home. He bought me a beer, I bought him one! He got me another, and shortly thereafter, I did the same.

"Kampai," he said, raising his glass. Not wishing to disclose I didn't know what 'Kampai' meant, I raised my glass with a flourish. "Kampai," I said loudly. "Kampai," chorused the group at the next table. Four 'Kampais' later, I said my goodbyes to Moto and left.

Weeks later, I met another Japanese gentleman on a flight. We chatted about various trivia. In passing, I inquired if 'Kampai' was a Japanese form of saying 'Cheers'. He looked puzzled, then smiled. "Where did you have the drink?" I told him it was in The Ginza.

"Oh, it probably meant 'Company's paying."

I can't think of a better way to describe The Ginza.

With Tokyo being host to a lip-smacking cornucopia of food flavours and textures, you are left asking the million yen question — how does one tackle Japanese food? Japanese cuisine has always received 'mixed reviews' beyond its shores, with most foreigners considering it being exotic in the extreme: either visually too artistic to be of relevance to the stomach, or composed of ingredients too alien. The mere mention of 'raw fish', 'eel', or 'bean curd' conjures up visions of something 'foreign', best left untried.

Don't fret. The first thing to remember is that Japanese cuisine is like the Japanese people themselves — simple yet complex at the same time, but very pleasant. It's an elegant intersection of the culinary world, as eclectic in its tastes as the culture from which it springs. It offers palate-tickling sensations that range from the subtle joys of 'sashimi' to the hearty basics of noodles. Ocean-fresh seafood, tasty cuts of young pork loin, succulent fillet of beefsteak, tender chicken, and farm-fresh vegetables and herbs are just some of the ingredients used.

The essential idea is to enhance the food's natural taste, not camouflage it with rich sauces. Freshness borders on fanaticism. While *gohan* (rice) usually boiled till sticky, is the staple ingredient — indeed, the word for meal in Japanese 'gohan' means rice — Japanese cuisine goes far beyond *tempuras, sukiyaki,* and *sushi.*

A bowl of soup, either made from soybean paste *(miso)* or a clear fish stock, accompanies all meals, as do pickled cucumbers, cabbage, daikon radishes, which are usually eaten with the rice at the end of the meal. A variety of vegetables ranging from carrots, cucumbers and peas, to wild mountain roots and grasses are served in an assortment of ways ranging from fresh, boiled, pickled, or deep-fried. Meats are normally chopped into bite-sized pieces, or thin slices easily picked up by chopsticks. These are mostly dipped into a tiny dish of sauce, usually with a soy sauce base and fresh ingredients like ginger, onions, or grated radish. *Soba* and *udon* are two kinds of noodle.

Meats are rarely overcooked, and often served raw. And as for *sushi!* All I can say after all these years is that it's a question of personal taste! Taste apart, it's intriguing to see the way food is served. Crockery is selected to suit the food's colour and texture.

The most exquisite culinary refinement and ultimate Japanese eating experience is 'Kaisek Ryori,' which originated in Japan's Zen temples, where meat was shunned. Each course is served in gorgeous lacquerware or china. Though expensive, it's an experience to be tried at least once.

From tiny kiosks the size of walk-in closets to deluxe establishments a quarter size of football fields, the variety of eateries is as staggering as it is exciting. There are exclusive restaurants with impeccable service, sober décor and sobering rates; there are racy ones with louder, bolder music, but there are also more modest establishments that serve sumptuous cuisine at affordable rates, at least by Tokyo standards.

To scratch the surface of Japan's vast selection of culinary variety, take a walk in the vicinity of any Tokyo subway or train station. For non-Japanese speakers, some restaurants display plastic and wax replicas of their dishes in front windows, or provide a menu with colour photos. Tipping is neither expected, nor encouraged.

There are other cities around the world that offer non-stop commercial, artistic and entertainment activity, but they don't quite match up to what you get to experience here. Topping things off is the fact that the city is totally safe. So make bold. Venture out without fear. You'll always stumble upon a 'koban' (police box) and an obliging 'omawari-san' (security personnel) will help out at the slightest hint of trouble.

Huge, bustling, almost awesome, Tokyo does defy comparison. It does demand exclusive attention. It's simply gigantic in all forms and proportions. Yet alongside bustling thoroughfares lie quiet neighbourhoods where the traditional pattern of Japanese life still ebbs and flows.

This is what makes a visit and stay so enriching. And it all becomes so much better if 'company's paying'.

# The Puszta

In a sense, it was exactly as imagined. Or maybe it's just me.

What was more endearing — the sweet smell of plums and apricots that was all-pervading, or the ghost-like riders in the failing light, their shrill cries echoing across the countryside. Perhaps it was a bit of both.

In fading light, we had driven in amidst a swirl of dust and been welcomed with apricot and plum brandies at the Old Tanyacsarda premises in Lajosmizse, a remote country ranch which is home to some of Europe's most prized horses and skilled riders, and lots of folklore.

We had driven out of Budapest for the Puszta — the Hungarian Great Plain, considered the very heart and soul of the country, the real Hungary if you please, the historic region where the country's foundations were laid centuries ago by fierce, battling tribes. Where it all began.

The Puszta and the Great Plain are Hungary's great heartland, lovingly cared for and preserved, a national showpiece of immense geographical, historical and heritage value. And its stories and legends are those on which the foundations of an entire society rest. The land is enmeshed in local folklore, its vast expanses fostering much of the country's romantic literature. Several noble legends have been born and nurtured in this remarkable stretch of country.

Literally, Puszta translates into an 'empty, bare, grassy plain', and is considered to be a distant cousin of the prairies, the steppes, and the pampas. Compare it to whatever you like, it's bare all right, and barren to the point of being hauntingly beautiful.

This is image country, and among the images that come thick and fast, perhaps the most endearing is that of the daring 'csikos' (horse riders), astride five horses, racing across a lonely track of barren land, a feat known as the 'Koch five-in-hand' after the German artist who painted this as an imaginary scene, little realising how famous his work would become.

Personalities move on, memories fade. But some remain. Like those of the famous outlaw, Sandor Rozsa, the noble-spirited brigand who robbed the rich to help the poor, and became a cult hero in the bargain.

It is such legends of the land that are its major attraction. Add to all this cheerful inns and taverns oozing with atmosphere, robust and friendly people, and a congenial atmosphere, and it explains why the region is being looked at so closely now, and becoming a major international tourist centre.

The flat country on both sides of the Tisza River is actually quite diverse in landscape, with sand drifts in one area, plum orchards in another. And though not blessed with Hungary's otherwise temperate weather — the summers are hot and baking and winters extremely chilling — the Puszta is home to some of the richest flora and fauna in the region, as resilient as the people with whom it shares the land. This isn't a land for softies. It's hardy folk you get to rub shoulders with here, and you better believe it.

The terrain is vast and varied, hard and forbidding, with imagination and reality blending together, best personified by the '*delihab*' — a rare mirage-like natural phenomenon where images of far-flung objects float upside down over the horizon. Sometimes what you see as the '*delihab*' are tiny villages, at other times it could be inns thatched with reeds, or scattered countryside farms with sweep-pole wells and dazzling white walls.

I remember telling myself repeatedly how big the region was. Traversing the Puszta provides an overwhelming sense of space. All the towns dotting the Great Plain happen to be set exactly 27 kilometres apart, which is a story by itself. It appears that in the Middle Ages, this was the average daily distance merchants could cover on foot. At the end of the day they pitched camp at suitably sheltered places, which in time drew people who held markets, built churches, and collected tolls. And a town was born. It is these towns you get to visit today.

Late afternoon found us in Szeged, the economic and cultural capital of the Southern Great Plain. Szeged has a history all its own. A flood in AD 1879 that washed half the town away, prompted inhabitants to opt for modern town-planning. The result is boulevards and avenues not unlike the ones gracing Budapest and Paris.

A tour of the town can be a delightful experience. The main town landmark is the Neo-Romanesque Votive Church, an honour it shares with the adjoining 13th-century Romanesque Demetruis Tower, the town's oldest monument. The statues of 100 Great Hungarians stand in the National Memorial Hall around the Cathedral Square. Szechenyi Square is among Hungary's biggest and liveliest parks with tastefully laid out, charming statues and fountains. Flanking it are the Neo-Classical Zsoter House and the Zopf-Art-Nouveau style Town Hall. It's here that the town's history was chartered, and here that tourists congregate.

183

But monuments and boulevards apart, Szeged, I was told to my delight, is famous for its cuisine, and is home to the famed Fisherman's Soup, and some of Europe's tastiest salamis. The salamis are prepared with pork with flavouring spices known only to a few salami masters. And you don't have to be an expert of Hungarian cuisine to enjoy dishes like the Puszta Porkolt and the Great Plain Sirloin. While nationally popular, Hungarian goulash isn't quite the main choice of local gourmets, but is readily served if asked for.

This is the place to spice up your life. Literally. Embellishing the food are the famous Szeged and Kalocsa red peppers, an intrinsic ingredient, imbibed with generous helpings of onions. And alongside local favourites like the fragrant, ultra-potent Kecskemet plum and apricot brandies, is a choice of several light table wines.

The golden sunshine of early morning found us once again on the road, arrow-straight, stretching ahead and merging with the horizon. We were driving through country as flat as a billiards table, mainly scrubs, shrubs, and occasional patches of agriculture. Once again, we pulled into a town full of surprises.

Kecskemet is a veritable treasure house of historic buildings. The Hungarian Art-Nouveau style Cifra Palace — now an art gallery; the world-renowned Zoltan Kodaly Teaching Institute; and the beautifully refurbished 19th-century Town Hall, are all notable landmarks in their own right. The town owes much of its charm to its spacious main square with its promenades and churches of various denominations, existing side-by-side with imperious dignity.

How can I not mention the local apricot brandy, which remains exactly the way it has been for generations. Strong, fruity, sweet, pale in colour — there's also a darker version — and fiery in spirit, you either like it instantly, or never get used to its rich taste and flavour. Served in small glasses, this renowned alcoholic beverage has been the city's signature aperitif and goodwill ambassador.

Hesitating over the first glass, I found myself a little keener with each sip, until I reached that nebulous stage where I was actually 'merry' with the stuff. Relatively speaking, of course!

It was another day and another city. And another dimension of the show. The first thing that strikes you when you drive into Hungary's second city after Budapest, are the shades of imperial opulence. Debrecen is a major city, famous for its sundry tourist establishments, upscale restaurants, and the world-renowned thermal baths reputed to cure several ailments, which have become an industry on their own. The local architectural lineage extends to the Town Hall and the nationally famous building of the Reformed College. Also noteworthy is Nagytemplom — The Big Church — a beautiful Classical structure. And it's definitely worth the effort finding the time to visit Nagyerdo — The Great Forest.

The next day found us back on the road, chugging along, seemingly in the middle of nowhere. But this wasn't 'nowhere'. Quite the opposite, in fact! Nothing personifies the Puszta's rugged spirit and character better than the Opusztaszer National Memorial Park. Built as a tribute to Hungary's conquest by the Magyar tribes over 1,100 years ago, Opusztaszer is a first-class cultural centre and major tourist attraction.

This is the country's exact spot of origin, Hungary's heart. This is where it all began in those 'guts and glory' days. Various sections of the complex preserve those momentous memories. A most attractive feature and undisputed showpiece is Arpad Feszty's 'cyclorama', a stunning 15-metre high and 120-metre long work of art that has drawn international praise and is counted among Europe's biggest and best paintings.

The hauntingly life-like, moving painting narrates in superb detail the region's invasion and conquest, a prelude to its becoming a nation.

I have never really been an art buff and never fully understood how anyone in his right mind could go crazy admiring what someone has painted, but this one was different. This one was special. Very special.

Our daylong sojourn at Opusztaszer had put things in proper perspective. It was fascinating to see the birth, early days and gradual development of a nation whose history is as eventful as it is colourful.

The week had gone by quickly and pleasantly. It was time to say goodbye to this beautiful region of history and folklore. It was time to move on.

As the sun sets over the Puszta, the mist quietly moves in, turning everything pale and ghostly. It is now time to partake of the sweet bread of the peasants and drink their strong brandy, before sitting back to listen to music that recounts the birth and history of the country.

# Pokhara

We had kept pace with each other for quite a while now, and I must say it was pretty good company.

Things were under control. No problems as far as we could see. It was a question of complete compatibility and total harmony.

Far below, on the thin silver ribbon that was the meandering river, three rafts bobbed and bumped along, hidden from view, then reappeared, then hid again as we rounded corner after corner. This went gone on for almost half an hour. They waved at us. In fact, they waved so much that I wondered how they were managing the raft in the swirling waters. Finally, the road forked off and we lost visual contact with our rafting friends.

But the river stayed with us. I had noticed two things: the hills had become progressively higher and more forested as we travelled along the 'highway' from Kathmandu; in three hours, we had passed a mere four villages, testimony to the fact that sustenance in this hard region isn't everyone's cup of Himalayan tea, and that people in these parts didn't talk much. Not that I am complaining. It was just fine with me, actually.

It was lunchtime when we arrived at Pokhara, just a little more tired than we should have been. "It was all those bends on the way," I told our motley little group, but they didn't seem particularly interested.

The first thing that struck me was the paradox of nature presented in such splendid fashion. While there was a cool breeze blowing, the sun's rays were strong enough to make any patch of shade desirable. Inviting, snow-covered peaks looked down on us from a distance. These are some of the world's highest summits, the undisputed pride of the high Himalayas. They seemed to brood, but were truly magnificent in their white plumage. There was total silence, the air was crisp, and all was well out here in this remote part of the world.

Unspoilt and beautiful, Pokhara is Nepal's western gateway and stronghold, the closest the country has to a resort, and a town of immense value in terms of its location and natural richness. Nestled at the foot of high mountains in a valley of great geographical diversity, the town and region's strong point has always been the bounties of nature so lavishly bestowed on them. Enhancing this further and adding value and beauty to the region are its seven lakes, notably the three 'biggies', Phewa Tal, Rupa Tal, and Begnas Tal.

In early days, adventurers who chanced upon the spot lavished praise on the region, describing it as one where tropical flowers bloomed on the shore of a blue lake, with Himalayan peaks filling the skyline. They talked of the tranquillity, and of the complete sense of solitude.

Within an hour of arriving, we were at one of the regional landmarks, with a packed hamper lunch to keep us in good humour and out of mischief. Petale Chhango is the Nepali name for Davids Falls, and let me tell you that while it isn't exactly Victoria Falls, it's quite a sight and has a fair bit of rushing water that glistens brightly in the sunlight before disappearing into an underground chasm.

Though relatively scarce, water plays a pivotal role in Pokhara's fortunes. Cutting through the valley and the town in an impressive gorge, the Seti Gandaki River must surely be among the world's coldest, and I can definitely vouch for this. Called Seti or White Gandaki because of the limestone floor which gives it a milky sort of look, the river has always been immensely important. For the residents of the valley, it's the very basis of existence, providing precious water and food in the form of a variety of freshwater fish.

As in most of Nepal, religion is alive and thriving in the region. Nepalese believe strongly in their deities and have done their bit to build shrines wherever they could in their honour. To the north of town lies the venerated Mahendra Cave, while Bindhyabasini Temple, also located nearby, is the oldest and most important shrine in the valley with a constant stream of devotees. There's also the hill-perched Buddhist monastery in Matepani, sporting an air of serenity and providing excellent views of the valley.

Talking of views, they are actually a local mainstay and invaluable asset, perhaps the greatest asset in terms of tourism. Pokhara features magnificent views of Dhaulagiri, Manaslu, Machhapuchhre, and Annapurna. If they take my advice, they should classify 'views' as an industry in its own right. More than anything else, this is what brings people here. And it's an asset with a permanent shelf-life. No matter what, those views won't disappear. They'll be around for as long as the planet is there. How's that for some philosophical musing.

It was time for a cultural diversion, and a nice little one it turned out to be too. For an insight into the Annapurna area's people, geography, birds, plants, animals, and to see one of Asia's largest butterfly collections, drop in at the ACAP Natural History Museum located in the Prithvi Campus. By no means a large institution, it does, however, serve a very useful purpose in terms of its educational value, especially if you are interested in butterflies, and makes for a pleasant stopover. More generously bestowed is the Pokhara Museum which has exhibits of ethnic jewellery, musical instruments, and costumes, among other items.

Came evening and we escaped to the lake, very much the thing to do here. This is where the so-called local action is to be found. The downtown area, if you please. Offering great lakeside scenery, Phewa Tal, as the three kilometre-long lake is known, is Pokhara's most famous landmark and the popular rendezvous of all visitors, the place for some sun, fun and the next meal. The setting is beautiful, and things are almost always quiet. In fact, about the only noise around is courtesy of the shopkeepers who tend to sit outside their shops playing with their children while awaiting customers.

Set in this idyllic location, Boomerang Restaurant at Lakeside, is the premier local eatery establishment, long famous for its breakfasts, candlelight dinners, barbeques, and international cuisine. Weather permitting, the luxurious garden on the lake is a fine place to relax. For night owls, the Kangaroo Pub in the same complex is a genuine watering hole, a nice place for a drink or dance. Also popular is the wood-fired German Bakery and Café Damside.

Boats, canoes and sailboats can be hired in Lakeside and Damside, and you can visit the island temple dedicated to the goddess Barahi, and explore the opposite shoreline dotted with little villages like Gurung, Brahmin, Chetri and Jalari.

Walking along the main street just before the lake's edge, I was accosted by a man on a bicycle who asked me if I wanted to buy some "really good hashish". Before a "no" had actually left my mouth, he was gone, cycling away furiously. I guess that's what experience is all about. Having sensed that I wasn't a customer, there was no point in his hanging around. 'He's a professional,' I told myself. Later, I learnt that he had approached two other colleagues from our group and then lost interest in them about as quickly as he had in me.

The town itself is laid-back almost to the point of disbelief. There isn't much vehicular traffic; water buffaloes wander the streets at will; women carrying loads of fodder pass you by, and the sound of the giant pipal trees' rustling leaves fill the air. Quite the kind of scene you would like to encounter if you are seeking an escape from big-city existence.

If the outdoors attract you and your energy levels are up to scratch, this is the place for you. This is the place. Pokhara and its valley excel in offering the great outdoors in a pleasant way throughout the year. With several diverse and interesting treks and rafting expedition options available at its doorstep, the town and its environs spoil you for choice if you are keen on stretching your legs. The 'nature lover's and outdoorsman's paradise' tag is fittingly apt and well-merited.

A day walk to the surrounding hills offers panoramic Himalayan views over the beautiful valley and the chance to pass little villages which have ignored the passage of time. For a wonderful walk, head for the former fort at Sarankot, directly to the north of Phewa Tal. Other options are the ruins of the fort at Tulakot; Kahun Danda, and the World Peace Pagoda. If time or energy levels are in short supply, just walk around Phewa Tal. It's a very pleasant walk and guaranteed to lift your mood.

There are also several day village-tour options. Lumle, a traditional Gurung village, is an hour's drive from town and the countryside scenery is as pretty as you would want. An hour's walk from here is Chandrakhot that offers good views of Modi Khola and the Himalayas. There are also the villages of Kaskikhot with its ancient fort and palace, and Dampus, which features impressive views of the Annapurna Range.

Also within relatively easy reach are other famous spots like Annapurna, Mustang, Manaslu, Chitwan, Dolpa, Jumla, Humla, the holy Mount Kailash, Lumbini, Tansen and Gorkha.

When it was time to leave, I took a stroll on my own to get a last look at those magnificent mountain peaks in the distance. And to breathe in some more fresh air. This business of getting fresh air into my lungs was something I had always wanted to do, but never really been able to for any great length of time. Well, here, it's on offer all the time.

It had been an easy, tranquil two days, heavy on fresh air and superb views. Pokhara is just one of those places where you are forced to slow down.

If you don't, you are missing the whole point.

# Johor Bahru

Where is the real Malaysia?

Or shouldn't I ask?

My curiosity stems from my perceived notions of the country that had always been presented to me as a 'melting pot' of different cultures, as indeed it is.

There's Kuala Lumpur of course, which I have always found to be a fine city with generous amounts of greenery and fine dining. But it's basically just another large capital and too cosmopolitan, by half. So, is it typically Malaysian? What is typically Malaysian? The answer obviously lies in looking elsewhere and I found what I was seeking in Johor Bahru, capital of the state of Johor, its regional administrative and commercial centre, and the southern gateway to the country.

"There's only one place I call home, and that's Malaysia." How can any self-respecting man forget Michael Yeo's passionate remark that lies at the heart of 'Malaysia, truly Asia' — till recently Tourism Malaysia's highly visible global advertising campaign. Well, it worked! I went to check it out!

For years I knew it only by its exotic-sounding name. Even when I decided to visit it, the build-up hadn't been all that great, so it was with mixed feelings that I arrived here one summer night.

Wedged in at the southern tip of Peninsular Malaysia, Johor Bahru's diverse ethnic mix of Malays, Chinese, Indians, and Eurasians who collectively make up its population of one million, makes it a fascinating place to visit. The resultant mixed heritage on display has several social layers, offering a cross-cultural scenario that percolates down to dining, shopping and day-to-day living. Adding to all this is the fact that Singapore is literally a 'short walk across the bridge'.

There's this thing about Malaysia! It took me a while to put my finger on it, but finally I found the source of the country's charm to stem largely from the fact that it has become an amalgam of different cultures, fused into one over the years. Thanks to its diverse resident communities, you get a whiff of 'different' aspects in everything from the goods for sale to the culinary treats that await you in diverse eateries.

The city itself is a bit non-conformist in nature. I found it greener, more spacious, and more relaxed than I had imagined. The sense of space comes through mainly because things are spread out, giving an uncluttered look, proving that exotic seaside resorts don't have to be small, noisy, and overcrowded with boisterous sailors, exuberant tourists, and beaches littered with discarded beer cans.

Awaiting you is a high-rise skyline that seems etched against a green foreground of parks and gardens. If there's one thing that emerges clearly and quickly here, it's the slow pace of life. Things sort of shift into low gear in a pleasant manner, to the point where you are lulled into imagining that's the way it's meant to be. I settled in and slowly began to absorb the local flavour.

If you are doing the typical tourist type of visit, start by taking in the famous sites. For an upscale initiation, visit the Royal Abu Bakar Museum and the Grand Palace, set in spacious gardens that taper down to the Straits of Johor, a strip of seawater that cuts the city off from Singapore. They ask you to take off your shoes and carry them around with you in plastic bags. Barefoot, my guide Sisi and I walked the length and breath of the ancient, grand building with priceless treasures and heirlooms of the Johor royal family, displayed in glass cabinets. The museum also has a retail outlet called the Mawar Gift Shop, and the in-house Johor Art Gallery displays an array of traditional and historical items ranging from silverware to weapons.

An hour later I found myself staring at the Sultan Abu Bakar Mosque, the other grand structure in town. Set in spacious, manicured gardens that overlook the Straits, the site provides a panoramic view of the waterway and beyond. The mosque itself came as a bit of a surprise because of its extraordinary European style dome, quite unlike other Islamic shrines you'll get to see.

Sisi then drove me to Dataram Bandaraya which features official parades and cultural events from time to time, duly informing me that it wasn't always so empty and quiet. Sisi liked quiet environs and didn't talk much. But he went about his job with quiet vigour.

For authentic local flavour, drop in at the Kampung Mohommed Amin Cultural Garden located in the city centre. Here you get the flavour of local life as it really is, with indigenous Malay music, local dishes like 'roti canai' (chappati) and 'nasi lemak' (fish), and with a bit of luck, you may even catch a Malay wedding or two.

It wasn't at all part of my itinerary, and it certainly wasn't my top priority, but then I didn't know the facts. To say that local shopping is an attraction is to put it rather mildly. Thanks to Malaysia's almost frenetic 'shoppers' paradise' tag what awaits shoppers is an exciting experience, with the prices being competitive in most retail outlets, be they big malls, arcades, or bazaars. Devaluation of the local currency has made shopping here highly attractive for Singaporeans who now just hop across for most of their shopping. While the world itself is for sale, the best buys are select electrical goods, designer clothing, batiks and pewterware.

The '*Pasar Malam*' or night markets, offer a unique shopping experience. Try the Monday Kampung Melayu Majidee Night Market for a variety of goods available at very reasonable prices, and also sample freshly cooked local dishes and top-quality fried bananas. Taman Pelangi every Tuesday, or Kampung Setangi and Jalan Kebun Teh every Wednesday, are definitely worth trying out.

The cutting-edge in shopping comes in the form of the Johor Bahru Duty-Free Complex located at the International Ferry terminal, a huge local tourist draw as I saw for myself. With some 163 retail outlets, a hypermarket, and assorted curio outlets, this large duty-free department store is the place to allow indulgence for international designer ware, glassware, porcelain, cosmetics, and electronic goods.

My lack of interest in shopping is matched by my deep interest in all matters related to cuisine. The 'foodie' in me denied long enough, it was time to get down to brass tacks. And we did, with great gusto.

Awaiting the gourmet is the best of Malaysian cuisine served without fuss at several restaurants that range from the highly sophisticated to the most basic. And food stalls and vendors seem to come out of nowhere at night and serve up delicious local dishes at amazingly low prices. There's plenty to tickle those taste buds. No matter what, don't miss trying *satay* (barbequed skewered chicken, lamb or beef), *lontong* (rice cubes in creamy coconut sauce), *rojake* (local salad), *mee rebus* (noodles in gravy), and the highly-rated *laksa* Johor (flaked fish and gravy cooked with coconut milk).

Venturing out in my quest for authentic local cuisine turned out to be quite a ball. The stalls at Lido Beach and Stuland Laut feature hawkers who conjure up an amazing variety of dishes seemingly out of nowhere. Half an hour's drive got us to Kukup where the seafood is of unmatched quality. For classier dining and quality Malaysian Chinese cuisine, board the Eden Floating Restaurant, anchored off the Duty-Free Complex, which offers a unique mix of dining and entertainment for some 1100 guests. Abalons and scallop are specialities of the house, and diners can pick their raw seafood and vegetables from a market-style setting and have it prepared to order. More authentic Malay cuisine awaited me at the daily buffet of local specialities served at Mawar Complex restaurant at Jalan Sungai Chat.

The day's gone, let the action begin! Came nightfall and I decided to prowl around for action, not knowing what to expect. Unburdened by overdue local knowledge and my guide's overpowering protectiveness, I managed things rather well. You can get disappointed if you fall into the comparisons trap, but there's plenty happening by way of entertainment in select corners of the city. The trick is to know where, and how to join in. You can choose from several discos, pubs, and karaoke lounges, but for something special, it just has to be a Kuda Kepang dance, which originated here and features dancers imitating the movements of horses, to the music of a traditional orchestra. Kuda Kepang is normally performed at select, special occasions like cultural fairs, but with a bit of luck you can sometimes see a performance in the city itself. So look out for it.

The great thing about all this is the fact that it's safe for you to venture out at any time of the day or night. So take your cue and get those limbs moving.

And discover something of the real Malaysia.

# A Piece of Kandy

It lives in a different time-warp.

That's about the only way I would like to describe it. What you get when you visit is an experience laced with simple charm. Plenty of simple charm, as it turns out.

A scenic hill resort-cum-cultural centre-cum religious spot rolled into one, Kandy manages to do what places around the world proclaim to, but can't quite manage today. It slows you down. That's it. Slows you down to the point of being totally relaxed in a pleasant sort of way. 465 metres above sea-level means it's hilly enough. But it's also forested enough, isolated enough, and original enough, which all translates into making it a genuinely charming destination. Nestling on low hills, the town is looped by Sri Lanka's largest river, the Mahaweli, with nature's bounties further reflected through green valleys between the low hills; rivers; lakes, and cascading waterfalls.

Within a couple of hours of arriving, I had started to unwind, even if I didn't immediately notice it. In fact, I had started to feel at home and I am convinced this was at least partly owing to the fact that the hotel's staff had singled me out for attention, inquired if my room had a nice view, and if I wanted a cup of tea to get over my long journey. They were chatty and thoroughly nosey, but obviously meant well, so that was that. I was pleased.

The bus journey from Colombo had been scenic but hard. The conversation had been jarring. But entering the resort had put things in perspective, to the point where, within 20 minutes of my check-in, I had wandered off from my hotel in an exploratory mode, braving the drizzle that had been our companion for hours now.

A few minutes and a few short steps, and I found myself standing at the entrance of the town's most famous, most-visited site — The Temple of the Sacred Tooth (Dalada Maligawa) is truly worthy of all its fame. If you are spiritually inclined, you'll feel the special atmosphere of the shrine. If you are not, you'll get charmed by the varied art forms wrought into the structure.

I decided to ignore the rain that seemed to be getting heavier by the second. But none of the 200-odd tourists who thronged the place seemed to notice it, let alone mind it, so why did I have to be the odd man out. "It's only rain," I told myself as I rinsed my scarf for the second time in two minutes, and inched my way closer to the shrine's main courtyard, joining a queue that was moving at a snail's pace.

The famed 16th-century temple is the lodestar of the Buddhists. Though not very big in physical proportions, it is, nevertheless, a priceless, highly revered shrine. One of the temple's most spectacular sections, the *patthirippuwa* or the octagon, was added by the king of Kandy in the early 19th century, and a golden canopy was recently constructed over the relic chamber. To the accompaniment of flute and drum music, rituals are conducted daily in the temple to venerate the relic. July and August each year sees public honouring the temple on Esala Perahera or Procession of the Month of Esala.

The next hour was spiritual and blissful and its memories have stayed with me. With the incessant sound of the flute keeping me company as a soundtrack, I traversed the length and breadth of the shrine, entered most of its rooms and chambers, saw the sacred tooth, exchanged pleasantries with a group of European tourists who smilingly mentioned "You're obviously not from these parts," and soaked in more rain than I can ever remember doing wilfully.

The temple had soothed me and set my mood. I am quite sure it was my visit here that had something to do with the fact that I ended up liking Kandy, to the point that I consider it to be the high point of my Sri Lanka visits. My liking grew to the extent that I ignored the rain that kept us company for most of our stay, ignored the fact that mine was probably the only room at the Hilltop Hotel that didn't have a frontal view, and didn't miss my all-important mid-morning cup of coffee. That's something I need every day of my life, wherever in the world I am. But I ignored its absence and instead relished the local tea.

The town itself has an interesting history. Born in the 14th century, Kandy became the capital of the Kandayan kingdom in the 16th century, and was the seat of much of Sri Lanka's culture. The Royal City fell into the hands of the British when the last Kandayan king, Sri Vikrama Rajasinha was captured by them in AD 1815. The British called it Kandy for Kanda in Sinhala, meaning a 'hill'.

The region lent itself to religion, which over the years has had a strong influence on the people here. Dotting the city and its environs are several hallowed and living shrines of Buddhists, Hindus, Christians, and Muslims. The Temple of the Sacred Tooth is particularly important for Buddhists. Visiting temples is not only a pleasant task, but highly informative, and with a little guidance, fairly easy to do.

Straddling two sides of the lake are Sri Lanka's two most important Buddhist Monasteries, their chief incumbents being the senior monks of the Buddhist Order in Sri Lanka. The Malwatta Monastery on the lake's southern side is embellished with 18th-century architectural design and planning, while the Asigriya Temple situated on the city's western side at Asgiriya, contains a giant statue of the Recumbent Buddha, and also the cremation ground of the Kandayan royalty. The higher ordination of the *sangha*, the monks, takes place annually in both these temples.

Known as the Western Shrines, the 14th-century Gadaladeniya; Lankatilaka, and Embekke Temples are situated close together on the Kadugannawa-Peradeniya Road, 16 kilometres west of Kandy. Set on a rock, Gadaladeniya is built of stone and has a seated Buddha image, lacquered doors, wall murals and carved stone friezes. Lankatilaka is a magnificent though peculiarly designed, white, three-storeyed brick building that shines against the blue background. Amidst the painted wooden doors and wall and ceiling frescoes in the shrine room is a superb seated image of the Buddha. The Embekke Temple is a deistic shrine dedicated to God Kataragama, and is famous for its intricately designed carved wooden pillars that leap to life with dancers, musicians, wrestlers, legendary beasts and birds.

There's also Dodanwela Devale that's of historic interest as the site where King Rajasinha of Kandy offered his crown to the presiding god after his great victory over the Portuguese in the 17th century. The 15th-century Suriyagoda Vihara, the rock-perched Hindagala Temple; Gangarama and Degaldoruwa Temples, both famous for Kandayan murals and Buddha images; Galmadauwa, and Medawela Viharas, are other notable shrines in the region.

Housed in what were once the quarters of the royal concubines, amidst the remains of the splendid royal palace of the Kandayan Kings, the National Museum and the Archaeological Museum both contain interesting exhibits and definitely merit a visit. The Audience Hall is a unique example of wooden architecture of the Kandayan period, and the site of the memorable AD 1815 Kandayan Convention, ceding the territories of the once-impregnable kingdom to the British, thus ending the 2,500 year old rule by kings in Sri Lanka.

Accompanied by the drizzle, I found myself entering the confines of the Royal Botanical Gardens, a local highlight and tourist delight, the 'green lungs of a green city'. Once the pleasure gardens of a Kandayan queen, the gardens are a 150-acre oasis, with landmarks like the Great Palm Avenue; the Orchid House; the Pergola, and the Octagon House.

"Guess how heavy," our young guide asked me with a grin as wide as the sweeping hills that ringed the city. I picked one up. "Five kilos," I told him, trying to gamefully hang on to it. "Yes, maybe, but sometimes you get one that weighs ten kilos," the good man informed me with his trademark grin. They were strewn around the place, the giant coconuts that had fallen down on the pathways. With due flourish he sliced the top of the giant coconut in question, and its juice was about as sweet as any I have tasted anywhere. The 'drinks break' over, we walked on and saw the variety of vegetation on display. Lush with hibiscus, cannas, bougainvilleas, and crotons, the gardens are a 'must-see'.

Its geographical setting apart, Kandy has this great distinction of not changing and losing its character. The town is still the home of the arts and crafts, music, dance and song that flourished during the reign of the patron king. At the Kandayan Art Association, you can buy the work of skilled craftsmen, and also see weavers, coppersmiths, brasssmiths and silversmiths at work. Laksala, the government handicrafts shop, is another good sales outlet. At Kalapuraya Nattarampota, seven kilometres from Kandy, is a settlement of craftsmen who produce their work in their own homes, at their own rhythms, like in olden times.

Nature has been kind. Much of Kandy's beauty comes from its lake, and there's scenic splendour all around. The Dumbara Valley; the tea-plantation heights of Hantane; Hunnasgiriya Falls; the mountain plateau of Hanguranketa, Katugastota, and Halloluwa where the road winds past precipitous heights; all feature immense natural beauty. There's lush greenery all around throughout the year — tea, rubber and coconut crops merge into the forested hillsides of Udawattakele, and at Bahirawakanda, the untamed mountain abode of the Guardian deity of the land.

It's all quite soothing. And quite lovely in its own, inimitable way! And to top things off, there's always that cup of high-quality tea to come back to.

# Santa's Snowy Playground

From the air it had resembled a giant park alternating with vegetation and open spaces, leaves fallen off golden yellow trees forming a huge carpet. At ground level it's nature at its most abundant.

Layer upon layer of birch stood etched against the landscape as I drove along a broad road that snaked through valleys and up gently undulating hills. Ahead, vast stretches of open country greeted me with their solitude. There was complete silence except for the wind whistling through the forested hills crisscrossed by ski and hiking trails, and through the wilderness with its shining riverbeds. There was silence and there was a sense of peace.

I had arrived in the 'north'. That's the best way to describe it. Capital of the province of Finnish Lapland, Rovaniemi is a town of immense natural beauty and wide, open spaces, as seen from the fact that its population of 55,000 is spread across an area of 8,000 square kilometres. On offer are the unique, geographical and natural delights of the Arctic Region, with nature being the biggest asset. During summer, activity revolves around exploring the region's forests and lakes, while winter offers a freezing but pleasant experience and a chance to ski cross-country across a barren, beautiful landscape that appears to stretch till eternity.

Everywhere things are quiet, but almost everyone is engaged in something constructive, be it chiseling handicrafts out of giant trees, or reindeer farming. And yes, the town does have a world celebrity.

Ancient local history records that the first 'tourists' arrived here some 8,000 years ago, and the permanent settlement began with visitors from the west and southeast, and the appearance of the Sami — Lapland's own indigenous population. For centuries Rovaniemi was a remote outpost, till the 1800s, when Lapland's natural resources were tapped and logging became an industry. Then came the 'gold fever' that attracted thousands to the region. The town developed and became Lapland's business centre, and so it has stayed.

It isn't Manhattan, but it's the centre of things in this part of the world, at least by Lap standards. Spread expansively and neatly at the confluence of Lapland's mighty Ounasjoki and Kemijoki Rivers, Rovaniemi boasts a distinct city-centre appearance with large public buildings in the middle of vast stretches of wild country. Trade apart, it's also a cultural centre, adventure-sports hub, university town, and major tourist destination.

While lumberjacks, gold miners, and hunters drifted here once from different parts of the Northern hemisphere, today you rub shoulders with tourists from the world over, seeking a unique Arctic experience comprising nature, culture, adventure sports, and fine shopping and dining. Tourism has found Rovaniemi.

The sense of space apart, the first thing that struck me was the complete absence of any shadow of the past, and for good reason. They don't exist, the town having been completely destroyed during World War II, and rebuilt from the foundations upwards, into an ultra-modern, functional capital of Lapland.

There are several contemporary urban landmarks to keep you interested: Arktikum House; the Jatkankynttila Bridge with its eternal flame, spanning the Kemijoki River; the Town Hall, and Lappia House that serves as a congress centre, concert hall, and library.

All else apart, you get a close look at the unique people who have made this harsh region their home. A good picture of loggers' lives and work — a colourful forestry tradition — is presented in the indoor and outdoor exhibitions at the Lapland Forestry Museum. The Ethnograph Museum with its open yard setting rich in provincial Southern Lapland culture, pays tribute to nature and the countryside. And the Provincial Museum of Lapland shows the life of the local Samis and their unceasing struggle to adapt to their harsh natural surroundings.

Ounasvaara, a year-round recreation centre, offers the delights of winter sports, courtesy the in-house sports park, jogging tracks, ski centre, and ski tracks. A firm believer of the theory that exercise is for those with nothing else to do, I politely turned down all invitations to take a shot at jogging and skiing, and settled down in the restaurant, which provided a diversion more suited to my psyche. It was worth it. Not only does the establishment serve good, authentic Finnish and Lapp food, it features stunning views of the river and the landscape gleaming in the distance.

In terms of sightseeing and discovery, nothing's more charming or educative than Arktikum, the Arctic Centre, a modern, multi-display science institute engaged in observing and researching Arctic region phenomenon. In a setting making skilful use of natural light, and with the aid of interactive computer and film programmes, the museum highlights the traditions and future of mankind.

Our sightseeing done, it was time to call on Rovaniemi's most famous citizen. Santa Claus, *the* Santa Claus, is the town's great attraction. In Rovaniemi, one can meet him and his reindeer every day of the week, throughout the year, visit him in his home and office (Santa's Cave), and have a photo taken with him. You can send letters and gift parcels from his Main Post Office and shop in his Workshop Village, a cheerful complex of shops, restaurants and offices.

Then came what turned out to be the first of my two famous encounters.

Our first meeting was against the backdrop of softly falling snow. His 'office' was bright and cheery, with bright lighting, furniture neatly laid out, and streamers and posters gently perched on the walls, adding colour to things. And there he sat regally on his chair, as visitors streamed in and queued up to sit by his side for the famous, customary photograph.

I now realise how fortunate I was to be singled out in my group. Singled out I was, and found myself exchanging pleasantries and discussing the weather with Santa. He bade me sit down, asked me what I did for a living, and we chatted on for a bit, holding up the queue. But I wasn't going to hurry this one along for it isn't everyday in one's life that one gets to meet Santa Claus himself in his very own office, in his very own town. No Sir, this wasn't my everyday routine, but rather, a special journey to a special place to meet a rather special person.

Nonchalantly, I introduced myself, explained what I was doing so far away from home, and tried to look and sound 'super cool' as we exchanged pleasantries. Outside, the snow was falling silently, shrouding everything gently.

Eager to silence all my critics back home who constantly accused me of not ever doing an honest day's work, I thought I wouldd interview him. A 'scoop of sorts', I thought. The untiring journalist at the right place at the right time, all the time, working away for glory!

Exactly the reverse happened. He shook my hand graciously and started to talk. Then came the 'interview'. Who was I? What did I do? Did I travel a lot? Did I enjoy my work? Seeing the queue behind me getting longer and its members progressively more irritated, I was eager to move on and out of the limelight. Unfazed, he continued for another couple of minutes (or was it an hour?) before he deigned to look at the unfortunate souls behind me.

"Come again," he invited me grandly, shook my hand again, and I was history.

Stepping out of his office, I felt a rare sense of elation. "It's my unique personality, of course," I told myself smugly. But time was short in Rovaniemi. There were places to visit, things to do. Off we went on our special tour that included a visit to a reindeer farm, and then to a husky farm, before indulging ourselves with generous helpings of salmon and white wine.

A year later, I was back in Rovaniemi. As I crossed the 'threshold' into what was by now familiar territory, it was like returning home.

There he sat in his office exactly like the last time. He hadn't changed a bit (a year isn't enough to change someone like him). As I approached him for the photo, out came his hand, "You've been here before." "Yes," I said. He inquired about my health, I asked about his. "Good to see you again," he declared grandly. Once again I was holding up the queue!

"It's my endearing personality, of course," I told myself smugly, avoiding the angry gaze of those behind me in the queue.

Christmas is festivity time here. There is general bonhomie, especially in the 'village' which welcomes thousands of visitors in festive fashion. There's a host of special activities including Arctic Christmas plays, puppet theatre and concerts, and 'Christmas Fantasia'. The place comes alive with a delightful vengeance.

Tourism and commerce have spawned a large local hospitality industry, with several hotels and eateries offering everything from quick snacks to gala dinners. And it may surprise you to know that there's vibrant fun and entertainment in nightclubs, but that's modern-day Lapland for you. A real treat is the local Lappi *à la carte* menu that features delicacies that offer Lapland's best and most exotic harvest, with salmon and reindeer specialities being particularly recommended.

Excitement ran high as we crossed the Arctic Circle a little way north of town. For 20 Finnish Marks, they give you a certificate to prove it, and the two that I have remain among my cherished documents.

Rovaniemi offers a holiday with a difference. And depending on your luck, you just might hear the jingle of bells and see a reindeer sledge passing by, ridden by... You guessed it!

Looking back at my two visits to Rovaniemi, and seeing the two photos with Santa and the 'Arctic certificates', I realise just how important my meetings with him really were.

The other day I was showing the certificates and photos to a lady friend. "They're just wonderful," she said, looking first at the photos, then at me, then at the photos again. "They're just wonderful, and you're so lucky, and I'm so proud of you," she said again, peering at the photos.

"Oh, by the way, I'm the one on the left and Santa's on the right," I told her.

This time she really gave me the 'eye' before pouring over the photos again, and purred, "I'll take your word for it."

# Gateway to the Fjords

Way up in cold, grey Scandinavia they don't get too excited about little things in life.

Life here is mostly about serious stuff, plain and simple. But there are subjects that are quintessential to Scandinavians' psyche. The trick is to know which ones. And then to hone in on where to find them! Once you do, you have enhanced the value of your visit far beyond what a tour operator could have done for you.

Talk seafood. Or rather, talk salmon, and you have got their attention. Scandinavians take their seafood almost as seriously as they take life itself, and an hour spent browsing around little stalls selling shrimps, herring, mackerel, and the redoubtable salmon itself, told me why. There were as many tourists out that morning as there were traders, all fighting the icy wind and the smell that was almost an assault on the senses. This wasn't really a tourist spot, just the 'fish market', the most important place in town.

Every tourist town has a claim to fame. Bergen has several. And we aren't talking salmon now. Nature's been more than kind! It's quite a package, with snow-clad mountains mirrored in clear lakes; waterfalls cascading from rocky knolls; emerald green fields etched against rugged granite, and the stunning majesty of the fjords. Especially the fjords, arguably, the single best reason to visit Norway.

Bergen's year-round tourist popularity stems from the fact that it is the gateway to Norway's legendary fjords — Hardangerfjord, Sognefjord, and Geirangerfjord. Hemmed in by seven mountains, the little coastal town literally clambours up the mountainsides, offering spectacular views. And an upfront encounter with ceaseless rain and icy winds!

History records that Bergen's been a busy little town for quite a while now. Located in the northern seas, it was a calling point for foreigners for a thousand years. Today, the sailors and traders of old have been replaced by tourists who flock here from the world over to see the fjords, walk around the little town and its environs, try some bread rolls and salmon, and savour genuine Nordic marine flavour. I was one of a crowd.

But first, the history! Ever since King Olav Kyrre bestowed 'town status' on this Viking harbour in AD 1070, cultural traditions, trading, and shipping have predominated, with the city being part of local history, cultural history, and Norwegian history all rolled into one. Today, you roam through living history in a modern setting that's just a whisper away from Norway's mightiest and most scenic fjords.

With corn brought here from the south and fish from the north, to be traded and shipped worldwide, Bergen was born, cradled, nurtured and seasoned by the sea. Once the North's largest harbour city, it still has its face turned towards the sea that has given it so much for so long, without really asking for anything in return.

Times change. So do trends. Dried fish and cod liver oil have swapped places with hi-tech know-how. Coiled rope has given way to steel girders, old sailing ships have made way for oil rigs equipped in the city's harbour. The 'here and now' part of life is present. But the flavour of old lingers, hanging over things like a historical shroud, especially on the seafront.

Talking of flavour, nothing charmed me more than Bryggen, the old trading wharf nestling by the inner harbour of Vagen, destroyed and lovingly rebuilt. This is the famous old face of Bergen and the key part of its cultural heritage, quite fittingly featuring in UNESCO's World Heritage List.

Bryggen was formerly the local commercial heart, where Bergensers and Hanseatic League merchants thrived and prospered commercially. The Hansa's distinct lifestyle is reflected in this 'town within a town' that features old timber buildings and a distinctly laid-back atmosphere. Quite simply, Bryggen is special.

Bergen was recently chosen as being amongst Europe's three tidiest cities. I did the recommended thing and walked, taking in sights waiting to be explored. There's this perennial rain that can play spoilsport and ruin what would otherwise be very pleasant walks. But I had already decided not to let little things like the weather bother me, and that must have helped, because I ended up walking more than I had planned. 'Singing in the rain' I certainly wasn't, but it was extremely pleasant.

The fragrance of flowers spills over everything, especially the rhododendrons that appear everywhere in a burst of colours. My leisurely, winding tour took me meandering around old streets and alleyways made for browsing, past small wooden houses that lie higgledy-piggledy, and up cobble-stoned stepways that climbed steeply. I stopped by at the aquarium with its penguin, fish, and seal species, and, of course, at the fish market. Everyone does. It's mandatory.

The town isn't short on views, but the one from the Ulriken, the city's highest mountain, is about as good as it gets. Those who don't want to go up can just sit on the quay and gaze at the tall sailing ship, *Statsraad Lehmkuk*, the local pride and joy. I did, briefly. But there were other things to do. Into the funicular I went, and up to the top of Mount Floien and its summer restaurant for a much-needed beer and another superb view.

All this behind me, I finally put out to sea, bound for the fjords, those broad and narrow, deep and sheltered inlets from the sea that are a geographical wonder, attracting tourists from the world over. Behind us the town faded mistily into a cluster of houses haphazardly spread across the hill. Ahead, and to the left was the sea, starting to get a bit choppy, and to my right, the fjords, rising majestically sheer out of the water, stunningly beautiful, dwarfing the tourist boats and fishing vessels that tried to ease up and kiss their base. You have to be there to appreciate the sheer impact and beauty of these awesome natural wonders.

A little time spent here told me that Bergen boasts more than just the fjords and the sea. There is also rich local culture, well portrayed at several notable outlets. There is the world's oldest symphony orchestra founded in AD 1765; the famous Natural History Museum; and Norway's first national theatre, both founded in AD 1850. Visitors can enjoy the International Festival of Music — Norway's largest annual cultural event — and also the local ballet ensemble, excellent pop, jazz, choirs, and the local 'drummer-boy's brigade'.

Several art galleries exhibit paintings by Edvard Munch and other artists. The Grieg Concert Hall pays tribute to Edvard Grieg, the famous composer who lived and worked here, brought fame to the city, and whose home at Troldhaugen is now a museum and tourist haunt. The great landscape artist J.C. Dahl; writer Henrik Ibsen, and the well-known playwright Ludwig Holberg were all famous sons of the town.

If there's one thing I have learnt to take seriously on my travels, its local food. The fact that I like eating may or may not have anything to do with it, but it's a pastime that has yielded rich dividends, never mind the little pressure on my waistline.

The local dining experience, and most restaurants' joy and prized offering is fresh seafood. And fresh *means* fresh. While the salmon here is the world's best, the fish market offers the sea's bounties with rows of red lobster, assorted mackerel and caviar, and mounds of shrimps. I didn't need much persuading to try out the various delicacies around, and whole-heartedly recommend the fried fish cakes, the ever-popular fish soup, and the Shilling Bun, a coil of crisply baked dough smothered in cinnamon and sugar. Complimenting everything is the bread selection, especially the dark, icing sugar-moist bread cake. Restaurants like Lousiana Creole and Dickens offer surprises in their menus.

A bracing climate, trendy restaurants and boutiques, and the tag of 'Fjord's capital city', all create a situation where Bergen doesn't have to waste time trying to be modest.

And it isn't! And that's just fine!

# Little India, Big Images

Home away from home!

It's all so familiar to Indians, you can be excused for thinking you never really left home.

In the land of sizzling satays, you can also savour a *dosa* (crepe or pancake made from fermented rice and lentils) or *parantha* (Indian flat bread) complete with Indian ground spices, and a glass of sherbet or *lassi* (yoghurt-based drink). If the heat, humidity, tension or a nagging sweet tooth compels you, try a *kulfi* (ice cream).

I had spent an hour with my friend Magdelene Low walking around, browsing in little shops, and stopping by at a café for a quick meal of tandoori chicken, *daal* (lentils) and *naan* (Indian bread). I then opted for the *kulfi,* but declined the *paan* (betel leaf).

Magdelene is Singapore-based and works for Leading Hotels of the World, and when she asked me if there was any particular place I wanted to visit, I was quick on the trigger. So here we were.

A traveller to Singapore had written in AD 1879 of the "tall, graceful women gliding along the pavement, exquisite in movement and artistic in colouring." His fantasy-like writing was actually based on what he saw and admired. And the rest was left to imagination. But it's all there, exactly as advertised.

Welcome to Little India — as Singapore's Serangoon Road area is known — where the aroma of spices hangs thick in the air, and Western dresses are out of place, while all things Indian are firmly in the saddle. Little India embodies the vibrant and colourful culture of Singapore's large Indian community that hasn't lost touch with its roots.

Women in graceful saris shop for fruit and vegetables, and mango leaves frame doorways. The dull sheen of brass, the earthy hues of terracotta, and the faint glitter of gold catch the eye. Strings of jasmine sway in the breeze at every corner, nose-tickling spices and gossamer greet you at every turn, fine lengths of silk slither across shop counters. The shops sell everything imaginable. There are sweetmeats, spices, temple garlands, gold jewellery, furniture, utensils, and household goods.

If all this isn't enough, you find tongue-singeing chutneys, and sweet savouries that leave the stomach crying "encore". As for the people themselves, they could have stepped right out of Chennai. In fact, that's exactly what their forefathers did. So if you were planning to brush up on your Tamil, here's your chance.

This self-contained Indian township lives to its own distinct rhythm, its sights and sounds pure Indian. From the clinically clean boulevards of the rest of the city, you enter a labyrinth of streets and alleys that look a little more weather-beaten, and are a little less clean. At least by Singapore standards!

The next day I was back, alone, in an exploratory mood. I stopped by at the Zhujjiao Centre, a major shopping area of the district, with several typical outlets selling a mind-boggling array of merchandise. On the lower floor is a great Singapore institution — the wet market, where locals go for fresh fruit, vegetables, fish, and meat, sometimes slipping on the wet floors. Upstairs is a booming hawker stall that seems to ignore the time of day when it comes to doing business. Go up to the second floor and you will literally stumble upon little shops crammed to the ceiling with everything from cheap clothes to not-so-cheap electronics, jewellery, and bric-à-brac.

Cross the busy street, and you come to the Govindasamy Store, another regional landmark. Founded by one G. Pillai, a patriarch of the local Indian community, the store has several floors frenetically selling cotton polyester, silks and brocades, and a host of consumer items in its supermarket section.

But there's more to the Serangoon shopping experience than visiting large stores, as my brief forays taught me. There are spice-sellers with bags full of the choicest Indian herbs and spices. There are jewellery outlets selling heavy gold and jewellery that constitutes a bride's dowry. There's henna for decorating ladies' hands and feet, turmeric powder, perfumed oils, and kohl for the eyes. A feature of the area is the '*mamak* man' (roadside vendor) selling everything from cigarettes to cold drinks, magazines to toothpaste, incense to cough medicine.

Wherever you go, the smell of jasmine follows you. In case you missed having your fortune read in India, there are plenty of parrot horoscopists thronging the streets, eager to 'show you the way', and help you along in the pursuit of health, wealth and happiness.

Hastings Road; Clive Street; Campbell Lane — no, we haven't left for England! These are side and back streets named after colonial soldiers and politicians who served in Imperial India. But here again, while the names are English, everything else is Indian.

"Do not settle in a land without temples," an old Tamil saying has it. True to their belief, many settlers helped in the construction of several temples that dot the area and have become regional landmarks. The Sri Veerama Kaliamman and Sri Srinivasa Perumal Temples are the main Hindu shrines, boasting intricate workmanship. On Race Course Road is the Buddhist Temple of 1,000 lights, and Dunlop Street has the Abdul Gafoor Mosque.

Food is reason by itself to visit Little India. Fiery with chilli, red with spices, fragrant with curry leaf, the food's always served piping hot, without undue fuss and ceremony, and is generally considered value for money. The Zhujjiao Centre stocks a bewildering selection of food items, and on Race Course Road you find excellent restaurants including the famous Banana Leaf Apollo with its renowned fish-head curry. The restaurants on Serangoon Road and Upper Dickson Road specialise in vegetarian food, and trying out their *thali* (food platter) is well worth the effort.

Little India fascinates. For Indians, it's an extension of home with familiar sights, sounds and smells. For visitors in general, it's an off-track, offbeat, more fragranced, more colourful and noisier part of Singapore.

Have a meal, and you get to enjoy a *paan*. Enter a shop, and photographs of gods and deities stare down at you. Walk the streets, and familiar Hindi film music greets you. Visit a temple and incense fragrance predominates.

You are left expecting to see rajas and elephants around the next corner.

Before I let you get Singapore out of your head, I would like to share one of its culinary traditions with you. Let's call it 'Feasting Without Tears in Singapore' — Barbequed king prawns resting on banana leaves, *murtabak* and sizzling satays on the grill, succulent pork ribs with 'gunpowder' chilli powder, sumptuous Indian pancakes, lamb chops with cucumber, fried carrot cake, washed down with pineapple juice, or Chinese tea perhaps. All this amidst plenty of activity, plenty of noise, and sometimes, plenty of fresh air under the stars.

If, as they say, food is quintessential to the Singaporean psyche, where does one go to discover its real secrets? Chances are you'll stumble onto it anywhere in the city, every day of the year. The trick is to know what it really is.

Just drop in at one of the hawker stalls or food centres as they are known, which excel in achieving the difficult task of serving up good food quickly, and at low rates. These are special places serving special food, the watchword being simplicity. There is a fine mix of Chinese, Peranakan, Malay, Indonesian and Indian food fads. This is feasting without fuss, heartburn, or tears, with nothing to regret except one's fancies.

History and tradition support hawker food, making it completely intrinsic to local heritage and lifestyles. In the past, the hawkers actually sold their wares travelling around from place to place, and many a client was known to wait at select spots for his ice creams or rice-and-noodle soup. The mobile hawkers of old have since been honoured in the food centres where they have been putting their culinary skills to good use and commercial value.

Your typical food centre might comprise an assortment of stalls, most selling diverse dishes, but strong on a particular one. This offers a 'mix and match' possibility so one can pick different items from different stalls.

This isn't your conventional club lounge type of scenario. Noisy, smoky, and lively, the centres' food is complimented with a distinct ambience and atmosphere hard to imitate. Some prominent centres are Chinatown Food Street, Smith Street, Chinatown Complex Hawker Centre, Newton Market, Lau Pa Sat Festival Markets, Hill Street and Maxwell Road Food Centre.

Hawker food differs from both home cooking and restaurant food. Learning their trade from their parents, hawkers jealously guard their secrets and pass them down from generation to generation. With a lifetime spent perfecting a dish or two, it's no surprise that for many Singaporeans, the humble hawker food often ranks as more delectable and epicurean than anything served in upscale restaurants.

From celebrities to common folk, from jet-set millionaires to the humblest blue-collar workers, everyone occasionally drops in at the centres to enjoy 'simple feasts with a thousand flavours'. No matter that the setting is simple to the point of being basic — often a plain stall — or that the crockery is melamine or plastic and the tables are formica-topped, or that service is at an absolute minimum without coiffeured waiters awaiting your leisure. Noticing such trivial details would offend a good Singaporean. The food and atmosphere ensure that just a roof above and a table below are enough.

Sit anywhere, note your table number and order from any stall, all of which display menus and prices. If not comfortable with chopsticks, just reach out for a fork. The hawkers proudly display their raw ingredients in their glass-cabinets stalls. Many traditional stalls offer facilities for brewing Chinese tea on the side, and one can brew it in miniscule teapots and sip away from dollhouse tea cups. Tipping is unheard of.

Brusque and businesslike, the hawkers will bring food to the table, astonishing everyone with their photographic memory. Be daring and ask for the 'gunpowder' chilli powder, (to be sprinkled prudently to avoid gastronomical regrets). Or just play safe and have what they bandy around as 'bland' food. No other ground rule applies. It's what it's meant to be. Wholesome eating without fuss or ceremony!

The food is always served piping hot and the quality always up to scratch. And the choice can extend far beyond the humble noodle. There's Indian *Rojak* (a mix of eggs, prawns, and boiled potatoes, served with a large variety of fritters); *Hokkien Hay Mee*, the prawn noodle soup that's considered something of a modern classic; *Char Kway Teow*, flat white noodles stir-fried along with Chinese sausages, cockles and eggs in a large wok; *Popiah*, the Chinese spring rolls filled with cooked strips of turnip, meat and bean sprouts in egg-based wrap; *Nasi Lemak*, fragrant rice cooked in coconut milk, had with pan-fried omelette, deep fried chicken wings, fish, or *sambal* chilli. Or just steamed rice with peanut-sized pork pieces.

Hawker centres' food is for the purist, with good, simple, old-fashioned delicacies. They bring to the people the abundance of the seas, fields, and orchards, cooked with simplicity and skill, minus any needless frills.

Quite the way it should be!

# Smorgasbord & Smart Pants

"Spring is in the air and I'm happy again…"

The lone singer had made his way down the promenade, settling himself into a comfortable position, careful to see that his head was in the shade, his legs soaked up the sun, and his rather ample posterior was wedged just right onto the bench that was going to be his 'headquarters' for a couple of hours and a couple of beers, at the very least.

During the 'high season', it would have been longer, but for now, a couple of hours of soulful singing would suffice. After all, there were other things to be done, or at least that's the way it was supposed to be. As the crowds swirled around, his voice got a little louder, renewed strength flowing through his throat, his spirit buoyed. The customary applause, a few coins tossed into the large black hat that rested at his feet, and yet another scene had been enacted in this dignified little drama.

I had spent an hour idling around languorously. Coiling through the medieval heart of the city and forming the backbone of its commercial district, Storget is one of the world's longest pedestrian streets. Shoppers find it is 'easy street', thanks to outlets specialising in contemporary Euro-fashions, crystal, antiques, and Danish design, and large department stores and intimate boutiques with friendly staff, even if the prices aren't. Tucked away into side streets are some really cosy bars, breathing distance from some excellent restaurants and cafés. Day and night, tourists throng the street, creating a constant carnival-type atmosphere that doesn't go down badly with locals either. You might say things are nice and easy.

It comes as a surprise to learn that Copenhagen was founded over 800 years ago. The city's character is shaped by myriad charms and delights, subtly disguised in day-to-day nuances within easy reach of tourists, regardless of their budgets. Entertainment stretches from opera to theatre, musicals, cinema, and late-night bawdy cabarets and floorshows. And the dining-out pleases everyone from Arabs to Asians and Europeans, and budgeting is just that tiny little bit kinder than in other Scandinavian capitals. The ability to welcome and adopt diverse cultural demands without visible strain is the local strength.

Blame it on the milling crowds around the waterfront bistros and cafés, but my first reaction was that Copenhagen didn't quite look Scandinavian. But this city of 1.7 million is Scandinavian to the hilt, as seen from its international airport which functions with the uncomplicated precision synonymous with Scandinavians, through beautiful buildings that reflect the best of Scandinavian design and flair, and in the parks, canals, harbours and boulevards that dominate the local landscape.

This is a 'hang-loose' type of city, mostly easy-going and informal. This means your time can be well spent on discovering and imbibing things local. There is plenty to see and do. The famous Royal Theatre is a well-known city landmark, but there are over 50 museums that hold regular exhibitions.

Local entertainment flows from outlets like the Modern Art Museum, the National Art Gallery, Louisiana, Legoland, the Frederiksborg Palace, and New Carlsberg Glyptotek. You can see Danish history at the changing of the guard ceremony at Amalienborg Palace, for Queen Margrethe II. A modern woman with family and a career, the Queen traces her lineage through Europe's oldest ruling dynasty — some 1000 years — to the time of the Viking.

On the waterfront is the place to be, so that's where I went, and what a treat it turned out to be. Gateway to the Baltic countries, Copenhagen Harbour is Europe's biggest cruise port. Ships churn back and forth between Danish ports and across the Baltic to St Petersburg, connecting Western and Eastern Europe.

Like many before me, I was quickly seduced by the Old Port Quarter that has got pure atmosphere coming out of the cracks. The area is a living legacy of former maritime days, and a popular tourist haunt today, and for pure atmosphere, it takes some beating. I did it all: explored the narrow streets, admired the little buildings, and heard some really interesting sailors' tales in some really smoky taverns.

A whiff of history comes through in Nyhavn Canal, choked with its quayside taverns, schooners, yachts, even a theatre boat, and lined with 18th-century merchants' houses in blues, russets, and gold. (The name 'Copenhagen' means 'merchants harbour'). The waterfront area's historical landmarks include the Danish Resistance Museum, the Baroque Gefion Fountain, and the Danish Royal Family's elegant Amalienborg Palace. Explore historic warehouse buildings with inviting shops and cafés, and see the Little Mermaid of Hans Christian Andersen fame sitting perched on a boulder at Langelinie Quay.

You have two contrasting but interesting tour choices. You can take a harbour cruise that includes the impressive local skyline of towers, spires and green roofs, and also, maybe, the 'Little Mermaid' at Langeline. Or you can explore some famous old places, like Amalienborg and Fredensborg, for instance.

All this apart is always that simplest option for biding time — a leisurely walk through the streets and avenues of the city, savouring the special flavour of little shops and cafés, and the ever-present street musicians.

I had often wondered about all the hype surrounding the Tivoli Gardens, but it seems well-founded. Featuring a large Taj Mahal-like pavilion, restaurants like Balkoven, lit at night by thousands of coloured bulbs, and a multi-layered Chinese Tower, the gardens are a top-drawer amusement park, attracting thousands of daily visitors to their salubrious surroundings. Trees and flowers provide a peaceful backdrop for the park's restaurants, cafés, and snack bars. Red-coated Tivoli Boys' Guards watch over you as you enjoy fireworks, puppet shows, rides and funhouse mirrors, a Hans Christian Andersen castle, a concert that features symphony performances, and a Commedia dell' Arte theatre.

The city is kind to gourmets! Eat traditional. The Danes' absolute favourite is smorgasbord — a selection of open-faced sandwiches put together from the basic building blocks of rye, black or French bread spread with fresh butter, fish, meat, or cheese. Fried flounder, marinated herring, roast beef, and a mix of hard and soft cheeses are usual components of the selection. A typical hot meal comprises salmon, pork, pheasant or beef. Christmas time sees roast duck doing the rounds.

By an old tradition that dates back to the time of the Vikings, Danes usually toast continually while eating their smorgasbord, by raising their glass, looking one in the eye, and wishing good heath with a merry 'Skal'. All of which is grist to the mill for diehard epicureans like me.

Copenhagen tends to expose its charms one at a time. For best value, sign on for a conducted tour.

At Elsinore, you can stand, like Hamlet, on the ramparts of Kronborg Castle, and enjoy a panoramic view of the countryside. And, typically, take your time deciding what to do next.

It's got official sanction.

# Two For The Road

Want to know something about cardinal overseas driving rules?

If you have got company, avoid being the driver. Consider the advantages. You can sit back and enjoy the scenery, give directions, offer advice, nap off, and most significantly, have a beer or two. Or three.

My friend Alison just happened to be the driver, I the navigator. And we planned to tour as much as possible of Southwest England in a week, the weather be damned.

When it was time to leave, the first surprise was the sunshine. "Odd," I thought to myself as I got into the crimson red Nissan rented from 'Budget Rent A Car', bags in the hold, seat belt secured, road map of Britain safely in place, all set to go.

Day One: We left London bathed in pale gold morning sunshine. Being British, Alison felt at home behind the wheel, though she did find the traffic "a little heavier than it had been two years back". The fact is that on Saturday mornings, Britain's motorways resemble runways. Everyone wants to 'take off'. So did we, as we exited the metropolis, cruising along the M3 towards the sprawling, sleepy town of Farnborough, where we hit the M3 motorway again, headed westwards for Salisbury, our jaunt's first official stop.

Steeped in history, Salisbury was the perfect curtain-raiser. The town features one of Britain's finest gothic Norman cathedrals, with the highest spire (123 metres); the best preserved Magna Carta (1215); a unique 13th-century frieze of Bible stories (Chapter House); the largest cloisters and close in Britain; and Europe's oldest working clock (1386). Not bad for a little town with a 'fruitish' sounding name.

We did our tourist bit and set out exploring. Situated in Cathedral Close and dating back to AD 1254, The Wardrobe now houses the Salisbury Museum of the Royal Gloucestershire, Berkshire and Wiltshire Regiment. Mompesson House, The House in the Close, is a perfect example of Queen Anne architecture dating to AD 1701. And there is the multiple award-winning Salisbury Museum that holds all those interesting collections of national significance.

A welcome coffee break (Alison opted for a hot chocolate), and we somehow managed to find the grey monolithic structure where we had parked our car. It had been a wonderful day and it was two educated tourists who headed out of town in fading light.

Day Two: Fifty minutes driving and we were in another historical landmark. Winchester oozes history. We discovered the town's pleasures the way they should be — on foot! The magnificent cathedral apart, there are medieval buildings, galleries and museums, and tranquil green spaces, ideal for strolling and soaking up the local atmosphere. Once the Romans' east to west route through the town, the historic High Street is today a lively, pedestrianised shopping precinct, as are the nearby side streets and The Square — site of William the Conqueror's treasury — which features boutiques, speciality shops and cafés.

We threaded the heritage trail across Winchester's historic heart, with its world-famous and lovely Cathedral Close;

Winchester College; and the house where Jane Austen died. Then we followed in the footsteps of the poet John Keats through the Water Meadows to St Cross to see the remains of the powerful medieval Bishops' Palace.

The Cathedral is quite special. A place of worship for over 900 years, it contains the tombs of the early English kings; the longest nave in Europe; Jane Austen's grave, and other treasures including the world-famous Winchester Bible.

Day Three: The next stop on our jaunt was a town greatly endeared to the English. And with good reason! With 11 museums that contain an assortment of exhibits, and Southsea featuring almost 6.5 kilometres of promenade offering sweeping views across the Solent to the Isle of Wight, Portsmouth Harbour shows true pedigree. Start off at Charles Dickens' birthplace, then go museum exploring. The City Museum unfolds the city's fascinating history, from a Saxon fishing village to a thriving commercial centre; the D-Day Museum with its magnificent Overlord embroidery, records the largest invasion force ever assembled on earth, and the Royal Marines Museum is a celebration of over 300 years of the elite naval fighting corp. One can explore the infamous dungeons and amazing time tunnel in Southsea Castle of Henry VIII fame, and see guns, gunpowder, and more, at the Royal Armouries at Fort Nelson.

Anchored at Flagship Portsmouth — a world-class marine heritage centre — are some of Britain's greatest historic ships that have now acquire folklore status. And Gunwharf Quays, Portsmouth Harbour's relatively new attraction, is a lively shopping and leisure complex featuring in a superb waterfront location, some 85 designer shops, over 20 restaurants and bars, outdoor ice-skating rink and bowling centre, a 14-screen multiplex cinema, and loads of atmosphere.

Take a guided tour of HMS *Victory*, Lord Nelson's flagship and one of Britain's most famous warships, lovingly restored and maintained, still in commission today, basking in eternal glory. Stand at the spot where Nelson died, then go below the deck and see vividly recreated life at sea for the 820 men and boys who lived, worked, fought and died during battle. Then take in the Trafalgar experience — a unique insight into what the Battle of Trafalgar was like. Then see the pride of Queen Victoria's fleet, HMS *Warrior*. Bigger and faster than any other ship then afloat, this was the world's first iron-hulled armoured battleship. Powered by steam as well as sail, she drove fear into the enemy, so much so that she never went into battle. Move on to another legend. Raised from a watery grave in 1982, Henry VIII's *Mary Rose* is everything an old ship should be. The ship sank in AD 1545 with 700 men on board. 437 years later, the world held its breath when she was finally recovered from the seabed.

The afternoon shadows had lengthened when we left this famous port and hit the road again.

Day Four: A point to ponder! Does a driving holiday get stale after three days? Well, this one didn't. The morning sun still resembled a huge orange when we pulled up at what must surely rank among Britain's most picturesque and quaint villages. Aptly called 'Heart of the Cotswolds', Stow-on-the-Wold belongs to the picture-postcard category. Situated beside the Roman Fosseway and set on a rounded hill, this ancient Cotswold wool town saw Iron Age people first settle on the hill, and is dotted with Stone and Bronze-Age burial mounds. The houses were built with the mellow Cotswold stone from local quarries.

In the centre of town, in the shadow of the Church, I sat and ate my hasty-tasty budget lunch (a pork pie and banana). Facing me was The King's Arms, *the* pub in town, a good example of a coaching inn where the main entrance was through the arch leading to the stables. Behind me was Talbot, renowned for wines and traditional ales. Racing Green, a trendy boutique, and The Cotswold Cobbler were other notable names. On Digbeth Street stands the Royalist Hotel, said to be England's oldest inn, since AD 947. The buildings are just stone. No paint, and all light brown. And the effect is highly soothing. "An impressionist's delight," I said to myself.

Another short drive yielded another delight! The Gateway to the Cotswolds is how they describe Broadway, one of Britain's most beautiful villages, its houses of honey-coloured Cotswold stone having lured visitors for centuries. Local history is reflected in the architecture, some buildings built in the grand Georgian style, others of a more lowly origin. St Eadburgha's Church has been a place of Christian worship for almost a thousand years. Abbots Grange dates back to the 14th century. Tudor House dates back to AD 1660. And parts of the Lygon Arms Hotel go back to the mid 16th century.

Beyond the village, the skyline is dominated by Broadway Tower, a folly built by the Sixth Earl of Coventry in the 18th century. It was with utmost reluctance that I climbed to the top of its 65-feet tower, but was rewarded with a spectacular view. And Broadway Hotel, where we bedded down, must surely be among Britain's most charming, illustrating a quaint style of half-timber and Cotswold stone, merry fireplaces, and home-style cooking served up with a smile.

Broadway's location makes it an ideal base to tour the Cotswolds. Within easy reach are several interesting places including Shakespeare country and the Vales, Warwick, Cheltenham, Stratford, Worcester, Oxford and Birmingham.

Day Five: A blissful day! Hemmed in by the beautiful West Country and Cotswolds countryside, Bath continues to bask in the splendour of its past, its strong intellectual legacy providing a captivating setting for some of Britain's finest cultural performances.

For centuries, the town provided inspiration for several great musicians, poets, artists, and writers. Today, theatre lovers are spoilt for choice in this thriving centre of creativity that is home to internationally renowned art centres, theatres, and galleries hosting a wide range of festivals and performances.

There were only two problems — I am not a theatre person at heart, and we couldn't find parking space. "Let's skip it," I told Alison as she frantically turned into every little street seeking a parking lot. "No one at home need know we didn't see the blessed place," I added for good measure.

As it happened, we found parking space and the energy to step out and go exploring the town, and a very pleasant experience it turned out to be.

We happened to be near the Museum of Costume and Royal Victoria Art Gallery, and stepped in and saw a pretty face of Britain through the ages. While in the museum mode, we also stopped by at the Holburne Museum. Set in one of Bath's most elegant Georgian buildings, it features 18th-century decorative art juxtaposed with works by leading British 20th-century craftsmen.

The mood sort of 'on', we arrived at the local highlight. The Roman Baths Museum brings to life the magnificent Roman Temple of Sulis Minerva and the 2,000-year-old bathing complex built around the town's natural hot springs. For £7.50 each, we took a guided tour of the complex, and with the aid of an audio set and running commentary, saw the hot-water pools and different sections with their collection of ancient heirlooms and artefacts. It was all quite impressive, the strong smell of sulphur, notwithstanding.

Day Six: The bubble burst! We might have known it was too good to be true. The day dawned grey and gloomy with a broad hint of rain. Now, in England when there's a broad hint of rain, it means there is rain. And it comes sooner rather than later. Pity, but that's how it goes. We bashed on regardless. And soon forgot about the weather.

The birthplace of polo, Cirencester is quiet, sleepy, and liable to be missed out on a driving tour. In fact, we almost missed it, then almost skipped it thinking it wouldn't be worth the effort, but then backtracked and dropped in. And we were glad we did. The fact is that it shouldn't be missed out. The Cirencester Park Polo Club is among the most renowned in the game, and several Indians have featured in the list of celebrities who have played the 'game of kings' on its hallowed grounds. April through September is tournament season. The rest of the time is for a laid-back, quiet existence.

Polo apart, Cirencester sports an easy ambience and is small enough to be an intimate place to live in or visit. In the shadow of the cathedral, a mug full of steaming latté coffee in hand, I sat and watched the world go by. Trendy boutiques edge the sidewalks of the town's main boulevard. One solitary half-timbered building stood out, but overall, the architecture is staid.

The weather cleared and mellow afternoon sunshine gave a golden tint to oaks that flanked the road, as we drove into the town I like to call the 'bard's backyard'. And indeed it is. Shakespeare's shadow looms large around Stratford-Upon-Avon, at quaint little corners and in quaint little ways. Bearing direct association with the poet are a host of symbols; statues of his famous tragic heroes decorating local parks; the Falstaff Restaurant; the Shakespeare Hotel (for honeymooners); the Encore Inn; the Birthplace Coach Terminal; Mary Arden's House; New Place; the Shakespeare

Centre; Anne Hathaway's Cottage, and Hollscroft-Suzzane Shakespeare and her husband Dr John Hall's house.

Its rooms intact, Anne Hathaway's Cottage and Farm allows one to actually go into the sitting-room where Shakespeare used to court Anne, and see the courting settee and various other items of domicile like utensils, chairs and beds.

As a student of English literature, I relived some of the scenes from the bard's famous works. Though regretting not being able to see the famed local theatre, it was a fulfilling experience all the same, and one that stays in my mind.

It was time to move on once again, and move on we did.

Once there was activity here. Today, it stands all by itself, desolate and mysterious, showing visitors the remains of a prehistoric monument that was in use thousands of years ago.

A two-hour drive took us back thousands of years. If you are anywhere in Southwest England, don't miss out on seeing Stonehenge. A marvel of English heritage, Stonehenge is the British Isles' most outstanding monument, a World Heritage Site, and definitely a place for those with a vivid imagination or sense of the surreal.

Imagine walking among the ancient people who mapped the course of the sun and the moon to build this monument. Look for the burial grounds in the landscape where they buried their leaders. Courtesy an audio tour, we learnt about the monument and its surroundings' history, and that some 8,000 years ago, the area was mixed pine and hazel woodland before becoming down land. The larger stones in the circle are Sarsen stones from the Marlborough Downs, and the smaller ones known as the Bluestones are from the mystical Preseli Mountains in Wales.

We would have stayed longer but for the icy wind that blew across the meadows and cut through our clothes like a scalpel. We fled.

235

A kilometre and half out, I looked back. The giant rocks stood starkly exposed in the fading light. The further away we went, the thinner they appeared, tapering off in girth until finally they resembled needles on a green patchwork.

It was eerie. And it was beautiful.

# St Moritz Serenading

Rhapsody in blue! Snow crystal and sunshine! The art of life!

It is a 'clockwork orange'. The sun actually shines on 322 days annually, contributing to the region's legendary sparkling dry 'champagne climate'. The few remaining days are given to downing warm drinks before cheerful fireplaces.

Given this munificence, few complain about the cold, crisp breeze on the Southern Alps.

I didn't. I couldn't.

I had made a quiet entry into the world's most famous and upscale holiday and ski resort. I had come burdened with knowledge. They had extolled the resort's numerous virtues, explained its fame, and prepared me for 'an experience beyond compare'. It was almost more than my journalistic mind was willing to accept at face value. So I was on a sort of judgment warpath, keen to see if the place really did measure up.

Bedding down at the Hotel Stefani, I got my first inkling of local status, or at least what is perceived as local status. "Just a couple of hundred metres down the road you'll find the chalets of the world's rich and famous," the girl at the reception desk had mentioned casually, partly because she sized me up as a first-time visitor, and partly because, as I later learnt, they all — the locals, I mean — like to put in a word or two in praise of their town. "Nature has blessed this town. I hope you'll be pleased."

"Oh sure, I'll be pleased. I'm easy to please," I replied, nodding my head politely. This seemed to go down well with her, and she promptly started to give me useful tips on just about everything from local dining to excursions in the region. With the verbal advice came maps and pamphlets of the resort and the region.

Was I 'pleased'? Well, the fact is that to not be pleased in a place like this would amount to pure cynicism. It's as simple as that. I mean, let's talk about just nature first! Not only has it blessed the town, it has actually embraced it, and the world wants to be a part of it all.

Hemmed in by snowy mountains in the Engadine Valley on the southern stretch of the Swiss Alps adjoining Italy, the town nestles by a pretty lake, with giant conifers as part of its green and white landscape of trees and snow. If the life-blood of the pretty lake country of the Engadine is vacationing, St Moritz is its glittering hub, geographically and otherwise. Each year, through the seasons, its classy hotels and chic boutiques open their doors to upscale international tourists who flock here to enjoy nature's richly offered bounties and a lifestyle stretched to the limits of elegance.

Aptly titled Top of the World, St Moritz remains at the top of the holiday resorts pyramid, having had more praise lavished on it than any other holiday centre in the world. Generations have passed, and the world's rich and famous continue to gather here for the ultimate luxury holiday. A few leisurely walks around town took me past not just the proverbial Swiss mountain chalets of the super-rich and super-famous, but also the sports cars of world celebrities.

Not that it needs to establish or reaffirm its credentials, but St Moritz boasts a list of firsts as long as my arm. It was here that winter tourism in the Alps started in AD 1864, here that the first modern winter sports — the Cresta (Skeleton) Run — were developed, and here that the first European golf tournament to be staged in the Alps was held. The first polo tournament on snow and the first horse races on snow and frozen lake were also held here.

The region has hosted the Winter Olympic Games twice, and the Alpine Ski World Championships thrice. Switzerland's first ski school was set up here, and the world's very first Palace Hotel opened its famous doors in town. Over the years, a galaxy of celebrities came and went, stayed here and played here, and the stories and legends were born. And things have stayed pretty much that way.

Sooner or later, you are bound to get tired of hearing how munificent nature has been to the region. But it's true. Such is the abundance of nature's bounties that the great outdoors is right at your doorstep. Within a 30-minute radius is everything outdoorsmen yearn for. Summer and autumn offer a variety of treks, hikes, and natural sights that include glaciers, panoramic walking trails, and the 25-odd lakes of the Upper Engadine. Tennis and squash centres, two summer skiing areas, a track and field centre for altitude training, an artificial ice rink, and a beautifully landscaped 18-hole golf course, enhance the outdoor experience almost to the point of indulgence.

As the seasons change, so does the lifestyle, and so does the 'mood'. With winter comes the famous local 'snow-how'. With the entire valley snowbound, the world converges here for all manner of activities that include doing the Cresta and the Bob runs, skiing downhill or cross-country, horse racing, skating, golf and polo on the frozen lake (with red balls on 'white greens'). Some come for the sports, some for the pretty snowy landscapes, and some just to be here and to be seen. This is the 'high season' and they don't let you forget it.

One thing you understand quickly enough is that the town has made no bones about the fact that all the praise that's been lavished on it is deserved. I had already had a sample of this. If they hadn't been quite the professionals they are, they would have put up signboards proclaiming that the town isn't for 'everyone'. Seriously though, this is a world of caviar on toast; designer labels; hefty tips, and champagne breakfasts. Nothing comes cheap in this ritzy resort, nothing comes second-hand, and nothing is ever recycled. Only the best will do. That's the large picture. That's the picture.

To its credit, it must be said that while you share space with the world's movers and shakers, the town is subdued and quiet, not one bit glitzy. Aware of its exalted status, but not glitzy, and much of the credit for this must go to the basic nature of the Swiss.

How would you like to share a bath with the world's movers and shakers? It's easily done here. Skilfully exploiting the region's rich mineral sources to pamper privileged clients, the upscale local health centre has spawned from St Moritz's long and celebrated tradition of health springs and spas, and is typically exclusive and efficient. It is believed that the chalybeate water with natural carbonic acid tapped here has been effectively used for medicinal purposes for some 3,000 years now. The deluxe, modern spa centre offers complete hydrotherapy from drinking cures to peat baths and packs; physical therapy; strain cures, and the Kneipp cure.

While the bounties of the glorious outdoors is what brings the world here, nestled amidst all this is a slice of authentic local culture, vividly displayed in two small but interesting museums that pay tribute to the region in their own little way.

From my hotel, it was a mere 10-minutes walk to the Segantini Museum, dedicated to Giovanni Segantini, the Italian painter whose works were inspired by the local countryside, and who spent his last years here. Among the 50-odd works of his life exhibited here, is his most memorable painting, an alpine triptych made up of *Birth, Life,* and *Death.* If you have got an eye for art, chances are this piece will catch your fancy.

Impressed, I decided to carry on in this vein and dropped in at the other local museum. Engadine Museum (which from the outside could be mistaken for a chalet) is a very interesting place, featuring a comprehensive collection of artefacts that reflect the region's history and social and domestic cultures. Founded by antique collector, Richard Campbell, the museum has everything one would find in a patrician home, right from an ostentatious living room and kitchen, to fine quality period furniture.

As I was leaving, I took stock. Of all the resorts I had visited, St Moritz came out tops. The town has never harboured any pretensions of mediocrity. This is haloed holiday turf. But while it certainly is the 'Top of the World', it does have a 'human' face.

With just a hint of champagne!

# Redoudtable Redang

From Kayu Manis, the restaurant on the first floor, the view was about as good as it could get that sunny morning.

Now that's a lot for me to say, because I've seen a view or two in my life. I still remember most of them with utmost clarity. And they still excite me. As for this one, it ranked right up there.

If you haven't got my drift, I'll spell it out good and proper. Right in front of me was something not seen in too many places around the world, and as often happens to me, I guess I was in the mood: three islands stood as sentinels against the blue expanse of the sky and sea, framing things in their own inimitable way. Green, blue and turquoise, the water seemed as still as a millpond, lapping the golden sand on the beach almost delicately. Somehow, that stuck in my mind — that the water was so gentle. No waves, no seagulls, no sound. Just a pretty stillness! Almost picture-postcard perfect, the kind that stays with you long after you've left the place.

That did it! That was my cue to do what I do best. Laze around as if it were going out of fashion. I couldn't think of a better reason in the world to linger over my coffee, and that's just what I did. Linger and gaze. In a bizarre sort of way, this sums up my visit here, really. Because the truly beautiful sites on this planet invite lingering. Well, that's my take on the matter, anyway.

In a way, I had been forewarned about the seduction by none other than Tan Sri Datuk Seri Panglima Abdul Kadir bin Haji Sheikh Fadzir, former Malaysian Tourism Minister, and currently, Executive Chairman, Sazean Group, which operates four quality resorts in Malaysia.

I doubt if anyone else could be better qualified to pass judgement of this nature than this gentleman. Having been at the helm of affairs of Malaysian tourism for several years, and being responsible for steering national tourism policy during the period in which the country was placed firmly on the global tourism map, Tan Sri Fadzir knows what he is talking about. In his inimitable, charming manner, he had revealed the true strength of the Sari Pacifica brand. "I think you're going to like the place and the experience," he had said to me with a smile.

And here I was, and this certainly *was* the place. Sari Pacifica Resort & Spa, Redang Island, is just the kind of place I would recommend to those who have had it with the urban bustle, or those who need a total unwind and mental refurbish, or those who are in love!

"It seems to be as nice as you had wanted me to imagine it to be," I said to Chandra Sehgaran, who as a Deputy Director with Tourism Malaysia, was our host-cum-escort. And my friend! Somewhere, in the not too distant past — three days before, to be precise — Chandra had casually mentioned the beauties of Malaysia's East Coast, and the fact that they were still relatively little known compared to other parts of the country.

Getting here was an interesting journey. We hopped into our van at Charating Beach, and drove along a superb highway for some three hours before arriving in Kuala Trengganu, the State's main city and hub of commercial activity. It is a city of fair proportions, but hurried that we were, sadly, we missed seeing its sights. What we didn't miss out on, however, was a stop for lunch at a traditional café that coincidentally, served as many as three of my favourite dishes — thin chicken curry; deep fried fish, and spicy salad. The deal is simple. The food is stocked and displayed in glass counters. You just pick out what you want, and it is served piping hot at your table.

Somewhat satiated and in a jolly sort of mood, we said goodbye to our guide and driver, and hopped on to a ferry. Five minutes later, we were out on the high seas, making good speed for Redang Island. The sea was choppy, but no one seemed to notice or care.

And now, here I was. The 70-room property sprawls across one of the world's finest sea-face areas. The long, golden stretch of beach is common property and shared with other resorts. And the structure itself is of imposing proportions, with an impressive façade, and seems to have been built brick-by-brick to offer total seduction.

"I'm glad you like it," Jassin Sulaiman, the resort's Operations Manager, said to me with a polite smile. While I was trying to figure out how he had assumed I liked it, he drove the point home by mentioning myriad reasons for one to be charmed by what he termed 'island living'.

Now, this 'island living' is a story by itself, with a distinct identity and character. Innumerable comments make the rounds about the so-called 'islander mentality' compared to 'others'. Without going into details, suffice it is to say that most islanders are protective towards their environment, and don't always take to strangers.

They wanted me to feel at home and really get to know the place, and that's what I endeavoured to do. My conducted tour of the resort meant a walk in the sun to the spa, which is conceived exactly the way spas should be and sports a tranquil atmosphere. I promised to treat myself to a massage, but never did get around to doing that.

They showed me their conference room, which looked like one nice place in which to conduct a meeting. I promised to return some day with a convention group, or to give a lecture, or some such thing.

The guest rooms are split into two lots: the ones on the beachfront that offer expansive sea views, and the others, clustered around a lily pond, with garden views. I must admit both had their plus points, though I was glad to be in one which commanded an excellent view of the beach, bay and sea.

The day had gone as quickly as it tends to in dreamy locations worldwide. It was sunset, which is always a special time. Somehow, sunsets have always got me thinking of what could have been. I mean in my private life. The fact is that they always bring with them a whiff of nostalgia, and always manage to make me a little morose. But then that's the way my life has panned out, and I suppose, that's the way 'single bingles' are meant to feel at sunset in paradise.

"It can get a bit lonely out here in these exotic locales if you are all by yourself," Chandra said to me in a matter-of-fact tone that suggested a bit of experience. "But that's life." He looked a bit thoughtful, and his mind seemed to be elsewhere. "Yes, that's life," I told him, trying to inject some personal 'experience' into my tone.

He then sprang a surprise on me. " Did I tell you that I'm crazy about fishing?" "No, you didn't tell me. Must have slipped your mind, what with your hectic work schedule and travel, etc." He could barely conceal his sense of elation. "I'm planning to go out for some deep-sea fishing tonight and you're welcome to join me if you like." He then went on to tell me that he loved the sport and wanted to try his hand at landing a big catch in these waters. He was hiring a boat to take him out to sea. "How big will the boat be?" I asked with a degree of concern I didn't want to show. "Oh, big enough," he said with a grin. You can't pull one over Chandra that easily. "A boat is a boat," the good man added.

Eventually he went on his own, and as he told me later, had quite an outing, though he didn't manage to land a big fish. That is always the ultimate reward for fishing enthusiasts. But the important thing was that he got to give vent to his passion, and that is what I believe life's got to be all about — living out your passions.

Meanwhile, I was determined to make the most of this place, and didn't want to spend any time than absolutely necessary in my room, nice as it was.

So, what does one do here? Not much, really. You snorkel, scuba dive, deep-sea dive, fish, swim, island-hop, watch turtles, laze, eat and drink. Quite a tough regimen, you might say. Even my exceptional energy levels didn't allow me to indulge in all these wonderful pursuits, but I *did* laze, eat and drink.

Now that things had been put into proper perspective in this exceptional resort, it was time to sail out to discover the other gems of the island. And that is the only way I can describe Sari Pacifica Resort & Spa, Lang Tengah Island.

The ferry ride from Redang Island to Lang Tengah took all of 30 minutes, far too short for the plethora of visual delights thrown up. It was sea and sand at their very best and the resort is just what the doctor ordered for those who just want to 'escape' and lose themselves. It is a genuine hideout, tucked away from sight, completely removed from the conventional modes of day-to-day life.

43 rooms, a spacious, 100-covers restaurant also named Kayu Manis, a spa, and a stunning sea-front with clear waters, make this a genuine paradise for honeymooners and those inclined to relax and take in the beauty of the sea.

Mohamed Zaimi, the resort's manager, took me around the premises and filled me in on its salient features, its pristine beauty for those who appreciate the bounties of nature, and on the type of business and clientele they get.

A rather sumptuous lunch tucked in, our motley group hopped back into our boat for a bout of scuba diving. Everyone took the plunge except me, but then — as I was at pain to explain to anyone willing to listen — someone has to stay back and look after things while the boys and girls go out and frolic. And then there was also this little business of the beer to be guarded.

Before I knew, a couple of days had gone by. As often happens in such locales, time had slipped by too fast. But that's the way it is, and the experience had been rich and pleasant enough. I had breathed in the fresh air; walked along golden sand beaches; seen the sea in its myriad colours; inhaled the salt spray. And shamefully indulged in savouring the fresh seafood comprising an assortment of fish, crab, lobster, and prawns, served grilled, fried, sautéed, or curried. And I had told myself over and over again that I had been lucky to be at one of the world's most beautiful cluster of islands.

How's that to perk you up and recharge your batteries?

# Golden Temple: A Living Shrine

Coming home!

That's what it is.

It's payback time! And I am home! It has been a while coming, but I have made it. And now I know what it feels like to be truly at peace in an environment it's so easy to blend into.

Why do I feel that being here is like coming home? Good question! After all, there's a huge world out there and I have seen it, and I have felt at home in so many different places at so many different times. So why this feeling of supreme inner peace now, at this particular place?

You don't have to ask me. You can, of course, but I would prefer it if you 'walked the talk' and actually experienced what I did.

It stands there in simple majesty, the gilded splendour of its dome and panellings shining in the sunlight, silhouetted softly in the water of the surrounding 'pool of nectar' (holy tank). All around the pool, along the spotlessly clean marbled pavement that fringes the temple complex's vast amphitheatre like a mosaic border, walk the devotees in clockwise fashion, heads bowed in reverence, some praying, some listening to the hymns, others just reflecting.

And everywhere, resonating across the shrine and filtering through its various buildings and open spaces, forming a continuous, soothing background soundtrack is the nonstop chanting of the *kirtan* (religious hymns). It grows on you. It soothes. It calms. It makes you want to pause and listen. It makes you unwind.

I am humbled and awed at the same time. Not just because of the sheer physical and architectural splendour of the shrine complex, and the rich burden of history so gracefully carried, but also because of the total serenity at hand. The mood is tranquil. The atmosphere electric! It's just one of those things hard to explain, but easy to experience.

The most exalted of all Sikh *gurdwaras* (shrines), the Hari Mandir or Golden Temple in Amritsar is the ultimate Sikh pilgrimage — a journey's end, or beginning — depending on how one looks at it, and for the public in general, a 'must-visit' shrine and spiritual stop-over. For centuries pilgrims from near and far have been drawn here, and from the beginning, it has been the cradle of the city that grew around it and has been sustained and nurtured by its divine sanctity. Today, as yesterday, the city's signature institution is the main reason to visit.

A sense of reverence rather than a quest for tinsel richness shapes things here. The Sikh gurus encouraged everyone, irrespective of caste and creed, to come and reside in the city. The Hari Mandir was made open on all four sides, signifying open entry to all. As you queue up with hundreds of other devotees at the temple, you begin to sense the depth of the gurus' feelings.

The Golden Temple's noble story began some four centuries ago with the fourth Sikh guru, Guru Ram Das, sanctifying the 'Pool of Nectar' in the 16th century. The pool itself had long been associated with Indian legends. Lord Rama's twin sons had supposedly been taught the Ramayana here. In AD 1574, Guru Ram Das set up home by the side of the pool that was regarded as blessed with miraculous healing powers. His home came to be known as Guru-ka-Mahal. Shortly thereafter, the guru bought the pool and its surrounding land and excavated the tank to construct a shrine at its centre. That was the temple's simple and quiet beginning.

In AD 1588, the temple's foundation stone was ceremoniously laid by the Muslim Sufi divine, Hazrat Mian Mir of Lahore, at the request of the fifth Sikh guru, Guru Arjan Dev. Then things started to buzz, with the guru's followers settling down in the neighbourhood. A small town called Ramdaspur quickly emerged, deriving its later name, Amritsar, from the holy tank that encircles the Hari Mandir or Darbar Sahib, now known as the Golden Temple because of its gilded gold exterior.

As the followers of Sikhism grew in numbers, the town that grew around the temple during Guru Arjan Dev's lifetime, developed further in size, stature and importance. The first Sikh emperor, Maharaja Ranjit Singh made Amritsar his spiritual capital and oversaw the temple's future development. Wishing to do his bit for this holiest of holy shrines, he gilded the embossed plates, renewing the *pietra dura* and embellishing the interior with a floral designed, mirrored ceiling.

So much for the history!

As an eclectic monument that grew as much from people's devotion as from the guild craftsmen's skills, the Golden Temple has achieved the kind of romantic glory which defies conventional norms and compels humility before God. Hallowed over succeeding generations by the meditations of holy men and the blood of martyrs defending the Sikh faith against imperial oppression, the temple has always been a refuge for the sick and weary. As in the past, as always, many who throng the premises come with their personal problems, seeking divine blessings.

Regarded as one of the most tastefully decorated shrines in the world, the temple has had universal praise lavished on its art and architecture. For the purist, it is a collection of architectural symbols whose beauty is greatly enhanced by its simplicity. For the pilgrim, especially the Sikh pilgrim, it is simplicity and nobleness as manifest in religion.

I descend into the amphitheatre (unlike most temples, here you actually descend as the structure is built below the level of the surrounding area as an act of humility) and am confronted by the stunningly beautiful *sanctum sanctorum* glimmering in the water of the holy tank. This first view of the Golden Temple is something that stays with you. You may see it a thousand times in picture postcards or posters, but seeing it for yourself is a completely different experience.

I kneel to the ground and bow my forehead before the shrine, and join some hundred other devotees in a clockwise walk across the vast, square amphitheatre splayed out around the tank. In the first corner, two women seated behind a 'counter' are serving water, and I drink a cupful. I pass Dukhbanjani Beri (an ancient tree marking a very holy spot). Several devotees are taking a dip here and elsewhere in the tank. A dip here at this particular spot is considered especially significant. On my left is one of the complex's four gates. I walk on and turn the corner again past another water counter, and then yet again to arrive at the *'pershad'* (holy food) counter where I join the queue, collect the *pershad* and take it with me to offer at the designated point. I now reach the causeway that leads to the sanctum sanctorum.

Ten minutes. That's all that I have been here, but I am already in a 'groove'. I can sense the mood, feel the rhythm.

And I notice it isn't just me. I notice the other devotees' faces are calm. They are all calm. So I try to be calm too. It has never been easy for me, but here I am already as calm as I can imagine myself to be.

I move on and step on to the causeway. There is a queue and so I wait. The queue melts away and I make my way to the door of the shrine.

The main structure is 150 square metres, rising from the centre of the sacred pool, and is approached by a 60 metre-long causeway. The 52 square metres Hari Mandir stands on a 20 square metres platform, its lower part marble, its upper portion embellished with gilded copper plates.

I enter the stunningly beautiful confines of the *sanctum sanctorum,* and am in front of the *Guru Granth Sahib* (holy book of the Sikhs) reverentially placed under a jewel-studded canopy. For Sikhs, the *Guru Granth Sahib* is everything. It is the physical embodiment of the Gurus. It is in front of the *Guru Granth Sahib* that devotees bow and touch their forehead to the ground. I do the same.

There is now a queue behind me but I want to linger. So I stand in a corner to be a part of this for as long as I can. They like to have you move on to make place for those behind, and an attendant gives me the 'eye' but I ignore him and hold my spot. I am not ready to leave. Not just yet.

The ground level structure's interior is ornate, with intricate inlays on the ceiling and walls. The first floor pavilion is known as the Shish Mahal or Mirror Room, and above this is another small pavilion, and both contain the *Guru Granth Sahib.* The workmanship is exquisite, but apart from the murals, the emphasis is on simplicity.

The ceiling features a rich design ensemble but on the whole is relatively plain looking as there are no other colours apart from gold. Hanging by a gold threaded rope is a single, large chandelier.

I move out and climb the marble steps to enter the first-floor part of the structure. Behind me, little windows look out onto the amphitheatre, and I see hundreds of devotees treading the shining marble flooring, heading towards the shrine. Their clothing and turbans form a patchwork of colours. They'll do exactly what I did, and probably end up sitting at the very spot I am occupying at the moment.

But it's the scene below, in the ground floor of the *sanctum sanctorum* where I was just minutes ago, that's totally enrapturing, and which must rank among the most powerful and beautiful I have ever seen. A bird's eye view is something else. Before the *Guru Granth Sahib* is a floral pattern hewn together with several strings of flowers. The attendants keep replacing the strings, distributing them among the devotees, replacing them with fresh ones. This is almost a constant process. Fresh flower garlands being arranged in a pattern, then handed out to devotees minutes later, to be replaced by other fresh ones. Strewn around on the carpeted floor is offerings of money periodically collected and deposited in a *goluk* (strong box). To the left of the *Guru Granth Sahib* sit the *granthis* (hymn singers) who'll sing *shabads* and *kirtan* (devotional hymns) for perhaps an hour, before being replaced by another troupe. To the right, *pershad* is being sanctified and then distributed. Some devotees get *saropas* (saffron-coloured holy cloth), some get flowers if they ask for them. But they all get blessings, which is what they have come for. There's no shortage of blessings here.

Time means nothing as I see and experience all this. I find it hard to believe I have been here for an hour now. The *kirtan* has grown on me. I have never been more at peace. I have never felt so calm. Never! And then, for the first time in my life, I believe I went into a sort of trance. I don't know exactly how long it lasted, but it was there. Not given to flights of fancy, I don't know if I really went into a trance or was just lulled into a sense of total calm. Whatever it was, it will stay with me forever as one of my truly unique experiences.

Finally, I tell myself it's time to move on, and have to force myself to do so. I really do. I can't fully explain it, but that's how I felt at that moment.

I leave the *sanctum sanctorum* to see the complex's other notable landmarks. The *kirtan* accompanies me everywhere. On stepping off the causeway, I find myself right in front of the Akal Takht, a massive marble structure with a stunning façade, that's the night resting place for the *Guru Granth Sahib*, and that also fulfills other roles and functions. It is the podium for important Sikh religious discussions and issues.

I stop at the two giant *nishan sahibs* (flagpoles) that stand as silent, magnificent sentinels just by the side of the Akal Takht, turn the fourth corner, and am back at the main entrance to the shrine. But I am not leaving. Not just yet.

I want to partake of the *langar* (community meal) served at all big Sikh Gurudwara. *Langar* everywhere is special. Here, it's even more so. I walk to the nearby giant *langar* hall (community kitchen) and find hundreds, literally hundreds of devotees seated on the floor, partaking of the meal served caringly and lovingly to one and all.

I join them and am immediately served by two young Sikh volunteers. As always, the food is delicious. As always, I overeat just that little bit. Of course, it doesn't matter here for they would have continued to serve me for as long as I would have wanted. Having partaken of two helpings,

I politely decline when the attendants come around with more food. I get up and take my steel plate and glass to the wash basin to wash them myself which is the thing to do as a small token of service, but have them taken from me by a lady volunteer who's doing dishwashing along with some ten other ladies.

Housed within the temple complex are several other notable institutions. The Teja Singh Samudri Hall serves as a platform for significant meets. In the Guru Ram Das Sarai, devotees find basic but clean accommodation. The museum and library contain a collection of priceless Sikh relics and manuscripts.

A short walk from the Golden Temple brings you to a series of other, smaller shrines of importance and great architectural beauty. Baba Atal Sahib, Babek Sar, and the Shahidi (martyr's) Shrine — all trace their links to the Sikh Gurus. And all are architectural gems in their own right.

Amritsar played a pivotal role in India's independence struggle and no national monument is more significant to India's recent history than Jalianwala Bagh, a poignant, grim reminder of one of the bloodiest chapters of India's freedom movement. The 2,000 Indians killed and wounded here in the indiscriminate firing by General Dyer's British troops in 1919 was a carnage of unimaginable horror that had nation-wide ramifications, enraging the whole country. Jalianwala Bagh commemorates the martyrs and preserves the tragic episode in its historical context. A small gallery with photos of key personalities involved, the well into which the hapless crowds jumped to escape the murderous hail of bullets, and a simple memorial make up this site which shaped India's destiny.

People visit Amritsar not quite knowing what to expect. Not your conventional tourist city, it never fails to charm visitors with its simplicity, laid-back locals, and the pristine beauty of the Golden Temple.

Big but not huge, crowded but not suffocating, the city endears. There are bustling bazaars around the temple, stocked brimful with an assortment of items that range from crisps and savouries like *papads* (wafer thin salted bread) *vadis* (savouries) *ampapad* (salted, dried mango slices), and the most amazing array of spices, to durries and fabrics. These are the best local souvenirs, so don't miss out.

The visitor today finds a distinct 'frontier' atmosphere, enhanced by the fact that the city nestles within breathing distance of the Indo-Pakistan border. A robust, hard-working lot, the Amritsaris pride themselves on their high-quality food and dairy products, and are generous with their hospitality.

Prepare to indulge the palate. The *lassi* (yoghurt shake) served here, especially at Gyan's is considered the best in the world. The *dhaba* (roadside café) culture still predominates. True gourmet fare cooked in *asli ghee* (clarified butter) tempts visitors and is an assault on their waistline, with the renowned Kesar Dhaba being the numero uno. Delicious as ever is the *rabri* (boiled milk), and the world famous Amritsari fish (deep fried river fish) is an all-time favourite.

While in Amritsar, journey a little farther to take in other gurdwaras like Tarn Taran Sahib, Baba Bakala, and Goindwal Sahib, all within an hour's drive. Also less than an hour's drive is the Wagah Checkpoint on the Indo-Pakistan border, where you can see the two countries' flag-hoisting and lowering ceremonies.

The Golden Temple grows on you. Mirrored, are unforgettable images dear to the devout: the golden dome shimmering in the water; the *kirtan* resonating everywhere. Thousands of devotees, hands folded, praying and kneeling before the holy book, or sprinkling holy water over themselves, or seated at the *langar*-hall, or doing *seva,* (service) all lost in reverence.

Amritsar offers the chance to go on a pilgrimage and a cultural and gourmet trip, all at the same time, and a visit to the Golden Temple will probably leave you asking why you hadn't done it before.

Leaving is never easy.